BRITISH WOMEN'S HISTORY

British Women's History

A Documentary History from the Enlightenment to World War I

Alison Twells

I.B. TAURIS

LONDON · NEW YORK

Published in 2007 by I.B.Tauris & Co Ltd

6 Salem Road, London W2 4BU
175 Fifth Avenue, New York NY 10010
www.ibtauris.com

In the United States of America and Canada distributed by
Palgrave Macmillan a division of St. Martin's Press
175 Fifth Avenue, New York NY 10010

ISBN 978 1 86064 161 9
ISBN 978 1 86064 162 6 (PB)
International Library of Historical Studies 44

A full CIP record for this book is available from the British Library
A full CIP record is available from the Library of Congress

Library of Congress Catalog Card Number: available

Typeset in Sabon by RefineCatch Limited, Bungay, Suffolk
Printed and bound in Great Britain by
TJ International Ltd, Padstow, Cornwall

For Ruby and Madeleine

Contents

Acknowledgements

I should like to thank the librarians at Sheffield Hallam University Learning Centre, the British Library, Sheffield City Archives and Local Studies Library, Nottingham University Library, Nottingham Local Studies Library and Birmingham University Special Collections. Thanks also to my colleagues in History at Sheffield Hallam University for their continued support over the time that it has taken to complete this volume, and especially to John Baxendale, Merv Lewis and Nicola Verdon for their help with sources. I am also indebted to Lester Crook and Liz Friend-Smith at I.B.Tauris and Richard Willis at Swales & Willis for their patience and support.

This Reader is very much the product of the research undertaken by historians of British women over the past 30 years. I am particularly and personally indebted to Eileen Yeo and Jane Rendall for their pioneering and inspirational work over many years and for their contributions to this volume of sources relating to Jewish and Scottish women. Thanks also to Jane Aaron and Simon Morgan for their help with sources and to Sarah Richardson for her generosity in sharing her research on Anne Lister. I am indebted to Sian Rhiannon Williams, who hunted down the excerpt from *Y Gymraes* and supplied both the original Welsh version and English translation. Helen Rogers contributed key sources and read the entire manuscript; it has benefited immensely from her suggestions and critical commentary. Clare Midgley made invaluable comments on the introduction and the anonymous reader at I.B.Tauris made extremely helpful suggestions regarding the shape of the volume. My thanks and appreciation also to my family: to Sue Salaun for her rigorous reading of the manuscript; Jean Powditch and Tony Mancini for their generous support; and Ruby and Maddy Twells, for their great enthusiasm for all things female and of the 'olden days'. Finally, I should like to thank Penny Hardcastle and Molly Powell at Burton

Street Community History Project in Sheffield, for suggesting the photograph for the front cover. I am extremely grateful to the Burrell family for their enthusiastic response to my request to use this lovely picture of their grandmother. Clara Drinkwater (nee Green), c.1885–1959, lived in Owlerton, Sheffield, where she worked at Trebor-Bassetts. She married and became a mother to twin girls in 1917, and later a much-loved grandmother. Her mother Sarah Ann Green is peeping from behind the net curtains.

The authors and publishers would like to thank all the copyright holders of material reproduced in this volume for granting permission to include it. I would like to acknowledge the following for their kind permission to reproduce excerpts from texts: Everyman's Library, Northburgh House, 10 Northburgh Street, London EC1V 0AT (Rousseau, *Emile*); Oxford University Press (Austen, *Pride and Prejudice* and Thompson, *Lark Rise to Candleford*); Shepheard-Walwyn Publications (Foakes, *My Part of the River*); New York University Press (Nightingale, *Cassandra*); HarperCollins Publishers Ltd (Foreman, *Georgiana, the Duchess of Devonshire*); West Yorkshire Archive Service, Calderdale: SH: ML/E/14-18 (Anne Lister's election comments); Manchester University Centre for Continuing Education (Foley, *A Bolton Childhood*); Little, Brown Book Group Ltd ('Food: Chief Articles of Diet'); Faber & Faber (Mitchell, *The Hard Way Up*); Methuen, now Taylor & Francis (Newman, *Infant Mortality*); Continuum International Publishing Group (Coleman, *Maiden Voyages and Infant Colonies*); Dundee City Archives (Mary Slessor's letter); Sheffield City Archives and Local Studies Library (Sheffield Ladies' Anti-Slavery Society petition and the Empire Day photograph); University of Michigan Press (*The History of Mary Prince*); University of Toronto Press (J. S. Mill 1867 speech). Every effort was made to contact authors and copyright holders to secure appropriate permissions, but if proper acknowledgement has not been made, the copyright holder should contact the publishers.

Introduction

In 1791, when she was just 15 years of age, Jane Austen composed *The History of England from the reign of Henry the 4th to the death of Charles the 1st*, a parody of eighteenth-century history writing and, in particular, of Oliver Goldsmith's four-volume *History of England* (1771). Austen described herself as a 'partial, prejudiced, & ignorant Historian', declaring that '[t]here will be very few Dates in this History'. She then proceeded to trot through a list of English Kings and Queens, between 1399 and 1649. The short paragraphs sum up wittily the preoccupation of historians with wars, murders, beheadings, torture and long speeches. Austen is particularly sharp on both the absence of women from the historical account, and the irrelevance of their ill-treatment to society's posthumous appraisal of its rulers. 'It is to be supposed that Henry [4th] was married,' she wrote, 'since he had certainly four sons, but it is not in my power to inform the Reader who was his Wife.' Of Edward 4th she concluded sarcastically that 'This Monarch was famous only for his Beauty & his Courage, of which the Picture [an unflattering sketch drawn by her sister Cassandra] we have here given of him, & his undaunted Behaviour in marrying one Woman while he was engaged to another, are sufficient proofs.' Summing up the historical verdict on James I, she wrote sardonically that 'Though this King had some faults, among which & as the most principal, was his allowing his Mother's death, yet considered on the whole I cannot help liking him.'[1]

'The History of England' is an entertaining little book, with some sharp observations on the interests of (male) historians and their neglect of the significance of women in the lives of important men. In highlighting these points, Austen was not so far removed from the later twentieth-century critique of mainstream history, which has come, finally, to transform the practice of history in Britain and beyond. Women scarcely featured as subjects of many of the histories written throughout the nineteenth and first 70 years of the twentieth centuries.[2] This, as Austen suggests, was not for the want of consciousness among women of their exclusion. As Johanna Alberti has recently argued, women historians had for a long time posed questions about their sex's absence from the historical record.[3] But women as the writers of history were few and far between. Their proliferation as students, teachers and researchers of history as a result of the post-war educational expansion, alongside changes in the focus of professional history and the second-wave feminist movement of the 1970s, has seen a transformation of the place of women as both writers and subjects of history.

This documentary history draws upon 30 years of scholarship by historians of women to provide sources concerning women's lives in the 'long nineteenth century' (1780–1914). In the introduction, I provide an overview of the development of the discipline since the 1970s, emphasising its origins in the feminist movement and exploring its relationship to mainstream history.

The development of women's history

Women's history in Britain has its origins in the revolution in history writing which occurred during the 1960s and which saw a shift away from the almost exclusive concern with the histories of the elite towards the lives of ordinary people. 'Peoples' history' or 'history from below' was unleashed on academic and more popular history with the publication by Edward Thompson of his ground-breaking *The Making of the English Working Class* in 1963. Thompson, a historian of eighteenth- and nineteenth-century England, criticised traditionalist historians whose studies omitted consideration of the poor, evidence of conflict and exploitation and of the political movements of the period. He was also critical of cruder Marxists, for whom personal experience and reflection were not among the range of factors which led to a consciousness on the part of the poor of themselves as a social class. Focusing on the rescue of the poor 'from the enormous condescension of posterity', E. P. Thompson's work heralded a new departure within social history and inspired a desire among a new generation of historians to record and interpret the lives of people hitherto marginalised in dominant historical accounts.[4]

It might reasonably be imagined that a new movement peopled by historians with a commitment to the poor and dispossessed would hold a great deal of potential for the writing of women's history. Even within the new 'peoples' history', however, women struggled to find a voice. Indeed, in a tale which has gained in significance as the volume of women's history has increased, the proposal by Sally Alexander to study women's history at a History Workshop meeting at Ruskin College, Oxford, in 1970 was met with derisive laughter from some men.[5] Women, it was claimed, were not only absent from historical sources, but their lives as housewives and mothers were unchanging; neither were they agent in effecting change. But Alexander, Anna Davin, Juliet Mitchell and other women involved in History Workshop had not only been inspired by the new focus on hidden voices in history, but had received a new-found confidence from the politics of the emergent women's movement in Britain.[6]

Feminism is not popular today, and the second-wave 1970s feminist movement in particular is caricatured in the media and held responsible for a range of contemporary dissatisfactions and discontents. But women's history and, indeed, almost any subject in the Arts and Humanities that students may choose to study at degree-level in the twenty-first century, has been profoundly shaped by feminism. It was feminists who first challenged the absence of women: from history, from the literature studied on English degrees, from anthropology, psychology, and from any number of academic disciplines. Feminism posed further searching questions about women's hitherto neglect: who decided which historical topics, novels, aspects of society and experience, etc. were worthy of study? Arguments were made that the narrative of key historical events, like the largely-male canon of English literature, may not have been arrived at from a neutral assessment of intrinsic worth (that they just *are* the most significant events, just as men were the 'best' writers) but that they were shaped by the concerns and interests and beliefs of (mostly-male) academics. Moreover, feminists claimed that such a devaluation of things female mirrored a societal undervaluing of women's experience; the 'just a housewife' syndrome. It was this political analysis which led to the emergence of courses in women's history, women's writing, the psychology of women, anthropology of gender, the sociology of housework and more, and also women's studies degrees which combined such modules from across the range of disciplines.[7]

Women's history has developed in identifiable phases in the UK, although we should be wary of presenting them as being too discrete from one another.[8] Of iconic status at the beginnings of women's history in Britain is Sheila Rowbotham's *Hidden from History*

(1973). Rowbotham, who had been a student at Oxford in the early 1960s, commented on the sheer distance of the history she studied from most people's lives. It was, she stated, 'very difficult to study history which was not about Parliament and the growth of the treasury or about cabinets, treaties and coalitions' (presumably shaped by the desire to produce candidates for the Indian Civil Service or the Foreign Office).[9] The only women who warranted a mention in university history teaching were those who have been called 'women worthies': unusual women who had done extraordinary things and were thus deemed suitable subjects for a biographical or hagiographical account of their lives. Mary Queen of Scots, Elizabeth I, Queen Victoria, Florence Nightingale and Emmeline Pankhurst all find their way into this category. While this approach has perhaps been the most thoroughly disparaged as the least enlightened and least representative of most women's lives, it was, as Johanna Alberti has pointed out, consistent with a biographical approach to history-writing that remained a dominant form well into the twentieth century. In contrast, *Hidden from History*, written when Rowbotham was teaching with the Workers' Education Association (WEA) and engaged in research in the context of the wider group of socialist and Marxist historians associated with E. P. Thompson, explored the experiences of women in some of the social movements then popularly under study, from seventeenth-century Puritanism to early nineteenth-century radicalism, trade unionism and suffrage.[10]

While the 'hidden from history' approach has done much to identify the participation of women in social movements, its focus on the places where women's lives coincided with those of men does not tell us a great deal about the lives of women in general. What about the things that occupied women when they weren't at that trade union meeting, for example, or the lives of those who were not participant in such movements at all? While parts of women's days and weeks undoubtedly overlapped with the activities of men, they were also filled with quite different roles and concerns. Girls and boys were socialised and educated differently. Women took different jobs, and if they married, usually took responsibility for the home and for raising children. They had less time for commitments outside the home or even for leisure activities. Thus, what about the time spent cooking and cleaning and running a home, or the years spent carrying and giving birth to and caring for babies and children and hoping to not conceive any more? What of the various activities involved in 'making ends meet' and keeping the family together?

Out of these questions, there emerged a more 'woman-centred' approach to history, which was concerned with all of these womanly life events. Titles such as *Suffer and Be Still* (1972), edited by Martha Vicinus, Judith Walkowitz's *Prostitution in Victorian Society* (1980), *Labour and Love* (1986), edited by Jane Lewis and Ellen Ross's *Love and Toil: Motherhood in Outcast London* (1993) are suggestive of this new focus on women's domestic and maternal experiences, family life and sexuality.[11] Such work was inspired by a new generation of women's history in the United States which, grappling with women's domestic experience, had raised important questions about the extent of their oppression or empowerment, and the significance of the concept of 'patriarchy' in understanding women's lives.[12] Such studies – a number of them focused on British women's history – had theoretical implications for historians of women in Britain, many of whom had emerged from a socialist tradition and had been concerned with understanding the ways in which Marxism did not explain aspects of women's lives, including their place in the labour market, issues around reproduction, or domestic violence. The concept of 'patriarchy' and especially Joan Kelly's notion of a 'doubled vision' of patriarchy and capitalism, offered particular theoretical challenges to women's history, leading to much debate and the beginnings of a more intense focus on issues of sexuality and the process of the acquisition of a specifically female identity.[13]

The 1980s and early 1990s then were rich years for the development of women's history, witnessing an increase in the volume and intensity of research and writing. Alongside these came the appointment of lecturers in university history departments with specific expertise in women's history. The establishment of the Women's History Network saw regular conferences, while journals such as *Women's History Review* and the re-orientation of *History Workshop Journal* to that of socialist *and feminist* historians, have seen a concern not only to recover women's lives in the past but to explore the methodological issues concerned with their recovery. Women's history found its way onto the BBC in the 1990s. To take just three examples: the series 'A Skirt through History' was aired on BBC2 in 1994, with sketches about the lives of Anne Lister, Mary Prince, Hannah Cullwick and others (see documents below); Jane Rogers' novel *Mr Wroe's Virgins* (1991) became a BAFTA-nominated television production in 1993, and Sarah Waters' first novel *Tipping the Velvet* (1998), based around Victorian music hall and with a lesbian love story at its centre, was adapted into a drama serial by Andrew Davies and was shown on BBC TV in 2002.

Into such activity came a new strand of inquiry and debate in the 1980s and 1990s, as some feminist historians began to suggest that the study of 'gender history' rather than 'women's history' would further develop the subject, possibly enhancing its reception in the mainstream. The American historian Joan Scott in particular argued that the focus on 'women', while producing some excellent studies of women's lives, ultimately served merely to describe, and so to reinforce, the differences between men and women. The focus on women's role in the private sphere, for example, did little to explore the dynamics of gender which underpinned the organisation of society. Rather than just 'recovering' women's experiences in the past, Scott argued, historians needed to look at the relations between men and women, and to investigate what it meant to be a woman (or a man) at a particular historical moment.[14] Looking at an event through the lens of gender history might reveal a new understanding about particular historical problems or about society in general. Thus, a focus on gender and the French Revolution, for example, enabled a more critical exploration of the meaning of citizenship and rights: their denial to women allows consideration of the consequences of the revolution, the problems of 'gender' at the heart of democratic projects and the relationship of 'citizenship' to notions of the 'public' and the 'private'.[15] This was, Scott argued, a political project, which would enable the practice of women's history to contribute to women's liberation through an exploration of the changing and socially constructed nature of gender inequalities.

The new 'gender history' drew upon 'postmodern' analyses of culture, which were in the 1980s presenting challenges to all academic disciplines. The work of the French theorists Jacques Derrida and Michel Foucault in particular had emphasised the importance of language and discourse in shaping an individual's experience of the world. Rather than merely a reflection of the natural order of things, men's and women's experience of being men and women were, it was argued, socially constructed, produced in culture and not biologically determined.[16] 'Masculinity' and 'femininity' were two of the 'binary oppositions' through which culture was organised. Far from associated with fixed characteristics, both changed over time and were associated with other polarities, such as agency, control, strength and passivity, dependency and weakness. Gender historians maintained that binary oppositions could be 'deconstructed' to reveal the relationships of power implicit in their formulation. Gender roles then, were not just to be described, but needed to be 'interrogated' and undermined. To explore 'gender' as a category of analysis, Scott argued, allowed for a more radical approach to history.

The advent of 'gender history' made for a history which was at times exhilarating and at others, given the highly-jargonised language of post-structuralism, frustratingly theoretical and obtuse. But such issues certainly enthralled many feminist historians during the 1980s and early 1990s, and were debated in a number of forums, perhaps one of the most significant being the journal *Gender & History*, established as an Anglo-American collaboration in 1989.[17] Interest in 'difference' and 'identity' held considerable political and personal appeal for many feminists, inspired by the political challenges within feminism itself, principally over issues concerning the differences between women in terms of class, ethnicity and sexuality.[18] Research into lesbian identities and relationships in the nineteenth century has not only uncovered the lives of women subject to a particular censorship but has illuminated the construction and regulation of sexualities at different historical moments.[19] Black women's history has similarly called into question the use of general explanatory frameworks, or meta-narratives, such as the concept of patriarchy. For many 'black' women, for example, the family structure was not patriarchal, and men offered support rather than oppression in a hostile and racist world. Historians and feminists in nations which had been British colonies have also demonstrated that representations of 'third world women' as particularly passive and oppressed, were inaccurate and romanticised.[20] As has been shown by Clare Midgley's study of British abolitionists and their tendency to 'speak on behalf of' slave women, and by Antoinette Burton in her exploration of the significance of the figure of the Indian woman for British feminists' own claims for citizenship, nineteenth-century feminism itself emerged in an imperial context.[21] Recent challenges to the ethnic bias of 'British' history have further criticised the tendency of (English) historians to allow 'English' history to represent 'British' history to the exclusion of other peoples within the British Isles, and insisted that Englishness is (and should be treated as) another ethnic identity rather than the normative state.[22]

After the ferocious exchanges of the early-mid 1990s, the debate over the value of 'gender' history and an approach informed by post-structuralism seems to have settled.[23] This is in part due to the blurring of disciplinary boundaries, as the shift in historical studies towards a focus on language and discourse has been accompanied by the emergence within literary studies of the 'New Historicism', which stresses the study of texts in the contexts in which they were produced.[24] A pioneering study in this area is Leonore Davidoff and Catherine Hall's groundbreaking study, *Family Fortunes: Men and Women of the English Middle Class, 1780–1850* (1987), which combines a Marxist-inspired focus on class formation with a close reading of prescriptive literature and other texts to explore the importance of gender and, in particular, domestic ideology and separate spheres, to the 'new' middle class.[25] Three more recent studies illustrate developments in this field. John Tosh's *A Man's Place: Masculinity and the Middle-Class Home in Victorian England* (1999) has used family papers and correspondence, as well as prescriptive 'advice' texts, to explore the contradictions and the multiple meanings of masculinity in the 'lived experience' of men as husbands and fathers in the nineteenth century.[26] Helen Rogers' *Women and the People* (2000) engages with the debate about the linguistic construction of 'the People' and women's relationship to it, while also exploring the various, complex and often more material influences on women's involvement in radical politics: the demands on their time, the attitudes of those close to them, and the contingencies of women's lives as well as the roles and resources made available to them by political movements.[27] Catherine Hall in *Civilising Subjects* (2002) explores the place of ideas about gender and race in British imaginings of the post-emancipation Caribbean, and locates both very firmly in society in Birmingham in the mid-nineteenth century.[28]

There remain achievements to be made in the field of women's history. Some university departments remain untouched by developments in the field and it is still quite possible to study, for example, the French Revolution without reading the pioneering work of Joan Scott or Joan Landes;[29] or to look at the history of Jewish immigration to Britain, and not study Rickie Burman's ground-breaking work on the impact of migration on gender roles and identities in Jewish culture; or to study the history of London without reference to Ellen Ross's wonderful ethnography of late nineteenth-century domestic life; and to look at all of these without studying men as *men*. More commonly, students get the 'week on women' approach, where modules – on Nazi Germany or Soviet Russia, for example – might dedicate week 7 to 'women in . . .', but do not integrate women into the syllabus or explore the way in which 'gender' has developed that particular area of historical enquiry. Overall, however, despite an uneven development, women's history in Britain can only be described as a success story. Its integration into many history degrees has seen a profound transformation of the sorts of history students can do at degree level. The balance of journal articles and other publications, and the focus of conferences all suggest that women's and gender history is no longer on the margins.

Sources

This collection of documents consists of selected extracts from writing about women in the long nineteenth century. They include examples from the range of sources, written in a variety of traditions, including: prescriptive literature, didactic stories, political treatises, petitions, pamphlets and periodicals, lectures, poems, hymns, sermons, scientific papers, social surveys and investigative reports, Parliamentary papers, philosophical and psychological texts, novels, memoirs and diaries, travel journals, autobiographies, published and private letters, newspapers and visual evidence.

Written mainly by women, but including some contributions by men, many excerpts are from now 'classic' sources, although some are of a rather more obscure provenance. Such obscurity is often a feature of the uneven development of women's history itself: the history of Protestant English women has been more readily recovered than that of women in the rest of the British Isles,[30] and that of women who migrated to Britain as slaves and servants or as part of the major nineteenth-century diasporas from Ireland and eastern Europe. This collection tries in part to remedy that imbalance, although not always successfully. While Scottish women's history has seen great developments in recent years, for example, it has been a much more difficult task to locate sources on Welsh women's history.[31] Similarly, the absence of autobiographies by Irish women migrants has led me to draw upon sections about women – as mothers, cultural caretakers, workers – in more readily available autobiographies by Irish men.[32]

The internal organisation of the collection not only reflects key areas of women's domestic and social lives but also the historiography of women's history. It is to enable a fuller discussion of the historiography, therefore, that some documents are placed in one section rather than another: some excerpts concerning Irish and Jewish women, for example, could have been discussed in the general chapters on working women or women and politics, but have been placed in the chapter on diaspora to facilitate understanding of the development in women's history of consideration of issues of ethnicity. I am aware that this might seem a curious organisation, not least because placing 'other' women in a separate chapter can be seen as contrary to the process of considering Englishness as an ethnicity. I have chosen to organise the book in this way in order to facilitate teaching about historiography. The exception here is that of sexuality: while this subject should have warranted a chapter in its own right, the pressures of the word limit has meant that documents – concerning lesbianism, heterosexual sex, critiques of male sexuality – are dispersed within complementary chapters focused on domestic life and feminism.

The book is designed for teaching. The documents are deliberately lengthy; I find myself unsatisfied by heavily annotated collections, unsure as to why a particular selection – or cut – has been made, and desirous to see how the author had originally constructed her or his argument. The collection can, of course, be used in a variety of ways. It can be dipped into in order to find an 'illustrative' document for a particular topic. It might complement other anthologies, such as Maria Luddy's excellent *Women in Ireland, 1800–1918: A Documentary History*; Alison Oram and AnnMarie Turnbull's *The Lesbian History Sourcebook*; and collections on radical women by Ruth and Edmund Frow and, more recently, Kathryn Gleadle.[33] The documents may also be used to support a course of study of nineteenth-century women's history; or, as I have done, to develop a women's history module into a source-based module. The History Benchmarking specification states that 'students should carry out intensive critical work on' contemporary sources,[34] to develop critical historical skills, to encourage independent and self-motivated learning, to read critically, and to assess the problems of the historical record. Source work can also familiarise students with the past in a particularly intensive way. It encourages empathy and imaginative insight and understanding of past social structures and belief systems, of the complexity of historical situations, events and mentalities, language and idioms; a 'feel' for a period; and, it is to be hoped, inspires the same passion for women's history that has been a driving force for those of us who teach it.

Chapter One

Making Women
Enlightenment, evangelical and medical perspectives

Ideas about woman's nature – who she was, how she differed from men, who she might be, and the training and education appropriate to that end – were shaped by a range of intellectual and social movements during the late eighteenth and nineteenth centuries. Enlightenment and evangelical models of masculinity and femininity, despite their differences, roughly converged on the notions of essential difference and 'separate spheres'. Medical and scientific ideas about femininity gave further validation to ideas of woman's natural domesticity. The sources in the first part of this chapter focus upon the dominant ideas about femininity and women's role to emerge from these three broad and, at times, overlapping perspectives. The later part of the chapter looks at how these ideas were translated into practice, in the education of girls and women.

1.1 Jean-Jacques Rousseau, *Emile* (1762)

Enlightenment *philosophe* Jean-Jacques Rousseau (1712–1778) enthused about the new forms of education enabled by the Enlightenment beliefs that people were a product of their environment and had an extensive capacity for learning and improvement. He did not extend these principles to women, however. This excerpt from *Emile* (1762) reflects Rousseau's belief that girls and women, destined to be wives and mothers, should be educated to be companions of men and custodians of morality within a domestic setting. This is famously articulated by the female character, Sophy, who was to be educated to be modest, maternal and companionate, cultivating a desire to please.

1.2 John Millar, *The Origin of the Distinctions of Ranks* (1771)

French and, especially, Scottish Enlightenment philosophers developed a progressive understanding of social change, which saw all societies move from a state of savagery through barbarism to civilisation. This change involved a development in the economic base of society – from hunting and gathering, through pastorage and settled agriculture, to commerce – and in social and political institutions and cultural values and practices, including the relative roles of men and women. Women's participation in the same work as men was believed to occur in societies where women were enslaved and brutalised. In contrast, in civilised society, women were domestic creatures, responsible for the care of the home and children, the consumption of new goods made available by expanding markets, and the education of males to become responsible citizens. As this excerpt suggests, the organisation of the sexes into 'separate spheres' was a signifier of an advanced, civilised society.

1.3 Mary Wollstonecraft, *Vindication of the Rights of Woman* (1792)

In her *Vindication of the Rights of Woman* (1792), Mary Wollstonecraft (1759–1797) provided the most famous response to Rousseau. Wollstonecraft, who had been previously employed as a ladies' companion and governess, moved to London in 1787 to work as a journalist and translator, and began to mix in radical and liberal circles. She published her *Thoughts on the Education of Girls* in 1787, and in response to Edmund Burke's challenge to the principles of the French Revolution, *Vindication of the Rights of Man* in 1791. The second *Vindication* exposes the contradictions in Enlightenment thinking, whereby women, denied possession of a supposedly universal rationality, were deemed not to have full status as individuals in society. In this excerpt, Wollstonecraft compares women to slaves, and argues that their relationship to men reflects the despotic political systems and arbitrary monarchical power so criticised by Rousseau and others. Wollstonecraft's was not an altogether consistent position: she viewed women as needing rights as autonomous, individual subjects, on the same terms as men, and also as mothers and future mothers; therefore as simultaneously equal/the same and essentially different.

1.4 John Stuart Mill, *The Subjection of Women* (1869)

John Stuart Mill's classic text on nineteenth-century women's rights was influenced by his long intellectual friendship with Harriet Taylor, whom he married in the same year that she published *The Enfranchisement of Women* (1851). Mill's work ranged in subject from logic and metaphysics, history and literature, to economics and political theory. This excerpt expresses the argument that women's enfranchisement was essential to a civilised society in which men and women were friends and companions. Countering the argument that women were unfit to vote, Mill (1806–1873) claimed that woman's nature and true capabilities could not be known, because she had for so long been oppressed by society's norms and expectations.

1.5 Hannah More, *Strictures on Female Education* (1799)

Hannah More (1745–1833) was a key figure in the evangelical religious revival which swept Britain from the 1780s. She was associated with the 'Clapham Sect', a group of high-standing men and women, including William Wilberforce, Henry Thornton and Zachary Macaulay and their families, who led the loyalist response to (French) republican notions of social order in the 1790s. While her Cheap Repository Tracts targeted the poor, More's *Strictures on Female Education* (1799) urged middle- and upper-class women not to be taken in by talk of their 'imaginary rights', but to accept the equally vital 'smaller circle' of domestic life.

1.6 Sarah Stickney Ellis, *Women of England* (1839)

This classic text represents the popularization of evangelical formulations of gender roles during the mid-nineteenth century. Historians tend to agree that there was a hardening of attitudes in the 1830s about women's domestic role, encouraged by the anxiety surrounding the activities of Chartist and Owenite women. Yet, as can be seen in this excerpt, and despite her apologies at the use of the word 'preside', Sarah Ellis (1812–1872) was not advocating subservience for women, who were responsible for no less than the moral status of the nation. Some historians have argued that she was cleverly manipulating domestic ideology to empower women.[1]

1.7 Thomas Wright, The Journeyman Engineer 'Working Men's Homes and Wives' in *The Great Unwashed* (1868)

This excerpt from *The Great Unwashed* by Thomas Wright illustrates that while domesticity and separate spheres had a particular association with the middle class, they were also key characteristics of 'respectability' within the upper working and artisan classes. A man's ability to earn enough of a wage to keep his wife at home and her skill at keeping a clean and comfortable house were central to mid-Victorian respectability. This excerpt raises questions about how far these ideals permeated the working class, and the extent to which they were promoted from within rather than being foisted on the poor from above.

1.8 *Y Gymraes* ('The Welshwoman') (1850)

As well as being a mark of class pride, domesticity could also have a national dimension. *Y Gymraes* was the first Welsh periodical intended specifically for women. It appeared in January 1850 under the editorship of Evan Jones (Ieuan Gwynedd, 1820–1852), an eminent Baptist minister and poet.[2] Jones had been involved in the controversy that followed the publication of the 1847 *Reports of the Commissioners of Inquiry into the State of Education in Wales* (the infamous 'Blue Books'), which were critical of Welsh customs and the morality of the people, especially women. While rebutting such claims, Jones nonetheless believed that there was a need for women to be educated for the role of wife and mother. Jones's concern was with the creation of a virtuous Welsh nation, beyond reproach from the English.

1.9 John Ruskin, 'Of Queen's Gardens' (1865)

For Ruskin (1819–1900), women were 'relative creatures', existing to soothe the brows of men, to be responsive to men's moods and needs and to create the home as a 'haven in a hostile world'. It was natural that the world should be thus organised: men and women, he believed, were of distinct and opposite temperaments, and their education should allow them to develop their innate qualities. There is plenty of evidence to suggest that Ruskin was rather terrified of adult women; his feminine ideal, evident in 'Of Queen's Gardens', is infantile and innocent, inspiring men to chivalry.

1.10 Coventry Patmore, 'The Angel in the House' (1854–1863)

Coventry Patmore (1823–1896) represents women as passive, intuitive, virtuous and graceful. They are the opposite of men and complimentary to them. (Patmore believed his wife Emily was the perfect 'Angel in the House'.) Although the poem did not receive much attention when it was first published, it became increasingly popular, such that in the 1930s Virginia Woolf cited the continued potency of the ideal when she wrote in 'Professions for Women' that '[k]illing the Angel in the House was part of the occupation of a woman writer'.[3]

1.11 William Acton, *The Functions and Disorders of the Reproductive Organs* (1875)

By the middle of the century, it was widely believed that women were passionless beings whose role was primarily reproductive. William Acton (1813–1875), a London physician involved with the development of measures to regulate prostitution, made the distinction between the wife and mistress, endorsing the dominant ideology which saw women as either passive and good, or debased, depraved and corrupt. He believed that wives should consent to sexual intercourse to ensure the health and happiness of their husbands and beyond that, family and society. (See chapter 9 for the response to such ideas from Elizabeth Blackwell.)

1.12 Dr Henry Maudsley, 'Sex in Mind and Education' (1874)

Henry Maudsley (1835–1918), a London psychiatrist, claimed that women were governed by their biology, and those who failed to follow the path of nature and become wives and mothers were in danger of succumbing to hysteria and other 'female maladies'. Maudsley subscribed to the view, articulated by Dr Edward Clarke of Boston (USA) in *Sex in Education* (1873), that the body functioned as closed system, with all parts competing for finite resources. Depletion in one area could lead to exhaustion in another. Thus, women in their fertile years, and especially girls at the age of puberty, should conserve their energy to cope with the process of maturation, and so should avoid strenuous exercise, both physical and intellectual. If they failed to do this, they were likely to become victims of hysteria and other nervous complaints that might do irreversible damage to their reproductive systems. Any desires which deviated from the wifely and the maternal ideal threatened to create an 'unsexed' being. Education for women, in Maudsley's eyes, threatened the very future of the race. (The feminist rejoinder to Maudsley, from Dr Elizabeth Garrett Anderson, is included in chapter 9.)

1.13 Herbert Spencer, *The Principles of Ethics* (1892–1893)

As employment opportunities opened up for women towards the end of the nineteenth century, the possibility that they might choose not to marry alarmed many social theorists. Herbert Spencer (1820–1903), the influential philosopher and social evolutionist, supported the idea of marriage as woman's true vocation. Becoming a wife and mother would enable women to combine personal desires and duties to the nation. In conclusions that were not always consistent or supported by his evidence, he argued that women's rights were determined by their constitution. (The fact that they seemed to have different constitutions in different societies – women in 'primitive' societies worked and did heavy labour, for example – was not examined.) Physically weaker, 'taxed' by their biology, their development arrested because of the energy conserved for reproduction, women were mentally inferior and unstable, and not made for participation in the social and political sphere. Women wanting emancipation, and especially spinsters within the women's movement, were by definition deviant, embittered and unnatural.

1.14 Havelock Ellis, *Studies in the Psychology of Sex* (1901)

The emerging discipline of sexology gave further backing to the idea that marriage and motherhood were the only ways in which women could find health and happiness. Both single women and lesbians, the latter believed to be increasing in number due to the women's movement, became defined in sexological writing as medical and social problems. Havelock Ellis (1859–1939) developed the theory of sexual inversion, defined as 'sexual instinct turned by inborn constitutional abnormality towards persons of the same sex'. As this excerpt shows, sexologists saw 'natural' female sexuality as passive and lesbians as necessarily 'masculine'.

1.15 Dorothea Beale, 'On the Education of Girls' (1865)

For girls and women of the middle and upper classes, taught in private day schools or boarding schools or, if income allowed, by governesses at home, the emphasis was almost exclusively on the acquisition of 'accomplishments', such as singing, drawing and a smattering of modern languages. Dorothea Beale (1831–1906) here criticises the impoverished state of middle-class girls' education, focusing especially on the apathy of parents who were unwilling to make a commitment to the education of their daughters. These criticisms were supported by the 1869 Taunton Commission, which found that girls were usually ahead of boys until the age of 12, when their learning stalled and they made little further progress.

1.16 Harriet Martineau, *Autobiography* (1877)

In this excerpt from her *Autobiography*, Harriet Martineau (1802–1876) describes her passion for classical studies, kindled as a young girl at a local Norwich school run by a Unitarian minister. While his sermons were by her account excessively boring, with her sister Rachel and a few other girls in the class, she enjoyed learning Latin, composition and arithmetic. In her writing on the education of girls, Martineau argued that a wide-ranging education, including history and natural philosophy, was not incompatible with women's domestic duties. Indeed, she claimed in *Household Education* (1849), that the best housekeeper was an educated woman.

1.17 Mary Smith, *The Autobiography of Mary Smith, Schoolmistress and Nonconformist* (1892)

Working-class girls were taught either in dame schools or, from the 1810s, in the monitorial schools provided by the (Anglican) National Society for Promoting the Education of the Poor (1811) and the (Nonconformist) British and Foreign Schools Society (1814). The former emphasised basic literacy, while the latter emphasised religious education and domestic skills, to ensure that working-class girls were adequate wives and mothers and decent servants. Mary Smith, a future Sunday school teacher, claimed that she learned 'nothing or next to nothing' at a local dame school (in Oxfordshire). At her next school, she had to request to be taught mathematics, and resented the time spent doing needlework, as she explains in this excerpt. While many more girls attended Sunday schools, formal schooling remained a minority experience until after the introduction of compulsory elementary education in 1880.

1.18 Grace Foakes, *My Part of the River* (1972)

In this excerpt from *My Part of the River* (1972), Grace Foakes describes the emphasis on domestic skills in her schooling in London's East End in the early years of the twentieth century. In 1878 domestic economy was made compulsory, and girls learned needlework, home management and laundry skills ('cooking, cleaning and clothing'), alongside basic literacy. The moral panic about the health of the nation (see chapter 5) at the turn of the twentieth century saw domestic education extended to the secondary curriculum, as well as to Schools for Mothers. Many girls and their parents saw such instruction as of little use: needlework could easily be learned at home, and cleaning at school was sometimes perceived as skivvying for the headmistress.[4]

1.1   Jean-Jacques Rousseau, *Emile* (1762)

Sophy should be as truly a woman as Emile is a man, i.e., she must possess all those characters of her sex which are required to enable her to play her part in the physical and moral order. Let us inquire to begin with in what respects her sex differs from our own. But for her sex, a woman is a man; she has the same organs, the same needs, the same faculties. The machine is the same in its construction; its parts, its working, and its appearance are similar. Regard it as you will, the difference is only in degree. Yet where sex is concerned woman and man are unlike; each is the complement of the other; the difficulty in comparing them lies in our inability to decide, in either case, what is a matter of sex, and what is not . . .

The man should be strong and active; the woman should be weak and passive; the one must have both the power and the will; it is enough that the other should offer little resistance.

When this principle is admitted, it follows that woman is specifically made for man's delight. If man in his turn ought to be pleasing in her eyes, the necessity is less urgent, his virtue is in his strength, he pleases because he is strong. I grant you this is not the law of love, but it is the law of nature, which is older than love itself.

If woman is made to please and to be in subjection to man, she ought to make herself pleasing in his eyes and not provoke him to anger; her strength is in her charms, by their means she should compel him to discover and use his strength. . . .

The consequences of sex are wholly unlike for man and woman. The male is only a male now and again, the female is always a female, or at least all her youth; everything reminds her of her sex; the performance of her functions requires a special constitution. She needs care during pregnancy and freedom from work when her child is born; she must have a quiet, easy life while she nurses her children; their education calls for patience and gentleness, for a zeal and love which nothing can dismay; she forms a bond between father and child, she alone can win the father's love for his children and convince him that they are indeed his own. What loving care is required to preserve a united family! And there should be no question of virtue in all this, it must be a labour of love, without which the human race would be doomed to extinction.

The mutual duties of the two sexes are not, and cannot be, equally binding on both. Women do wrong to complain of the inequality of man-made laws; this inequality is not of man's making, or at any rate it is not the result of mere prejudice, but of reason. She to whom nature has entrusted the care of the children must hold herself responsible for them to their father. No doubt every breach of faith is wrong, and every faithless husband, who robs his wife of the sole reward of the stern duties of her sex, is cruel and unjust; but the faithless wife is worse; she destroys the family and breaks the bonds of nature; when she gives her husband children who are not his own, she is false both to him and them, her crime is not infidelity but treason . . .

Thus it is not enough that a wife should be faithful; her husband, along with his friends and neighbours, must believe in her fidelity; she must be modest, devoted, retiring; she should have the witness not only of a good conscience, but of a good reputation. In a word, if a father must love his children, he must be able to respect their mother. For these reasons it is not enough that the woman must be chaste, she must preserve her reputation and her good name. . . .

When once it is proved that men and women are and ought to be unlike in constitution and in temperament, it follows that their education should be different. . . .

A woman's education must therefore be planned in relation to man. To be pleasing in his sight, to win his respect and love, to train him in childhood, to tend him in manhood, to counsel and console, to make his life pleasant and happy, these are the duties of woman for all time, and this is what she should be taught while she is young. The further we depart from this principle, the further we shall be from our goal, and all our precepts will fail to secure her happiness or our own.

(Reprint: London: J. M. Dent, 2001, pp. 384–385, 388)

1.2   John Millar, *The Origin of the Distinction of Ranks; or, an inquiry into the circumstances which give rise to influence and authority in the different members of society* (1771)

. . . One of the most remarkable differences between men and other animals consists in that wonderful capacity for the improvement of his faculties with which he is endowed . . .

These improvements are the source of very important changes in the state of society, and particularly in relation to the woman. . . .

When men begin to disuse their ancient barbarous practices, when their attention is not wholly engrossed by the pursuit of military reputation, when they have made some progress in the arts, and have attained to a proportional degree of refinement, they are necessarily led to set a value upon those feminine accomplishments and virtues which have so much influence upon every species of improvement, and which contribute in so many ways to multiply the comforts of life. In this different situation, the women become, neither the slaves, nor the idols of the other sex, but the friends and companions. The wife obtains that rank and station which appears most agreeable to reason, being suited to her character and talents. Loaded by nature with the first and most immediate concern in rearing and maintaining the children, she is endowed with such dispositions which put her for the discharge of this important duty, and is at the same time particularly qualified for all such employments as require skill and dexterity more than strength, which are so necessary in the interior movement of the family. Possessed of peculiar delicacy, and sensibility, whether derived from original constitution, or from her way of life, she is capable of securing the esteem and affection of her husband by dividing his cares, by sharing his joys, and by soothing his misfortunes.

The regard, which is thus shown to the useful talents and accomplishments of the woman, cannot fail to operate in directing their education, and in forming their manners. They learn to suit their behaviour to the circumstances in which they are placed, and to that particular standard of propriety and excellence which is set before them. Being respected upon account of their diligence and proficiency in the various branches of domestic economy, they naturally endeavour to improve and extend those valuable qualifications. They are taught to apply with assiduity to those occupations which fall under their province, and to look upon idleness as the greatest blemish on the female character. They are instructed betimes in whatever will equal them for the duties of their station, and is thought conducive to the ornament of private life. Engaged in those solid pursuits they are less apt to be distinguished by such brilliant accomplishments as make a figure in the circle of gaiety and amusement. Accorded to live in retirement, and to keep company with their nearest realms and friends, they are inspired with all that modesty and diffidence which is natural to persons unacquainted with promiscuous conversation; and their affections are neither dissipated by pleasure, nor corrupted by the vicious customs of the world. As their attention is principally bestowed upon the members of their own family, they are led in a particular manner to improve those feelings of the heart which are excited by those tender connections, and they are trained up in the practice of all the domestic virtues.

(London: J. Murray, 1779, 3rd edition, pp. 107–111)

1.3 Mary Wollstonecraft, *Vindication of the Rights of Woman* (1792)

Women are everywhere in this deplorable state; for, in order to preserve their innocence, as ignorance is courteously termed, truth is hidden from them, and they are made to assume an artificial character before their faculties have acquired any strength. Taught from their infancy that beauty is woman's sceptre, the mind shapes itself to the body, and roaming around its gilt cage, only seeks to adorn its prison. Men have various employments and pursuits which engage their attention, and give a character to the opening mind; but women, confined to one, and having their thoughts constantly directed to the most insignificant part of themselves, seldom extend their views beyond the triumph of the hour. But were their understanding once emancipated from the slavery to which the pride and sensuality of man and their short-sighted desire, like that of dominion in tyrants, of present sway, has subjected them, we should probably read of their weaknesses with surprise . . .

Let not men then in the pride of power, use the same arguments that tyrannic kings and venal ministers have used, and fallaciously assert that woman ought to be subjected because she has always been so. But, when man, governed by reasonable laws, enjoys his natural freedom, let him despise woman, if she does not share it with him; and, till that glorious period arrives, in descanting on the folly of the sex, let him not overlook his own . . .

It is time to effect a revolution in female manners – time to restore to them their lost dignity – and make them, as a part of the human species, labour by reforming themselves to reform the world. It is time to separate unchangeable morals from local manners . . .

Besides, if a woman be educated for dependence, that is, to act according to the will of another fallible being, and submit, right or wrong, to power, where are we to stop? Are they to be considered as vicegerents allowed to reign over a small domain, and answerable for their conduct to a higher tribunal, liable to error?

It will not be difficult to prove that such delegates will act like men subjected by fear, and make their children and servants endure their tyrannical oppression. As they submit without reason, they will, having no fixed rules to square their conduct by, be kind, or cruel, just as the whim of the moment directs; and we ought not to wonder if sometimes, galled by their heavy yoke, they take a malignant pleasure in resting it on weaker shoulders.

But, supposing a woman, trained up to obedience, be married to a sensible man, who directs her judgement without making her feel the servility of her subjection, to act with as much propriety by this reflected light as can be expected when reason is taken at second-hand, yet she cannot ensure the life of her protector; he may die and leave her with a large family.

A double duty devolves on her; to educate them in the character of both father and mother; to form their principles and secure their property. But alas! she has never thought, much less acted for herself. She has only learned to please men, to depend gracefully on them; yet, encumbered with children, how is she to obtain another protector – a husband to supply the place of reason? A rational man, for we are not treading on romantic ground, though he may think her a pleasing docile creature, will not choose to marry a *family* for love, when the world contains many more pretty creatures. What is then to become of her? She either falls an easy prey to some mean fortune-hunter, who defrauds her children of their paternal inheritance, and renders her miserable; or becomes the victim of discontent and blind indulgence. Unable to educate her sons, or impress them with respect, – for it is not a play on words to assert, that people are never respected, though filling an important station, who are not respectable, – she pines under the anguish of unavailing impotent regret. The serpent's tooth enters into her very soul, and the vices of licentious youth bring her with sorrow, if not with poverty also, to the grave . . .

It does not require a lively pencil, or the discriminating outline of a caricature, to sketch the domestic miseries and petty vices which such a mistress of a family diffuses. Still she only acts as a woman ought to act, brought up according to Rousseau's system. She can never be reproached for being masculine, or turning out of her sphere; nay, she may observe another of his grand rules, and, cautiously preserving her reputation free from spot, be reckoned a good kind of woman. Yet in what respect can she be termed good? She abstains, it is true, without any great struggle, from committing gross crimes; but how does she fulfil her duties? Duties! In truth she has enough to think of to adorn her body and nurse a weak constitution.

(Reprint: Harmondsworth: Penguin, 1983, pp. 131–132, 135–137)

1.4   J. S. Mill, *The Subjection of Women* (1869)

All causes, social and natural, combine to make it unlikely that women should be collectively rebellious to the power of men. They are so far in a position different from all other subject classes, that their masters require something more from them than actual service. Men do not want solely the obedience of women, they want their sentiments. All men, except the most brutish, desire to have, in the woman most nearly connected with them, not a forced slave but a willing one, not a slave merely, but a favourite. They have therefore put everything in practice to enslave their minds. The masters of all other slaves rely, for maintaining obedience, on fear; either fear of themselves, or religious fears. The masters of women wanted more than simple obedience, and they turned the whole force of education to effect their purpose. All women are brought up from the very earliest years in the belief that their ideal of character is the very opposite to that of men; not self-will, and government by self-control, but submission, and yielding to the control of other. All the moralities tell them that it is the duty of women, and all the current sentimentalities that it is their nature, to live for others; to make complete abnegation of themselves, and to have no life but in their affections. And by their affections are meant the only ones they are allowed to have – those to the men with whom they are connected, or to the children who constitute an additional and indefeasible tie between them and a man. When we put together three things – first, the natural attraction between opposite sexes; secondly, the wife's entire dependence on the husband, every privilege or pleasure she has being either his gift, or depending entirely on his will; and lastly, that the principal object of human pursuit, consideration, and all objects of social ambition, can in general be sought or obtained by her only through him, it would be a miracle if the object of being attractive to men had not become the polar star of feminine education and formation of character. And, this great means of influence over the minds of women having been acquired, an instinct of selfishness made men avail themselves of it to the utmost as a means of holding women in subjection, by representing to them meekness, submissiveness, and resignation of all individual will into the hands of a man, as an essential part of sexual attractiveness. Can it be doubted that any of the other yokes which mankind have succeeded in breaking, would have subsisted till now if the same means had existed, and had been so sedulously used, to bow down their minds to it? . . .

Standing on the ground of common sense and the constitution of the human mind, I deny that anyone knows, or can know, the nature of the two sexes, as long as they have only been seen in their present relation to one another. If men had ever been found in society without women, or women without men, or if there had been a society of men and women in which the women were not under the control of the men, something might have been positively known about the mental and moral differences which may be inherent in the nature of each. What is now called the nature of women is an eminently artificial thing – the result of forced repression in some directions, unnatural stimulation in others. . . .
(London: Longman, Green, Reader and Dyer, 1869, pp. 26–29, 38–39)

1.5 Hannah More, *Strictures on the Modern System of Female Education with a view of the principles and conduct prevalent among women of rank and fortune, etc.*, Vol. II (1799)

But *they* little understand the true interests of women who would lift her from the duties of her allotted station, to fill with fantastic dignity a loftier but less appropriate niche. Nor do they understand her true happiness, who seek to annihilate distinctions from which she derives advantages, and to attempt innovations which would depreciate her real value. Each sex has its proper excellencies, which would be lost were they melted down into the common character by the fusion of the new philosophy. Why should we do away distinctions which increase the mutual benefits and satisfactions of life? Whence, but by carefully preserving the original marks of difference stamped by the hand of the Creator, would be denied the superior advantage of mixed society? Have men no need to have their rough angles filed off, and their harshness and asperities smoothed and polished by assimilating with beings of more softness and refinement? Are the ideas of women naturally so very judicious, are their principles so invincibly firm, are their views so perfectly correct, are their judgements so completely exact, that there is occasion for no additional weight, no superadded strength, no increased clearness, none of that enlargement of mind, none of that additional invigoration which may be derived from the aids of the stronger sex? What identity did advantageously supercede an enlivening and interesting variety of character? Is it not then more wise as well as more honourable to move contentedly in the plain path which Providence has obviously marked out to the sex, and in which custom has for the most part rationally confirmed them, rather than to stray awkwardly, unbecomingly, and unsuccessfully, in a forbidden road? to be the lawful professors of a lesser domestic territory rather than the turbulent usurpers of a wider foreign empire? to be good originals, rather than bad imitators? to be the best thing of one's own kind, rather than an inferior thing even if it were of an higher kind? to be excellent women rather than indifferent men?

Is the author then undervaluing her own sex? – No. It is her zeal for their true *interests* which leads her to oppose their imaginary *rights* . . .

In almost all that comes under the description of polite letters, in all that captivates by imagery, or warms by just and affecting sentiment, women are excellent. They possess in a high degree that delicacy and quickness of perception, and that nice discernment between the beautiful and defective, which comes under the denomination of taste. Both in composition and action they excel in details; but they do not so much generalize their ideas as men, nor do their minds seize a great subject with so large a grasp. They are acute observers, and accurate judges of life and manners, as far as their own sphere of observation extends; but they describe a smaller circle. A woman sees the world, as it were, from a little elevation in her own garden, whence she takes an exact survey of home scenes, but takes not in that wider range of distant prospects, which he who stands on a loftier eminence commands.

(London: T. Cadell and W. Davies, pp. 21–26)

1.6   Sarah Stickney Ellis, *The Women of England, their Social Duties, and Domestic Habits* (1839)

Every country has its peculiar characteristics, not only of climate and scenery, of public institutions, government, and laws; but every country also has its moral characteristics, upon which is founded its true title to a station, either high or low, in the scale of nations.

The national characteristics of England are the perpetual boast of her patriotic sons; and there is one especially, which it behoves all British subjects not only to exult in, but to cherish and maintain. Leaving the justice of her laws, the extent of her commerce, and the amount of her resources, to the orator, the statesman, and the political economist, there yet remains one of the noblest features in her national character, which may not improperly be regarded as within the compass of a woman's understanding, and the province of a woman's pen. It is the domestic character of England – the home comforts, and fireside virtues for which she is so justly celebrated. . . .

In other countries, where the domestic lamp is voluntarily put out, in order to allow the women to resort to the opera, or the public festival, they are not only careless about their home comforts, but necessarily ignorant of the high degree of excellence to which they might be raised. In England there is a kind of science of good household management, which, if it consisted merely in keeping the house respectable in its physical character, might be left to the effectual working out of the hired hands; but, happily for the women of England, there is a philosophy in this science, but which all their highest and best feelings are called into exercise. Not only must the house be neat and clean, but it must be so ordered as to suit the tastes of all, as far as may be, without arrogance or offence to any. Not only must a constant system of activity be established, but peace must be preserved, or happiness must be destroyed. Not only must elegance be called in, to adorn and beautify the whole, but strict integrity must be maintained by the minutest calculation as to lawful means, and self, and self-gratification, must be made the yielding point in every disputed case. Not only must an appearance of outward order and comfort be kept up, but around every domestic scene there must be a strong wall of confidence, which no internal suspicion can undermine, no external enemy break through.

Good household management, conducted on this plan, is indeed a science well worthy of attention. It comprises so much, as to invest it with an air of difficulty on first view; but no woman can reasonably complain of incapability; because nature has endowed the sex with perception so lively and acute, that where benevolence is the impulse, and principle the foundation upon which they act, experience will soon teach them by what means they may best accomplish the end they have in view.

It might form a subject of interesting inquiry, how far the manifold advantages of England as a country, derive their origin remotely from the cause already described; but the immediate object of the present work is to show how intimate is the connection which exists between the women of England and the moral character maintained by their country in the scale of nations. For a woman to undertake such a task, may at first sight appear like an act of presumption; yet when it is considered that the appropriate business of men is to direct, and expatiate upon, these expansive and important measures to which their capabilities are more peculiarly adapted, and that to women belongs the minute and particular observance of all those trifles which fill up the sum of human happiness or misery, it may surely be deemed pardonable for a woman to solicit the serious attention of her sex, while she endeavours to prove that it is the minor morals of domestic life which give the tone to English character, and that over this sphere of duty it is her peculiar province to preside.

Aware that the word preside, used as it is here, may prod a startling effect upon the ear of man, I must endeavour to bespeak his forbearance, by assuring him, that the highest aim of the writer does not extend beyond the act of warning the woman of England back to her domestic duties, in order that they become better wives, more useful daughters, and mothers, who by their example shall bequeath a rich inheritance to those who follow in their steps.

(London: Fisher, Son, and Co., 1839, pp. 9–10, 39–40)

1.7   The Journeyman Engineer (Thomas Wright), 'Working Men's Homes and Wives' in *The Great Unwashed* (1868)

Comfort is the one great essential to a home; without it there can be no home in the best sense of the word: and yet in numberless humble dwellings it has no place – mess and muddle reigning in its stead. That the houses of the working classes are not what they ought to be and might be, has long been notorious; and we have at length had some practical legislation with a view to their improvement. The general opinion seems to be, that the class of houses in which labouring men are compelled to live is solely to blame in this matter; and to this point – the only one indeed on which it could be brought to bear – legislative action has been directed. But the style of a house, though an important, is still a secondary element in the constitution of a home. As

> 'Stone walls do not a prison make,
> Nor iron bars a cage;'

so a house alone does not make a home. Among the working classes the wife makes the home. In no other rank of life are the home-influences so powerfully and directly felt. The working man's wife is also his housekeeper, cook, and several other single domestics rolled into one; and on her being a managing or mismanaging woman depends whether the dwelling will be a home proper, or house which is not a home. Whatever sanatory or architectural improvements may be made in artisans' dwellings, it will still be found, while wives remain as they are, that of homes supported upon like incomes, one will be a veritable 'little palace' in point of comfort, while another will be a domestic slough of despond.

(New York: Augustus M. Kelley, 1970 [1868]), pp. 30–32)

1.8   *Y Gymraes* ('The Welshwoman'), January 1850

... There is not a considerate man who does not want to see a great improvement among the women of Wales in all respects. The wish is for far more intelligent girls, maids, daughters, wives and mothers ...

How comfortable families would be if their *daughters* were intelligent and knowledgeable. If it were so there would be fewer complaints regarding pride at dress, attendance at fairs and straying from the path of virtue. Girls could control the anger of brothers, cheer up their fathers' minds, and bring joy to their mothers' hearts. Knowledge would create self-respect and self-respect would create respect for character. This would save families from having to drink from the many bitter cups which are placed in their hands at present ...

The happiness of the husband depends upon the *wife*. Upon her, to a considerable degree depends the success of their circumstances and their peace of mind. If the wife has not understood the importance of her situation, it is unlikely that she will fulfil her duties properly ... However excellent the wives of Wales are at present, they could be better, and their improvement would be a comfort to themselves and to those around them ...

As for the sphere of duty of the *mother*, it is evident that her importance is beyond description. Mothers are LIFE in all its meaning ... And who does not weep when they consider how often spirits are starved by the shameful ignorance of a mother. 'The language of the mother' will be the language of the child – the habits of the mother will be his habits; as she thinks, he will also think, for she is all in his education ...

We should not forget that there is one particular evil which blights the honourable character of the women of Wales. While we decry to the depths of our souls those who have endeavoured to portray the inchastity of Wales as though it were a frightening plague of which England and other countries are free; and while we are ready to prove that Wales stands higher than any other nation on the continent of Europe, yet, we cannot conceal our deep heartache that the enemy somtimes has cause to blaspheme. We would like to see Wales PURE. We would like to see all her children able to recite their parents' names without blushing . . . If we could achieve this [the disappearance of illegitimacy], we could consider Wales a paradise on earth. Until then, there is a serpent hiding in her bushes, poisoning her most beautiful flowers.

It is not our intention to tread the same path as that of other Welsh publications – religion will not be the main topic of our articles; our ambition is the elevation of the female sex in all respects – social, moral and religious. Our aim is to co-operate with the educational institutions of our age to produce faithful maids, virtuous daughters, provident wives and intelligent mothers . . .

It is understood, without our having to say so, that it will be our pleasure to nurture a national spirit among the Welsh. We do not wish to make Englishwomen of them. 'Cymru, Cymro a Chymraeg' [Wales, Welsh(man) and the Welsh language] are very dear to our hearts. Our wish is that our female readers will love the hills and vales, the rivers and springs of our land with 'a wife's love'. Our wish is that the next generation will be proud of their country, their language and full of determination truly to realise the motto,

'CYMRU FU, CYMRU FYDD'.
[Wales has been, Wales shall be' or 'Wales of the past, Wales for the future']

1.9   John Ruskin, 'Of Queen's Gardens', *Sesames and Lilies* (1865)

We are foolish, and without excuse, in speaking of the 'superiority' of one sex over the other, as if they could be compared in similar things. Each has what the other has not: each completes the other, and is completed by the other; they are in nothing alike, and the happiness and perfection of both depends on each asking and receiving from the other what the other only can give.

Now their separate characters are briefly this. The man's power is active, progressive, defensive. He is eminently the doer, the creator, the discoverer, the defender. His intellect is for speculation and invention; his energy for adventure, for war, and for conquest, wherever war is just, wherever conquest necessary. But the woman's power is for rule, not for battle, – and her intellect is not for invention or creation, but for sweet ordering, arrangement, and decision. She sees the qualities of things, their claims and their places. Her great function is praise: she enters into the contest, but infallibly judges the crown of contest. By her office, and place, she is protected from all danger and temptation. The man, in his rough work in open world, must encounter all peril and trial: – to him, therefore, the failure, the offence, the inevitable error: if he must be wounded, or subdued, often misled, and *always* hardened. But he guards the woman from all this; within his house, as ruled by her, unless she herself has sought it, need enter no danger, no temptation, no cause of error or offence. This is the true nature of home – it is the place of Peace; the shelter, not only from all injury, but from all terror, doubt and division. In so far as it is not this, it is not home; so far as the anxieties of the outer world is allowed by either husband or wife to cross the threshold, it ceases to be home; it is then only a part of that outer world which you have roofed over, and lighted fire in. But so far as it is a sacred place, a vestal temple, a temple of the hearth watched over by House Gods, before whose faces none may come but those whom they can receive with love, – so far as it is this, and roof and fire are types only of a nobler shade and light, – shades as if the rock in a weary land, and light as if the Pharos in the stormy seas – so far it vindicates the name, and fulfils the praise, of home . . .

This, then, I believe to be, – will you not admit it to be, – the woman's true place and power? But do you not see that to fulfil this, she must – as far as one can use such terms of a human creature – be incapable of error? So far as she rules, all must be right, or nothing is. She must be enduringly, incorruptibly good; instinctively, infallibly wise – wise, not for self-development, but for self-renunciation; wise, not that she may set herself above her husband, but that she may never fail from his side: wise, not with the narrowness of insolent and loveless pride, but with the passive gentleness of an infinitely variable, because infinitely applicable, modesty of service – the true changefulness of woman in that greatest sense – 'La donna e mobile', not 'Qual pium al vento'; no, nor yet 'Variable as the shade, by the light quivering aspen made'; but variable as the *light*, manifold in fair and serene division, that it may take the colour of all that it falls upon, and exalt it.

(New York: Wiley and Sons, 1865, pp. 90–92)

1.10   Coventry Patmore, *The Angel in the House* (1854–1863)

Canto X: Sahara

Preludes

I The Wife's Tragedy
Man must be pleased; but him to please
Is woman's pleasure; down the gulf
Of his condoled necessities
She casts her best, she flings herself.
How often flings for nought, and yokes
Her heart to an icicle or whim,
Whose each impatient word provokes
Another, not from her, but him;
While she, too gentle even to force
His penitence by kind replies,
Waits by, expecting his remorse,
With pardon in her pitying eyes;
And if he once, by shame oppress'd,
A comfortable word confers,
She leans and weeps against his breast,
And seems to think the sin was hers;
Or any eye to see her charms,
At any time, she's still his wife,
Dearly devoted to his arms;
She loves with love that cannot tire;
And when, ah woe, she loves alone,
Through passionate duty love springs higher,
As grass grows taller round a stone.

1.11 William Acton, *The Functions and Disorders of the Reproductive Organs, in Childhood, Youth, Adult Age, and Advanced Life, Considered in Their Physiological, Social, and Moral Relations* (1875)

. . . I should say that the majority of women (happily for society) are not very much troubled with sexual feeling of any kind. What men are habitually, women are only exceptionally. It is too true, I admit, and as the Divorce Court shows, that there are some few women who have sexual desires so strong that they surpass those of men, and shock public feeling by their consequences. I admit, of course, the existence of sexual excitement terminating even in nymphomania, a form of insanity that those accustomed to visit lunatic asylums must be fully conversant with; but, with these sad exceptions, there can be no doubt that sexual feeling in the female is in the majority of cases in abeyance, and that it requires positive and considerable excitement to be roused at all; and even if roused (which in many instances it never can be) it is very moderate compared with that of the male. . . .

I am ready to maintain that there are many females who never feel any sexual excitement whatever. Others, again, immediately after each period, do become, to a limited degree, capable of experiencing it; but this capacity is often temporary, and may entirely cease till the next menstrual period. Many of the best mothers, wives, and managers of households, know little of or are careless about sexual indulgences. Love of home, of children, and of domestic duties are the only passions they feel.

As a general rule, a modest woman seldom desires any sexual gratification for herself. She submits to her husband's embraces, but principally to gratify him; and, were it not for the desire of maternity, would far rather be relieved from his attentions. No nervous or feeble young man need, therefore, be deterred from marriage by an exaggerated notion of the arduous duties required from him. Let him be well assured, on my authority backed by the opinion of many, that the married woman has no wish to be placed on the footing of a mistress.

One instance may better illustrate the real state of the case than much description.

In ——, 185–, a barrister about thirty years of age, came to me on account of sexual debility. On cross-examination I found he had been married a twelve month, that an attempt at connection had taken place but once since the commencement of the year, and that even then there was some doubt as to the completion of the act. He brought his wife with him, as she was, he said, desirous of having some conversation with me.

I found the lady a refined but highly sensitive person. Speaking with a freedom equally removed from assurance, or *mauvaise honte*, she told me she thought it her duty to consult me. She neither blushed nor faltered in telling her story, and I regret that my words must fail to convey the delicacy with which her avowal was made.

Her husband and herself, she said, had been acquainted from childhood, had grown up together, became mutually attached, and married. She had reason to consider him debilitated, but – as she was fully convinced – from no indiscrete acts on his part. She believed it was his natural condition. She was dotingly attached to him, and would not have determined to consult me, but that she wished for his sake, to have a family, as it would, she hoped, conduce to their mutual happiness. She assured me that she felt no sexual passions whatever; that if she was capable of them they were dormant. Her passion for her husband was of a Platonic kind, and far from wishing to stimulate his frigid feelings, she doubted whether it would be right or not. She loved him as he was, and would not desire him to be otherwise except for the hope of having a family.

I believe this lady is a perfect example of an English wife and mother, kind, considerate, self-sacrificing, and sensible, so pure-hearted as to be utterly ignorant of and averse to any sensual indulgence, but so unselfishly attached to the man she loves, as to be willing to give up her own wishes and feelings for his sake.

(London: J. and A. Churchill, pp. 212–214)

1.12   Dr Henry Maudsley, 'Sex in Mind and Education', *The Fortnightly Review*, Vol. XV (1874)

Those who view without prejudice, or with some sympathy, the movements for improving the higher education of women, and for throwing open to them fields of activity from which they are now excluded, have a hard matter of it sometimes to prevent a feeling of reaction being aroused in their minds by the arguments of the most eager of those who advocate the reform. Carried away by their zeal into an enthusiasm which borders on or reaches fanaticism, they seem positively to ignore the fact that there are significant differences between the sexes, arguing in effect as if it were nothing more than an affair of clothes, and to be resolved, in their indignation at woman's wrongs, to refuse her the simple rights of her sex. . . .

It is quite evident that many of those who are foremost in their zeal for raising the education and social status of women, have not given proper consideration to the nature of her organization, and to the demands which its special functions make upon its strength . . . These are matters which it is not easy to discuss out of a medical journal; but, in view of the subject at the present stage of the question of female education, it becomes a duty to use plainer language than would otherwise be fitting in a literary journal. The gravity of the subject can hardly be exaggerated. Before sanctioning the proposal to submit woman to a system of mental training which has been framed and adapted for men, and under which they have become what they are, it is needful to consider whether this can be done without serious injury to her health and strength. It is not enough to point to exceptional instances of women who have undergone such a training, and have proved their capacities when tried by the same standard as men; without doubt there are women who can, and will, so distinguish themselves, if stimulus be applied and opportunity given; the question is, whether they may not do it at a cost which is too large a demand upon the resources of their nature. Is it well for them to contend on equal terms with men for the goal of man's ambition?

Let it be considered that the period of the real educational strain will commence about the time when, by the development of the sexual system, a great revolution takes place in the body and mind, and an extraordinary expenditure of vital energy is made, and will continue through those years after puberty when, by the establishment of periodical functions, a regularly recurring demand is made upon the resources of a constitution that is going through the final stages of its growth and development. The energy of a human body being a definite and not inexhaustible quantity, can it bear, without injury, an excessive mental drain as well as the natural physical drain which is so great at that time? Or, will the profit of the one be to the detriment of the other? . . .

When we thus look at the matter honestly in the face, it would seem plain that women are marked out by nature for very different offices in life from those of men, and that the healthy performance of her special function renders it improbable she will succeed, and unwise for her to persevere, in running over the same course at the same pace with him. For such a race she is certainly weighted unfairly. Nor is it a sufficient reply to this argument to allege, as is sometimes done, that there are many women who have not the opportunity of getting married, or who do not aspire to bear children; for whether they care to be mothers or not, they cannot dispense with those physiological functions of their nature that have reference to that aim, however much they might wish it, and they cannot disregard them in the labour of life without injury to their health. They cannot choose but to be women; cannot rebel success-fully against the tyranny of their organization, the complete develop-ment and function whereof must take place after its kind. This is not the expression of prejudice nor of false sentiment; it is the plain statement of a physiological fact. . . .

(London: Chapman and Hall, 1874, pp. 466–483)

1.13   Herbert Spencer, *The Principles of Ethics,* Vol. I (1892–1893)

All activities fall into two great groups – those which constitute and sustain the life of the individual, and those which further the life of the race; and it seems inferable that if for full health the structures conducive to the one must severally perform their functions, so must the functions conducive to the other. Such part of the organization as is devoted to the production of offspring, can scarcely be left inert and leave the rest of the organization unaffected. The not infrequent occurrence of hysteria and chlorosis shows that women, in whom the reproductive functions bears a larger ratio to the totality of the functions than it does in men, are apt to suffer grave consti-tutional evils from that incompleteness of life which celibacy implies: grave evils to which there probably correspond smaller and un-perceived evils in numerous cases. . . . That the physiological effects of a completely celibate life on either sex are to some extent injurious, seems an almost necessary implication of the natural conditions.

But whether or not there be disagreement on this point, there can be none respecting the effects of a celibate life as mentally injurious. A large part of the nature – partly intellectual but chiefly emotional – finds its sphere of action in the marital relation, and afterwards in the parental relation; and if this sphere be closed, some of the higher feelings must remain inactive and others but feebly active. . . .

The immediate cause of this greater energy is the increased quantity of emotion which the marital relation, and after it the parental relation, excite; and there is to be recognized both a greater body of emotion, and a higher form of emotion. To the lower egoistic feelings which previously formed the chief, if not only stimuli, are now added those higher egoistic feelings which find their satisfaction in the affections, together with those altruistic feelings which find their satisfaction in the happiness of others. What potent influences on character thus come into play, is shown in the moral transformation which marriage frequently effects. Often the vain and thoughtless girl, caring only for amusements, becomes changed into the devoted wife and mother; and often the man who is ill-tempered and unsympathetic, becomes changed into the self-sacrificing husband and father. To which add that there is usually exercised, more than before, the discipline of self-restraint.

Some effect, too, is wrought on the thinking faculties; not, perhaps, in their power, but in their balance. In women the intellectual activity is frequently diminished; for the antagonism between individuation and reproduction, which is in them most pronounced, tells more especially on the brain. But to both husband and wife there daily come many occasions for exercises of judgment, alike in their relations to domestic affairs, to one another, and to children – exercises of judgment which in the celibate state were not called for; and hence an increase of intellectual stability and sense of proportion.

(London: Williams and Norgate, 1892, pp. 534–536)

1.14   Havelock Ellis, *Studies in the Psychology of Sex*, Vol. II: *Sexual Inversion* (1901)

The commonest characteristic of the sexually inverted woman is a certain degree of masculinity or boyishness. . . .

When they still retain female garments, these usually show some traits of masculine simplicity, and there is nearly always a disdain for the petty feminine artifices of the toilet. Even when this is not obvious there are all sorts of instinctive gestures and habits which may suggest to female acquaintances the remark that such a person 'ought to have been a man'. The brusque, energetic movements, the attitude of the arms, the direct speech, the inflexions of the voice, the masculine straightforwardness and sense of honor, and especially the attitude towards men, free from any suggestion either of shyness or audacity, will often suggest the underlying psychic abnormality to a keen observer.

In the habits not only is there frequently a pronounced taste for smoking cigarettes, often found in quite feminine women, but also a decided taste for and toleration of cigars. There is also a dislike and sometimes an incapacity for needle-work and other domestic occupations, while there is often some capacity for athletics. . . .

The inverted woman is an enthusiastic admirer of feminine beauty, especially of the statuesque beauty of the body, unlike, in this, the normal woman, whose sexual emotion is but faintly tinged by aesthetic feeling. In her sexual habits we perhaps less often find the degree of promiscuity which is not uncommon among inverted men, and we may perhaps agree with Moll that homosexual women are more often apt to love faithfully and lastingly than homosexual men. . . .

Inverted women are not rarely married. Moll, from various confidences which he has received, believes that inverted women have not the same horror of normal coitus as inverted men; this is probably due to the fact that the woman under such circumstances can retain a certain passivity. In other cases there is some degree of psycho-sexual bisexuality, although, as among inverted men, the homosexual instinct seems usually to give the greater relief and gratification.

It has been stated by many observers – in America, in France, in Germany, and in England – that homosexuality is increasing among women. There are many influences in our civilization today which encourage such manifestations. The modern movement of emancipation – the movement to obtain the same rights and duties as men, the same freedom and responsibility, the same education and the same work – must be regarded as, on the whole, a wholesome and inevitable movement. But it carries with it certain disadvantages. Women are, very justly, coming to look upon knowledge and experience generally as their right as much as their brothers' right. But when this doctrine is applied to the sexual sphere it finds certain limitations. Intimacies of any kind between young men and young women are as much discouraged socially now as ever they were; as regards higher education, the mere association of the sexes in the lecture-room or the laboratory or the hospital is discouraged in England and in America. While men are allowed freedom, the sexual field of women is becoming restricted to trivial flirtation with the opposite sex, and to intimacy with their own sex; having been taught independence of men and disdain for the old theory which placed women in the moated grange of the home to sigh for a man who never comes, a tendency develops for women to carry this independence still further and to find love where they find work. These unquestionable influences of modern movements cannot directly cause sexual inversion, but they develop the germs of it, and they probably cause a spurious imitation. This spurious imitation is due to the fact that the congenital anomaly occurs with special frequency in women of high intelligence who, voluntarily or involuntarily, influence others.

(Reprint: Philadelphia: F. A. Davies, 1917, pp. 244–250, 260–263)

1.15 Dorothea Beale, 'On the Education of Girls' (1865)

First, then, I think that the education of girls has too often been made showy, rather than real and useful – that accomplishments have been made the main thing, because these would, it was thought, enable a girl to shine and attract, while those branches of study especially calculated to form the judgments, to cultivate the understanding, and to discipline the character (which would fit her to perform the *duties* of life), have been neglected; and thus, while temporary pleasure and profit have been sought, the great moral ends of education have too often been lost sight of.

To the poorer classes the daily toil and struggles of their early life do, to some extent, afford an education which gives earnestness, and strength, and reality; and if we would not have the daughters of the higher classes idle and frivolous, they too must be taught to appreciate the value of work. We must endeavour to give them, while young, such habits, studies, and occupations, as will brace the mind, improve the taste, and develop the moral character. They must learn, not for the sake of display, but from motives of duty. They must not choose the easy and agreeable, and neglect what is dull and inviting. They must not expect to speak languages without mastering the rudiments; not require to be finished in a year or two, but impatiently refuse to labour at a foundation . . .

I have a set of papers written by girls much younger in St Paul's district school here, which are greatly superior . . . We may well ask, how is such a state of things possible? How is it that the daughters of the higher middle classes are more ignorant and untrained than the children of the national schools? I think one cause is that parents have too often trusted, when they should have inquired; they frequently spend from £100 to £200 a year on sending their daughters from home; during the holidays they hear the piano, they see the drawings (not always the pupil's own) but how often do they institute any inquiry into the progress made in any other branches; or, if unable to undertake it themselves, how rarely do they care that there should be a system of examination to see whether the work is properly done. They are afraid of popular outcry, afraid of the excitement, afraid that their children should take a low place, forgetting that (if the examination be conducted without any of the improper excitement of publicity) it is also a test and means of moral training, since those who work from the right results simply do their best, and are not over-anxious about results. I do not desire that there should be a system of competitive examination, but a general testing of the work done, and if this cannot be responded to in a quiet lady-like manner, it does not speak well for the moral training of the school.

Another cause is that girls are often placed in an inferior school, or under incompetent governesses, or allowed to work in a desultory way until they are 14 or 15. Plans and governesses and schools are changed for a passing fancy, and then they are sent to one with a high reputation, this is thought will be enough for them, 'as they are not required to be learned ladies.'

I ask whether a boy educated on this plan would be good for much; would he or would he not be likely to have acquired habits of lazy self-indulgence? And is a girl so trained likely to prove a diligent and wise and thoughtful woman?

(A paper read at the Social Science Congress, October 1865,
reprinted from the *Transaction* (London:
Bell and Daldy, 1866), pp. 1–4)

1.16   Harriet Martineau, *Autobiography*, Vol. I (1877)

When I was young, it was not thought proper for young ladies to study very conspicuously; and especially with pen in hand. Young ladies (at least in provincial towns) were expected to sit down in the parlour to sew, – during which reading aloud was permitted, – or to practise their music; but so as to be fit to receive callers, without any signs of blue-stockingism which could be reported abroad. Jane

Austen herself, the Queen of novelists, the immortal creator of Anne Elliott, Mr. Knightley, and a score of two more of unrivalled intimate friends of the whole public, was compelled by the feelings of her family to cover up her manuscripts with a large piece of muslin work, kept on the table for the purpose, whenever any genteel people came in. So it was with other young ladies, for some time after Jane Austen was in her grace; and thus my first studies in philosophy were carried on with great care and reserve. I was at the work table regularly after breakfast, – making my own clothes, or the shirts of the household, or about some fancy work: I went out walking with the rest, – before dinner in winter, and after tea in summer: and if I ever shut myself into my own room for an hour of solitude, I knew it was at the risk of being sent for to join the sewing-circle, or to read aloud, – I being the reader, on account of my growing deafness. But I won time for what my heart was set upon, nonetheless, – either in the early morning, or late at night. I had a strange passion for translating, in those days; and a good preparation it proved for the subsequent work of my life. Now, it was meeting James at seven in the morning to read Loweth's Prelections in the Latin, after having been busy since five about something else, in my own room. Now it was translating Tactitus, in order to try what was the utmost compression of style that I could attain. . . . Our cousin J.M.L., then studying for his profession in Norwich, used to read Italian with Rachel and me, – also before breakfast. We made some considerable progress, through the usual course of prose authors and poets; and out of this grew a fit which Rachel and I at one time took, in concert with our companions and neighbours, the C's, to translate Petrarch. Nothing could be better as an exercise in composition than translating Petrarch's sonnets into English of the same limits. It was putting ourselves under compulsion to do with the Italian what I had set myself voluntarily to do with the Latin author. I believe we really succeeded pretty well; and I am sure that all these exercises were a singularly apt preparation for my after work. At the same time, I went on studying Blair's Rhetoric (for want of a better guide) and inclining mightily to every kind of book or process which could improve my literary skill, – really as if I had foreseen how I was to spend my life.

These were not, however, my most precious or serious studies. I studied the Bible incessantly and immensely; both by daily reading of chapters, after the approved but mischievous method, and by getting hold of all commentaries and works of elucidation that I could lay my hands on. A work of Dr Carpenter's, begun but never finished, called 'Notes and Observations on the Gospel History', which his catechumens used in class, first put me on this track of study, – the results of which appeared some years afterwards in my 'Traditions of Palestine' . . .

(Reprint: London: Virago, 1983, pp. 100–103)

1.17   Mary Smith, *The Autobiography of Mary Smith, Schoolmistress and Nonconformist. A Fragment of a Life. With Letters from Jane Welsh Carlyle and Thomas Carlyle* (1892)

It was indeed a very good school; thoroughness being the aim in the few things that were professed to be taught, as well as almost faultless discipline and good manners. A girl's education at that time consisted principally of needlework of various descriptions, from plain sewing to all manner of fancy work and embroidery, including muslin and net, on which we worked or flowered squares for the shoulders, veils, caps, collars, and borders; likewise a multitude of things not in wear now, but then considered very necessary. Parents were prouder then of their daughters' pieces of needlework than of their scholarship.

I believe my father would have wished it different, but it was usual to consign a pupil to the sole care of the governess, to direct and guide as she might deem fit and proper. So I was educated according to her idea, not his; the exception being made that I might be specially put forward in arithmetic, which was done accordingly. Every afternoon, therefore, Mrs H., my favourite teacher, came to the schoolroom door and called me to her in the sitting room, where she sat with her father, and there in that blessed quietude, with my kind teacher's help, I unravelled the mysteries of long division and compound addition, quite as much as it was then thought necessary for girls to know. Arithmetic was much more thoroughly taught to girls in Scotland and the North of England, and in most other branches of learning, as I found some years after. A blessing it was, that at this school we got no frivolous notions of life and its great duties, and that we had before us living examples of the sweet influences of religion and morality.

My special delight was in the learning, small as it was, that was then taught. I took much interest in flowering net and embroidering muslin, but less in canvas work, at which I was always slow. But we all traveled through one groove, however diverse our tastes might be. Thus I did an endless quantity of embroidery and flowering, children's caps, muslin aprons, and many other things; as well as a teapot stand, with a tiger in the middle! The canvas of this last article being very fine, I drew it up and spoilt it, and had to begin afresh, which cost me many tears.

What long months I worked at it – and how I hated it – but all was in vain! For long years Englishwomen's souls were almost as sorely crippled and cramped by the devices of the schoolroom, as the Chinese women's feet by their shoes. I had to go on with this hateful employment. 'It must be done, and done well', I was told, which I fully realized. I never remember to have been praised for any work I did, though I did a great deal.

But I had my delight in going early into the school room, while the rest were at play, sitting in its grateful quietude, reading over and over again such class books as the 'Pleasing Instructor', Magnall's 'Questions', Goldsmith's 'History of England', etc., all new to me. The 'Pleasing Instructor' I liked very much. It contained a selection of articles from the best English authors – Addison, Steel, Dryden, Young, Pope, the Taylors, etc. . . .

But here was a book I had a faculty for. These authors wrote from their hearts for humanity, and I could follow them fully and with delight, though but a child. They awakened my young nature, and I found for the first time that my pondering heart was akin to that of the whole human race. . . .

(London: Bemrose and Sons, 1983, pp. 100–103)

1.18   Grace Foakes, *My Part of the River* (1972)

. . . My teacher was Mrs Hamlyn. She was tall, thin and terrifying. If we misbehaved she would bring us out to the front of the class, stand behind us, fold our arms over our chest, and lean over us. Then pushing our sleeves up, she slapped us as hard as she could until our arms burned with the sting. We had a punishment book, kept by the Governess (Headmistress). If you were really naughty, you were sent to the Governess for the cane and to have your name put in red ink in the punishment book. This went against you when you left school, as each of us was given our 'character' (reference) when we left school. Without a good 'character' you could not get a job, as it was always asked for when applying for one. I still have my 'character'. It is one of my treasures, of which I am rather proud.

. . . In winter there was a very large coal fire lit before we came into class. In front of it was a large, iron fire-guard. The fire was lovely to look at but didn't seem to warm the classroom. My seat at the back of the class was always cold. I had so many chilblains on my fingers that I sometimes could not hold the pen. Not being able to afford gloves for us, my mother sewed up the legs of worn-out socks and threaded them through with elastic to keep them on. This was quite all right for going to school, but one cannot write with sewn-up socks on one's hands; and so, once at school, I had to go cold.

Most of us girls were very poorly shod, some coming to school with no boots or stockings at all. Those of us who did have them were lucky. Even so, most boots were made with cardboard soles which wore out very quickly, especially in wet weather . . .

Our teachers must have been heroines, for we were for the most part an ignorant and uncouth lot. They persevered, nevertheless, and, much to their credit, turned out some very good girls, who went on to sit for scholarships and, in quite a few cases, made good and were a credit to the school.

We had no homework, therefore no satchels were needed. We had no school milk and no school dinners. If a child was very poor, she could apply for a dinner ticket which entitled her to a free dinner at a coffee-shop. Not many applied for dinner tickets, for even the poor of the community were proud. The children went home for dinner, sometimes to a couple of slices of bread, cut thick to fill them up.

. . . We were taught hemming, sew and fell, top-sewing and gathering. Pieces of material were given to each girl and we would have to gather the material in, then stroke the gathers until they were all in a perfectly straight line. I could never see the sense of this, and as we never got any further than the piece of material I'm afraid I never tried very hard. We had no sewing-machines and were never encouraged to make a garment, and so there seemed to be a general dislike of the subject.

As we grew older, we were sent for one half-day a week to a central school for a course of either housewifery, laundry or cooking. We could not choose the course, it was chosen for us. At the laundry we were taught how to wash clothes, iron with a flat iron, goffer with a goffering iron, to starch and to smooth with a smoothing iron. All these processes are now things of the past, and I doubt very much if the young will have any idea what I am talking about. If we did the housewifery course, we were taught to sweep, dust, polish, make beds and bath a life-size doll. We had great fun on this course, for it was held in a house set aside for the purpose, and with only one teacher in charge we were quick to take advantage when she went to inspect some other part of the house. We jumped on the bed, threw pillows, drowned the doll and swept dirt under the mats. This was the highlight of the week, the one lesson that we never minded going to.

(London: Futura, 1988, pp. 136–139)

Chapter Two

Middle-class and elite women
Domesticity and 'separate spheres'

The ideology of 'separate spheres' was vigorously promoted in the nineteenth century as the ideal model for relations between men and women. As Davidoff and Hall have shown, it was an ideology most ardently supported from within the middle class.[1] The sources in this chapter will focus mainly on middle-class women's experience of marriage, motherhood and domesticity. Some consideration will also be given to elite women. Most women married and could expect to spend much of their adult life either pregnant or nursing small children: Kathryn Gleadle estimates that women of the elite classes spent eighteen years bearing and nursing babies and children in the nineteenth century, whereas this was reduced to thirteen years for women of the middle class.[2] With limited domestic help, middle-class women cared for, and in many cases educated, an average of eight children; they were also responsible for domestic management and the employment of servants.

Traditionally, historians have presented a negative view of domesticity, noting the legal situation of married women in which the husband had complete dominance and the wife had no separate legal existence of her own, and emphasising the limitations of the domestic sphere. More recently, however, historians have argued that domesticity might fruitfully be viewed, for some women at least, as overlapping with the religious public world and the social sphere, to provide a full life with expansive, even global, commitments.[3] The sources also raise questions about the problems of prescriptive literature; separate spheres as an analytical tool; and the relationship between the public, private and domestic spheres.

2.1 Ann Taylor Gilbert, 'Remonstance' (1810)

Ann Taylor Gilbert's poem 'Remonstance' is a classic statement of 'separate spheres'. The Taylors were Congregational evangelicals from near Colchester, Essex. Ann (1782–1866) and her sister Jane (1783–1824) wrote *Original Poems for Infant Minds* (1804, which included 'Twinkle, Twinkle, Little Star') and *Hymns for Infant Minds* (1810). 'Remonstrance' begins by rejecting antagonism between the sexes in what is undoubtedly a response to the ideas of Mary Wollstonecraft and other radicals of the 1790s. Taylor then goes on to outline women's and men's complementary characteristics. While women are weaker, softer and gentler than men, the reader is left in no doubt as to the value of their domestic role.

2.2 Jane Austen, *Pride and Prejudice* (1812)

This excerpt from Jane Austen's *Pride and Prejudice* highlights the tension between the 'prudent match' and the increasing idealisation of romantic love and conjugal companionship during the nineteenth century. While arranged marriages were less popular than in the 1700s, marriage was rarely just about romance. For most women, marriage was important for their economic well-being, for the bearing of children and, they hoped, for companionship. Whether they were elite women seeking husbands at balls and assemblies, or women from the middle class meeting prospective partners at private social occasions, church and chapel functions and, later in the century, at the theatre, dances and seaside holidays, all were concerned to make a 'good match'. Mrs Bennet's desire for a wealthy husband for her daughters was shared by Lizzie and Jane, but their appreciation of Mr Bingley's good humour and fine looks, as well as his ability to dance, are derived from more romantic feelings.

2.3 Mrs Ann Taylor of Ongar, *Practical Hints to Young Females, on the Duties of a Wife, a Mother and a Mistress of a Family* (1815)

This excerpt from Ann Martin Taylor's *Practical Hints to Young Females* emphasises the hard work required by a loving and companionate marriage. Taylor (1757–1830), mother of Ann and Jane (and six more surviving children) and the author of various conduct books, argued that a woman needed to be focused on her home if she was to make a successful family life. While she did not want to be 'too rigid' and consign young women 'to days of toil and drudgery', she felt sanctioned by Saint Paul when she said that women should 'be keepers at home'. Again, this account does not suggest a simple subservience; Ann Martin Taylor considered the wife as the 'head of the family', no less!

2.4 Isabella Beeton, *Beeton's Book of Household Management* (1861)

Beeton's Book of Household Management (1861), by the 24-year-old Isabella Beeton (1836–1865), became a bestseller, reflecting the general popularity of domestic manuals and conduct books in the mid-nineteenth century. This excerpt from the opening installment shows Beeton's lively and robust style, as she likens the job of the mistress of the house to that of the commander of an army. Other installments deal with a range of issues, including: choice of acquaintances, friendships, hospitality, evenings at home; the management of servants and role of the housekeeper; kitchen arrangements and an introduction to cookery, including an examination of French terminology used in modern cookery, plentiful recipes and ideas for menus; and the rearing of children, use of the doctor, and legal advice to women. Such topics are suggestive of the expanding role of the wife during the nineteenth century. The increasing adornment of the home was accompanied by higher standards of cleanliness, and hence responsibility for servants, who were seen to require moral as well as practical supervision and guidance. Entertaining and visiting were also important for setting and maintaining the standards of respectability so important to the delineation of the characteristics of the middle class (and the boundaries between them and those 'below').

2.5 Letter from Elizabeth Gaskell to Charles Eliot Norton (1858)

Many women enjoyed and derived considerable satisfaction from their domestic role. Elizabeth Gaskell (1810–1865) wrote her novels at a small desk in the drawing room, from which she could oversee the comings and goings of the house. This letter from Gaskell to Charles Eliot Norton (1858) conveys her immersion in the hustle and bustle of a busy domestic life and her good-humoured exasperation at the demands on her time. Other letters suggest a need for respite, however, and for her 'the hidden world of Art' was one in which writers could 'shelter themselves when too much pressed upon by daily small Lilliputian arrows of peddling cares'.[4]

2.6 Letter from Jane Welsh Carlyle to Mary Smith (1857)

While marriage was represented as companionate and as a partnership, for many women it involved the subordinating not only of their ambitions but of their sense of self. For Jane Welsh Carlyle (1801–1866), the witty and intelligent wife of the historian and writer Thomas Carlyle, the demands of marriage worked against her personal fulfilment, as expressed in this letter to Mary Smith, a single woman and a school teacher with limited resources who had written to Carlyle seeking support for her writing. Jane Carlyle's exasperation was not merely about her struggle to fulfil tasks that were unfamiliar to her, but the loss of her independence and self-determination, and the requirement that her primary role in life was to nurture her husband.

2.7 Florence Nightingale, *Cassandra* (1852)

In *Cassandra*, Florence Nightingale (1820–1910) describes with a terrifying vividness the suffocating nature of the tiresome and unfulfilling routines of women's domestic and social lives. She even extended her sympathy to women who wished to break limbs, or who took to their beds with spurious illnesses in order to get some time to themselves! After her experiences in the Crimean War and involvement in establishing the first school of nursing at St Thomas's Hospital, Nightingale spent years in seclusion, writing reports on health and sanitation.

2.8 Letters of Queen Victoria to her elder daughter, the Princess Royal (1858–1860)

Queen Victoria (1819–1901) was hardly representative of womankind as a whole, but shared her experience of a large family and experience of maternal suffering with women of all classes. Deaths of mothers and infants occurred more frequently among the poor, but childbirth was notoriously unsafe for all women, especially in Britain where (unlike much of northern Europe) there were no licensed midwives and childbirth was in the process of being taken over as an area of male medical expertise. (Victoria was one of the first women to use chloroform, for the birth of her eighth child, Leopold, in 1853.) These letters were written to her elder daughter, Princess 'Vicky', the Princess Royal, at around the time of the birth of her first child, Prince Wilhelm, in January 1859. Vicky had a long, frightening, agonising and life-threatening labour, which involved an attempt to 'turn' the breach baby boy in the birth canal. The Queen had wanted to be with her daughter at the time of her 'confinement', but was compelled to remain in England for state duties. Instead, she sent guidance in the form of notes that she had made at the time of each of her nine births. Historians have been keen to represent Victoria as an 'unmaternal' mother. Her comments about her 'ugly' and 'frog-like' babies are indeed amusingly frank. But her letters to her daughter are full of love and concern, and contain many recollections of her indulgences of her much-loved children, as well as an urgent repetition to the sensitive new mother that 'your child would delight me at any age'.[5] The excerpts also reveal Queen Victoria's anxieties at giving up her daughters in marriage; Vicky was just 17 when she married Frederick of Prussia. They also express her very fine anger at the powerlessness of even the most powerful and queenly of women in their marital relationships, even though she herself clearly enjoyed her intimate relationship with Prince Albert.

2.9 Letters of Dr Joseph Coats and Georgiana Coats (1883–1896)

The relationship between Joseph Coats and his wife Georgiana belies an outward appearance of a conventional Victorian marriage. Coats, a doctor and lecturer in Pathology at Glasgow University from 1894, leading figure in the Baptist Church and founder member of the Baptist Theological College of Scotland and the Scottish Mountaineering Club, certainly played the role of paterfamilias very convincingly; one of his daughters reported that people who did not know him well were often afraid of him.[6] Georgiana's life focused on her family and her children. Their letters reveal a loving relationship in which both parties expressed interest in the others' (very separate) activities, and in which they engaged in a good deal of teasing, self-mockery and irony. Coats, who took seriously his role in providing his daughters with moral instruction, engaged in plentiful paternal rough and tumble, as well as taking Olive Mary mountaineering.

2.10 Letters from Georgiana Devonshire (1783)

In this letter to her friend Bess, Georgiana Devonshire (1757–1806) describes the birth of her beloved 'Little G' in 1783. While her husband was disappointed at the arrival of a daughter, Georgiana soon fell in love with the child, to whom she felt a fiercer attachment than to her succeeding infants. It was customary for the aristocracy to put their babies to wet-nurse in this period, but Georgiana, horrified at the unclean and dissolute habits of the woman employed as maternity nurse, took the babe into her own bed and fed her herself. This was in the face of some opposition, particularly from her in-laws, as breast-feeding delays the return of fertility. Writing to her mother less than a month after the birth, she complained that 'what makes [them] abuse suckling is their impatience for my having a boy, and they fancying I shan't soon if I suckled . . .'.[7]

2.11 Maria and R. L. Edgeworth, *Practical Education* (1798)

Maria Edgeworth's (1767–1849) immensely influential *Practical Education* received its initial impetus from the teaching methods devised by her step-mother, Honora Edgeworth, to educate her children and unruly step-children at their home in Longford, Ireland. This was child-centred education, conducted within the household and family, devoid of rote memorization and beginning from the questions children ask, in order to encourage enquiry and engagement with everyday concerns.

2.12 Eliza Fletcher, *Autobiography* (1874)

Born in Tadcaster, near York, in 1770, Eliza (Dawson) married Archibald Fletcher, the Scottish advocate, in 1791, and moved to Edinburgh. She shared her husband's Whig principles and was hostess to many sociable occasions, in which Dugald Stewart and Henry Brougham and other members of Edinburgh's reforming and literary communities participated (see chapter 3 below). She was also mother to four daughters and two sons, and in this extract reflects upon their upbringing. 'Aunt Dawson', mentioned here, and with whom the elder Fletcher girls (Margaret, Grace and Mary) stayed in Tadcaster, had come to Scotland to be with her through her confinements.

2.13 Harriet Martineau, *Autobiography* (1877)

In her *Autobiography*, Harriet Martineau describes being thankful for her unmarried state. Like so many single women in the nineteenth century, Martineau was an active and productive woman whose life was far removed from the stereotype of the unfulfilled spinster. She was fortunate in that she could make a living from her writing. Single women were more likely to be poor, and it was from this group that demands for education and wider employment opportunities emerged from the 1850s and 1860s (see chapter 9).

2.14 The diaries of Anne Lister (1819)

Lesbians were unnamed and unrecognised by the law in the nineteenth century, a situation that was to remain unchanged until the advent of sexology in the 1890s (see chapter 1). As historians have discovered, it is difficult to determine the precise nature of a relationship. Many 'passionate friendships' were probably not sexual, but fulfilled emotional needs at a time of considerable emotional and mental distance between women and men; others most certainly were. Anne Lister (1791–1840), a landowner from Shibden Hall, near Halifax, is famous for her diaries in which she recorded in code her relationships with women, married and single. Lister's longstanding lover was Marianne, M. of this extract, who betrayed her to marry Charles Lawton, an elderly wealthy man whom both women assumed would not live too many years; Anne and M. carried on their affair in the hope that they would one day be free to live together.

2.15 The Ladies of Llangollen (1822)

The most famous 'female friendship' of the nineteenth century was that of Eleanor Butler and Sarah Ponsonby, the 'Ladies of Llangollen'. Both from Irish aristocratic families, Butler and Ponsonby had eloped to set up home together in North Wales in 1778. Their domesticity was celebrated by English commentators and literary visitors, as both a curiosity and as an epitome of the simplistic rural lifestyle promoted by Romanticism.[8] This discussion of the ladies comes from Anne Lister, who was very keen to meet the women on her visit to North Wales in 1822.

2.1   Ann Taylor Gilbert, 'Remonstrance' (1810)

'Women in the course of action describe a smaller circle than men; but the perfectness of a circle consists, not in its dimensions, but in its correctness.' (Hannah More, *Coelebs in Search of a Wife* (1809))

> Why this hopeless feud?
> This worse than civil strife.
> Which long with poison'd darts, hath strew'd
> The vale of social life?
>
> To each, an helpmeet was made
> Congenial but diverse:
> The rougher path was *his* to tread;
> The mild domestic, *hers*.
>
> His iron arm was braced for toil,
> Or danger's ruder shock;
> To win the curs'd, reluctant soil,
> Or fence the cavern'd rock.
>
> The watchful eye, the pliant hand,
> the gentler duties led:
> For *her* the rural rite was planned,
> The simple table spread.
>
> Composed, retiring, modest, she,
> Impetuous, *he*, and brave; –
> His passions boisterous as the sea,
> *Hers*, oil upon the wave.
>
> Wearied in far-extended chase,
> His ready meal she drest;
> With smiles illumed his dwelling place,
> With kindness soothed his breast. . . .
>
> Sure, 'twas a cold unmanly pride
> The harmony that broke:
> Why should the oak the lily chide,
> Because she's not an oak?

If all were lilies, where's the use,
Or strength the forest yields?
If oaks, the fragrancy we lose,
And beauty of the fields.

Through following ages, dark and drear,
Th' unnatural contest ran;
Nor generous feeling stole a tear
From hard, obdurate Man!

Woman, his haughty will consigned
In joyless paths to run:
No beam of day-light reached her mind,
And sages said she'd none.

At length, the brilliant western star
Of Knowledge 'gan to rise;
The mists of ignorance afar
Rolled sullen from the skies.

Neglected woman, from the night
Of dark oppression raised,
Caught the fair dawn of mental light,
And blest it as she gazed. . . .

The right that Nature gave, we claim, –
Just honours of our kind.
We envy not the manly frame
Of body, or of mind.

Man, in his way, perfection knows;
And we as much in ours:
The violet is not the rose,
Yet both alike are flowers. . . .

His soul is thoughtful and profound,
Hers brilliant and acute; –
Plants cultured, each, in different ground
And bearing different fruit.

Among the social duties led,
Where each excels his part,

Man's proudest glory is his head,
A Woman's, is her heart.

Unwearied by the toilsome course,
He climbs the hill of fame:
Takes immortality by force,
And wins a mighty name.

Along a cool, sequestered way,
Her quiet walk she winds;
Sheds milder sunshine on his day,
His brow with flowers binds.

Of art intuitive possest,
Her infant train she rears;
To virtue by her smiles carest,
Or chastened by her tears:

Besides the flitting midnight lamp,
With fond and wakeful eye,
Wipes gently off the dying damp,
Or sooths the parting sigh . . .

'Tis here that Woman brightest shines
(Though bright in other spheres):
Her name is drawn in fairest lines,
When written by her tears.
(Published in Josiah Conder (ed.), *The Associate Minstrels*, 1810)

2.2   Jane Austen, *Pride and Prejudice* (1812)

Not all that Mrs. Bennet however, with the assistance of her five daughters, could ask on the subject was sufficient to draw from her husband any satisfactory description of Mr. Bingley. They attacked him in various ways; with barefaced questions, ingenious supposi- tions, and distant surmises; but he eluded the skill of them all; and they were at last obliged to accept the second-hand intelligence of their neighbour Lady Lucas. Her report was highly favourable. Sir William had been delighted with him. He was quite young, wonder- fully handsome, extremely agreeable, and, to crown the whole, he meant to be at the next assembly with a large party. Nothing could be more delightful! To be fond of dancing was a certain step towards falling in love; and very lively hopes of Mr. Bingley's heart were entertained.

'If I can but see one of my daughters happily settled at Netherfield,' said Mrs. Bennet to her husband, 'and all the others equally well married, I shall have nothing to wish for.'

. . . A report soon followed that Mr. Bingley was to bring twelve ladies and seven gentlemen with him to the assembly. The girls grieved over such a number of ladies; but were comforted the day before the ball by hearing that, instead of twelve, he had brought only six with him from London, his five sisters and a cousin. And when the party entered the assembly room, it consisted of only five altogether; Mr. Bingley, his two sisters, the husband of the oldest, and another young man.

Mr. Bingley was good looking and gentlemanlike; he had a pleasant countenance, and easy, unaffected manners. His sisters were fine women, with an air of dedicated fashion. His brother-in-law, Mr. Hurst, merely looked the gentleman; but his friend Mr. Darcy soon drew the attention of the room by his fine, tall person, hand-some features, noble mien; and the report which was in general circulation within five minutes after his entrance, of his having ten thousand a year. The gentlemen pronounced him to be a fine figure of a man, the ladies declared he was much handsomer than Mr. Bingley, and he was looked at with great admiration for about half the evening, till his manners gave a disgust which turned the tide of his popularity; for he was discovered to be proud, to be above his company, and above being pleased; and not all his large estate in Derbyshire could then save him from having a most forbidding, dis-agreeable countenance, and being unworthy to be compared with his friend.

Mr. Bingley had soon made himself acquainted with all the principal people in the room; he was lively and unreserved, danced every dance, was angry that the ball closed so early, and talked of giving one himself at Netherfield. Such amiable qualities must speak for themselves. What a contrast between him and his friend! Mr. Darcy danced only once with Mrs Hurst and once with Miss Bingley, declined being introduced to any other lady, and spent the rest of the evening in walking about the room, speaking occasionally to one of his own party. His character was decided. He was the proudest, most disagreeable man in the world, and every body hoped that he would never come there again . . .

When Jane and Elizabeth were alone, the former, who had been cautious in her praise of Mr. Bingley before, expressed to her sister how very much she admired him.

'He is just what a young man ought to be,' said she, 'sensible, good humoured, lively; and I never saw such happy manners! – so much ease, with such perfect good breeding!'

'He is also handsome,' replied Elizabeth, 'which a young man ought likewise to be, if he possibly can. His character is thereby complete.'

(Reprint: Oxford: Oxford University Press, 1970, pp. 6–8, 11)

2.3   Mrs Ann Taylor of Ongar, *Practical Hints to Young Females, on the Duties of a Wife, a Mother and a Mistress of a Family* (1815)

No. II: Conduct to the husband

The first object that should claim your attention, is that being with whom you have united your fortunes. When he vowed to take you for better or worse, he staked the happiness of his future life; a treasure for which the most ample portion is insufficient to compensate. On your part, you promised to *love* as well as to honour and obey; and probably from the all-perfect being to whom you then surrendered yourself, you expected to derive such uninterrupted felicity as would render the fulfilment of this promise constantly easy and delightful. But, however discreet your choice has been, time and circumstances alone can sufficiently develop your husband's character: by degrees the discovery will be made that you have married a mortal, and that the object of your affections is not entirely free from the infirmities of human nature. Then it is, that by an impartial survey of your own character, your disappointment may be moderated; and your love, so far from declining, may acquire additional tenderness, from the consciousness that there is room for mutual forbearance . . .

As the head of a family, you must expect to meet with provocation, and to find your patience continually called to the proof: but you are utterly unfit to command others if you cannot command yourself; and that is a lesson which ought to have been previously learned, for it will be difficult to acquire when pressed by business and surrounded by vexations, which demand its immediate and perfect exercise. Destitute of a qualification so important, you cannot acquit yourself well; and possessing it, you will probably rule even over your husband with a sway which he will not be inclined to dispute, and of which you need not yourself be ashamed. There cannot, indeed, be a sight more uncouth, than that of a man and his wife struggling for power; for where it ought to be vested, nature, reason, and scripture, concur to declare: but the influence acquired by amiable conduct and self-command does not fall under this censure . . .

In order to cherish these kindly feelings, accustom yourself, in the contemplation of your husband's character, to dwell on the bright side; let his virtues occupy your thoughts more than his failings: this will impel you to honour him in the presence of others, and may eventually produce the happiest effects on his character; for most probably he will feel the value of that estimation in which you hold him, and be solicitous to preserve it. Do not expose his failings; no, not to your most confidential friend. If, unhappily, they are of the more flagrant kind, he divulges them himself; but if, on the contrary, they are merely such as to prove him to be a fallible creature, leave your friends to infer it for themselves, rather than furnish them with proofs of it from your complaints. Your own failings (should you have any) you would studiously conceal; and probably think it the duty of your husband to conceal them too: but the golden rule of doing unto others as you would they do unto you, does not apply, in this case, with sufficient force; because it is your very self, your better self, who would suffer by such an exposure; his honour and yours are inseparably one.

(London: Taylor and Hessey, 1815, 3rd edition, pp. 12–16)

2.4   Isabella Beeton, *Beeton's Book of Household Management* (1861)

Chapter One: The mistress

> Strength and honour are her clothing; and she shall rejoice in time to come – she openeth her mouth with wisdom; and in her tongue is the law of kindness. She looketh well to the way of her household; and eateth not the bread of idleness. Her children rise up, and call her blessed; her husband also, and he praiseth her.
>
> (Proverbs xxxi, 25–28)

1. As it is with the commander of an army, or the leader of any enterprise, so it is with the mistress of a house. Her spirit will be seen through the whole establishment; and just in proportion as she performs her duties intelligently and thoroughly, so will her domestics follow in her path. Of all these acquirements, which more particularly belong to the feminine character, there are none which take a higher rank, in our estimation, than such as enter into a knowledge of household duties; for on these are perpetually dependent the happiness, comfort and well being of a family. In this opinion we are borne out by the author of *The Vicar of Wakefield*, who says: 'The modest virgin, the prudent wife, and the careful matron, are much more serviceable in life than petticoated philosophers, blustering heroines, or virago queens. She who makes her home and her children happy, who reclaims the one from vice, and trains up the other to virtue, is a much greater character than ladies described in romances, whose whole occupation is to murder mankind with shafts from their quiver, or their eyes.'

2. Pursuing the picture, we may add, that to be a good housewife does not necessarily imply an abandonment of proper pleasures or amusing recreation; and we think it the more necessary to express this, as the performance of the duties of a mistress may, to some minds, perhaps seem to be incompatible with the enjoyment of life. Let us, however, now proceed to describe some of those home qualities and virtues which are necessary to the proper management of a Household, and then point out the plan which may be most profitably pursued for the daily regulation of its affairs.

3. EARLY RISING IS ONE OF THE MOST ESSENTIAL QUALITIES which enter into good Household Management, as it is not only the parent of health, but innumerable other advantages. Indeed, when a Mistress is an early riser, it is almost certain that her house will be orderly and well managed. On the contrary, if she remain in bed till a late hour, then the domestics, who, as we have before observed, invariably partake somewhat of their mistress's character, will surely become sluggards. To self-indulgence all are more or less disposed, and it is not to be expected that servants are freer from this fault than the heads of houses. The great Lord Chatham thus gave his advice on returning to this subject: – 'I would have inscribed on the curtains of your bed, and the walls of your chamber, "If you do not rise early, you can make progress in nothing." '

4. CLEANLINESS IS ALSO INDISPENSABLE TO HEALTH, and must be studied in regards to the person and the house, and all that it

contains. Cold or tepid baths should be employed every morning, unless, on account of illness or other circumstances, they should be deemed objectionable. The bathing of *children* will be treated under the head of MANAGEMENT OF CHILDREN.

5. FRUGALITY AND ECONOMY ARE HOME VIRTUES, without which no household can prosper ... The necessity of practising economy should be evident to everyone, whether in the possession of an income no more than sufficient for a family's requirements, or of a large fortune, which puts financial adversity out of the question. We must always remember that it is a great merit in housekeeping to manage a little well. 'He is a good waggoner', says Bishop Hall, 'that can turn in a little room. To live well in abundance is the praise of the estate, not the person. I will study more how to give a good account of my little, than how to make it more.' In this there is true wisdom, and it may be added, that those who can manage a little well, are most likely to succeed in their management of larger matters. Economy and frugality must never, however, be allowed to degenerate into parsimony and meanness.

(Serial: 1861, monthly, pp. 1–2)

2.5   Letter from Elizabeth Gaskell to Charles Eliot Norton, Plymouth Grove (1858)

I am sitting at the round writing table in the dining-room, – Marianne is mending me a pen, over the fire place, in order that the bits may drop into the fender; Meta is gone into the garden, to tell Joseph about the perennials for next year ... Thank you for telling us about your library. It sounds very pretty & pleasant, – and the views out of the windows make me have a kind of a Heimweh, – as if I had seen them once, & yearned to see them again, – instead of our dear old dull ugly smoky grim grey Manchester ... If I had a library like yours, all undisturbed for hours, how I would write! Mrs Chapone's letters should be nothing to mine! I would outdo Rasselas in fiction. But you see everybody comes to me perpetually. Now in this hour since breakfast I have had to decide on the following variety of important questions. Boiled beef – how long to boil? What perennials will do in Manchester smoke, & what colours our garden wants? Length of skirt for a gown? Salary of a nursery governess, & stipulations for a certain quantity of time to be left to herself. – Read letters on the state of the Indian army – lent me by a very agreeable neighbour & return them, with a proper note, & as many wise remarks as would come in a hurry. Settle 20 questions of dress for the girls, who are going out for the day; & want to look nice & yet not spoil their gowns with the mud &c &c – See a lady about a MS story of hers, & give her disheartening but very good advice. Arrange about selling two poor cows for one good one, – see purchasers, & show myself up to cattle questions, keep, & prices, – and it's not ½ past 10 yet!

(*The Letters of Mrs Gaskell*, ed. J. A. V. Chapple and
Arthur Pollard (Manchester: Manchester University Press,
1997 [1966]), pp. 487–490)

2.6   Letter from Jane Welsh Carlyle to Mary Smith, 11 January 1857

I can't think how people, who have any natural ambition, and any sense of power in them, escape going *mad* in a world like this, without the recognition of that! I know I was very near *mad* when I found it out for myself (as one has to find out for oneself *everything* that is to be of any real practical use to one). Shall I tell you how it came into my head? Perhaps it may be of comfort to you in similar moments of fatigue and disgust.

I had gone with my husband to live on a little estate of *peat bog*, that had descended to me, all the way down from John Welsh, the Covenanter, who married a daughter of John Knox. That didn't, I am ashamed to say, make me feel Craigenputtock a whit less of a peat bog, and most dreary, untoward place to live! In fact it was sixteen miles distant on every side from all the conveniences of life – shops and even post office!

Further, we were very poor; and further and worst, being an only child, and brought up to 'great prospects', I was sublimely ignorant of every branch of useful knowledge, though a capital Latin scholar and a very fair mathematician!! It behoved me in these astonishing circumstances to learn – to *sew*! Husbands, I was shocked to find, wore their stockings into holes! and were always losing buttons! and *I* was expected to 'look to all that'! Also, it behoved me to learn to *cook*! no *capable* servant choosing to live at 'such an out of the way place', and my husband having 'bad digestion', which complicated my difficulties dreadfully. The bread, above all, brought from Dumfries, 'soured on his stomach', (Oh,

Heavens!) and it was plainly my duty as a christian wife to bake at home!

So I sent for Cobbet's 'Cottage Economy,' and fell to work at a loaf of bread. But knowing nothing about the process of fermentation or the heat of ovens, it came to pass that my loaf got put into the oven at the same time *myself* ought to have put to bed, and I remained the only person not asleep, in the house in the middle of a desert! *One* o'clock struck, and then *two*, and then *three*; and still I was sitting there in an intense solitude, my whole body aching with weariness, my heart aching with a sense of forlorness and degradation. That I who had been so petted at home, whose comfort had been studied by everybody in the house, who had never been required to do anything but *cultivate my mind*, should have to pass all those hours of the night in watching *a loaf of bread!* which mightn't turn out bread after all!

Such thoughts maddened me, till I laid down my head on the table, and sobbed aloud. It was then that somehow the idea of Benvenuto Cellini, sitting up all night watching his Pericles in the oven, came into my head; and suddenly I asked myself, 'After all, in the sight of the upper powers, what is the difference between a statue of Pericles and a loaf of bread, so that each be the thing one's hand hath found to do?' The man's determined will, his energy, his patience, his resource, were the really admirable things, of which the status of Pericles was the mere chance expression. If he had been a woman, living at Craigenputtock, with a dyspeptic husband, sixteen miles from a baker, and *he a bad one* – all these qualities would have come out most fitly in a *good* loaf of bread!

I cannot express what consolation this germ of an idea spread over my uncongenial life, during five years we lived at that savage place; where my two immediate predecessors had gone *mad*, and the third had taken to drink!

(In *The Autobiography of Mary Smith, Schoolmistress and
Nonconformist, A Fragment of a Life. With Letters from
Jane Welsh Carlyle and Thomas Carlyle* (London:
Bemrose and Sons, 1892), pp, 309–311)

2.7 Florence Nightingale, *Cassandra* (1852)

... Women never have half an hour in all their lives (excepting before or after anybody is up in the house) that they can call their own, without fear of offending or hurting someone. Why do people sit up so late, or, more rarely, get up so early? Not because the day is not long enough, but because they have 'no time in the day to themselves'.

If we do attempt to do anything in company, what is the system of literary exercise which we pursue? Everybody reads aloud of their own book or newspaper – or, every five minutes, something is said. And what is it to be 'read aloud to'? The most miserable exercise of the human intellect. Or rather, is it any exercise at all? It is like lying on one's back, with one's hands tied and having liquid poured down one's throat. Worse than that, because suffocation would immediately ensue and put a stop to this operation. But no suffocation would stop the other.

So much for the satisfaction of the intellect. Yet for a married woman in society, it is even worse. A married woman was heard to wish that she could break a limb that she might have a little time to herself. Many take advantage of the fear of 'infection' to do the same.

It is a thing so accepted among women that they have nothing to do, that one woman has not the least scruple in saying to the other, 'I will come and spend the morning with you'. And you would be thought quite surly and absurd, if you were to refuse it on the plea of occupation. Nay, it is thought a mark of amiability and affection, if you are 'on such terms' that you can 'come in' 'any morning you please'.

In a country house, if there is a large party of young people, 'You will spend the morning with us', they say to the neighbours, 'we will drive together in the afternoon', 'tomorrow we will spend the evening together'. And this is thought friendly, and spending time in a pleasant manner. So women play through life. Yet time is the most valuable of all things. If they had come every morning and afternoon and robbed us of half-a-crown, we should have had redress from the police. But it is laid down, that our time is of no value. If you offer a morning visit to a professional man, and say, 'I will just stay an hour with you, if you will allow me, till so and so comes back to fetch me'; it costs him the earnings of an hour, and therefore he has a right to complain. But women have no right, because it is '*only* their time'.

Women have no means given them, whereby they *can* resist the 'claims of social life'. They are taught from their infancy upwards that it is wrong, ill-tempered, and a misunderstanding of 'woman's mission' (with a great M) if they do not allow themselves *willingly* to be interrupted at all hours. If a woman has once put in a claim to be treated as a man by some work of science or art or literature, which she can *show* as the 'fruit of her leisure', then she will be considered justified in *having* leisure (hardly, perhaps, even then). But if not, not. If she has nothing to show, she must resign herself to her fate.

(Published in *Suggestions for Thought to the Searchers after Truth Among the Artizans of England* (Reprint: New York: New York University Press, 1992 [1860]), pp. 213–214)

2.8 Letters from Queen Victoria to the Princess Royal (1858–1860)

Windsor Castle, October 27, 1858

... I hope Fritz is duly shocked at your sufferings, for those very selfish men would not bear for a minute what we poor slaves have to endure. But don't dread the denouement; there is no need of it; and don't talk to ladies about it, as they will only alarm you, particularly abroad, where so much more fuss is made of a very natural and usual thing.

Osborne, December 11, 1858.

... Some little further memoranda I will send you by the messenger. Mrs Innocent has likewise copies of all the notes I put down afterwards of all I did – during my confinements – as I know you will like to know – and this will be a guide. All this I have been particularly anxious about – as my first two confinements – for want of order – and from disputes and squabbles (chiefly owing to my poor old governess who would meddle) were far from comfortable or convenient and the doctors too had not found out quite how to treat me. I am therefore particularly anxious that you should profit from my experience (which resulted in my last five confinements being as quiet and comfortable as possible) and be spared as much (as possible) all the inconveniences arising from want of experience etc. which are natural in a first confinement. So you see, dear, that though alas far away (which I shall never console myself for) – I watch over you as if I were there.

Windsor Castle, January 29, 1859 [following the dangerous and difficult birth of Prince Wilhelm on January 27]

God be praised for all his mercies, and for bringing you safely through this awful time! Our joy, our gratitude, knows no bounds. My precious darling, you suffered much more than I ever did – and how I wish I could have lightened them for you! Poor dear Fritz – how he will have suffered for you! I think and feel much for him; the dear little boy if I could but see him for one minute, give him one kiss. It is hard, very hard. But we are so happy, so grateful! And people here are all in ecstasies – such pleasure, such delight – as if it was their own prince and so it is too! All the children so delighted! You will and must feel so thankful all is over! But don't be alarmed for the future, it can never be so bad again! ... How I do long to see my little grandson! I own it seems very funny to me to be a grandmama, and so many people tell me they can't believe it! That dear, dear locket gives me such pleasure! Not only because it was the dear little darling's hair, but because it shows me that you thought directly of poor absent Mama, who quite pines at times to be with you.

Windsor Castle, April 20, 1859

I have this very moment received your dear letter of the 18th and thank you much for it. I am glad you bear out what I said about our dear correspondence. It is an immense pleasure and comfort to me, for it is dreadful to live so far off and always separated. I really think I shall never let your sisters marry – certainly not to be so constantly away and see so little of their parents – as till now, you have done, contrary to all that I was originally promised and told. I am so glad to see that you so entirely enter into all my feelings as a mother. Yes, dearest, it is an awful moment to have to give one's innocent child up to a man, be he ever so kind and good – and to think of all that she must go through! I can't say what I suffered, what I felt – what struggles I had to go through – (indeed I have not quite got over it yet) and that last night when we took you to your room, and you cried so much, I said to Papa as we came back 'after all, it is like taking a poor lamb to be sacrificed'. You now know – what I meant, dear. I know that God has willed it so and that these are the trials which we poor women must go through; no father, no man can feel this! Papa never would enter into it at all! As in fact he seldom can in my very violent feelings. It really makes me shudder when I look around at all your sweet, happy, unconscious sisters – and think that I must give them up too – one by one!! Our dear Alice, has seen and heard more (of course not what no one ever can know before they marry and before they have had children) than you did, from your marriage – and quite enough to give her a horror rather of marrying.

Buckingham Palace, May 16, 1860.

[After a reference to Princess Alice's marriage] . . . all marriage is such a lottery – the happiness is always an exchange – though it may be a very happy one – still the poor woman is bodily and morally the husband's slave. That always sticks in my throat. When I think of a merry, happy, free young girl – and look at the ailing, aching state a young wife generally is doomed to – which you can't deny is the penalty of marriage.

(Roger Fulford, ed., *Dearest Child: Letters between Queen Victoria and the Princess Royal, 1858–1861* (London: Evans, 1964), pp. 141, 150–151, 159, 182, 254)

2.9 Dr & Mrs Joseph Coats, A Book of Remembrance, compiled by their daughters (1929)

From G.T.C.

Glasgow, 2–8–83

I was glad to get your small note this morning.

We went yesterday – the cavalcade – Janie, Mary, Baby, perambulator, Nurse and Moritz, to the Botanic gardens: tied Moritz at the gate and saw through Winter Gardens and Plant Houses – found the hour for Musical promenade changed from 4 till 7 – provoked: took cavalcade to Sophie's where we had tea, and returned at 7; heard three tunes by the pipes, etc., and returned . . .

I got a *new* key for you for gardens (good little woman!). I wrote to proprietor of Tummel Bridge Inn for terms and Post-Master at Braemar for information about lodgings with attendance for September (excellent small person!).

I sent off various parcels . . . all by *new* post, *just* over the 3lbs so had to pay 9d. instead of 6d. (But very good, Mrs. Coats – excellent!). I also sent off the 12/6 for old books and 3/- for wastepaper (so that I might not be tempted to spend it). (Wisdom far above rubies, young woman!).

And what else did I do? – Oh, yes.
I invited Minnie.
I wrote to A. Clark, Esq. (Insurance)
To Girls.
To Mrs. Fleming – a discourse about Isa.
To Mrs. H.S. Lamont.
To Shetland about account.

And what shall I more say?
. . . The cayenne has *nearly* killed the moths! But alas, what havoc they have made!
A *small wee* mouse was *drowned* this morning. His remains were committed to ashpit!
Further news in *Herald* of the day. With love.
Yours most intellectually and devotedly.

From G.T.C.

(Sent to Storie Street Church where Dr Coats was to give an address.)
Craigmore, 26–10–86

MY DEAR, – This is me. Two umbrellas, three sticks and one poker, come to inspire and applaud.
If you look up to the right hand corner (as you come in) just behind a person with a Black Bonnet trimmed with Crimson you will see my beaming face.
Look well – don't put your specs on, for they are lying on the chimney piece!
Don't pitch your voice too high.
Don't roar at your audience.
              and
Don't emphasize every fifth word!
. . . Now I am sure you have succeeded very well. . Did you hear the plaudits of the multitude – some of the 'External World'?
Was it very 'susceptible' to the flow of oratory so badly penned by the Secretarial Wife – or had the micro-organisms and the ill-ventilated condition of 'Storie Street' too depressing an influence?

Mind, I'm listening. Pull your cuffs well down and push your hair well up, take a sip of water – now go on. . . . This is a Bright (with a capital) Cold (with a capital) day. Put on your gloves and Button (with a capital) up your coat.

Good luck – Ta-Ta.

From J.C.

(On the eve of his 50th Birthday.)

Kilmalcolm, 3rd February, '96.

MY DEAR ONE, – 'Tis the end of another year in my journey. This day I finish 49 years of travel, of which over fifteen have been in your sweet company. We are getting older, if not old, and yet life is, to both of us, young and interesting as ever. The journey of fifteen years seems long and yet short. It does not seem so long since I was a sober bachelor in lodgings or with Kate as housekeeper. Yet it does seem long to think of a time when you were not there as my wife and there was no Olive Mary or Vicky. I say a sober bachelor, because I really seem to have more sportiveness as I get older, more freedom, at least, in expressing the sportiveness that is in me.

As to you, I rather fear that my respect and deference to your wisdom and understanding of people may lead me to leave you too much to follow your own way. You must be aware that you are, more and more, getting things arranged exactly as you want. Well and good; in the main your way is better than mine. This I freely acknowledge – but I wonder if it is always so and if I need to put the drag on a bit. Well, we shall not have any dispute about it and we will take the way together that either of us convinces the other to be the best. . . .

Your young old man,

J. COATS

(Glasgow: Jackson, Wylie & Co., 1929, pp. 225, 238, 250–251)

2.10   Letters from Georgiana, Duchess of Devonshire (1783)

Letter to Bess, July 1783

I was laid on a couch in the middle of the room. My Mother and Dennis supported me. Canis was at the door, and the Duchess of

Portland sometimes bending over me and screaming with me, and sometimes running to the end of the room and to him. I thought the pain I suffered was so great from being unusual to me, but I find since I had a very hard time. Towards the end, some symptoms made me think the child was dead. I said so, and Dr Denman only said there was no reason to think so but we must submit to providence. I then had no doubt and watching my mother's fine eyes ... I saw she thought it dead, which they all did except Denman who dared not say too much. When it came into the world I said, 'only let it be alive'. The little child seemed to move as it lay by me but I was not sure when all at once it cried. Oh, God, I cried and was quite hysterical. The Duchess and my mother were overcome and cried and all kissed me.

Letter to Lady Spencer, August 1783

My Dr little girl sleeps in bed with me after her first suckling as it is cold to move her, and the Rocker was to turn her dry and lay her down to sleep. I perceiv'd she had made the bed stink of wine and strong drink whenever she came near it, and that Mrs Smith was always wakeful and telling her to leave the child. This rather alarmed me, but this morning I learnt that she had been so drunk as to fall down and vomit ... I have therefore sent her 10 guineas and told her I would pay her journey up to town, and that I parted with her because I wanted her no longer.

(Amanda Foreman, *Georgiana: Duchess of Devonshire*
(London: HarperCollins, 1998), pp. 121–123)

2.11   Maria and R.L. Edgeworth, *Practical Education* (1798)

Several years ago a mother [a footnote asserts that this was Honora Edgeworth, step-mother of Maria], who had a large family to educate, and who had turned her attention with much solicitude to the subject of education, resolved to write notes from day to day of all the trifling things which mark the progress of the mind in childhood. She was of the opinion, that the art of education should be considered as an experimental science, and that many authors of great abilities had mistaken their road by following theory instead of practice. The title of 'Practical Education' was chosen by this lady, and prefixed to a little book for children, which she began, but did not live to finish. The few notes which remain of her writing are preserved, not only merely out of respect for her memory, but because it is thought that they may be useful. Her plan of keeping a register of the remarks of children has at intervals been pursued in her family; a number of these anecdotes have been interspersed in this work, a few which did not seem to suit the didactic nature of any of our chapters remain, and with much hesitation and diffidence are offered to the public. We have selected such anecdotes as may in some measure illustrate the principles that we have endeavoured to establish; and we hope that from these trifling, but genuine conversations of children and parents, the reader with distinctly perceive the difference between practical and theoretical education . . .

X – (a girl of five years old) asked why a piece of paper fell quickly to the ground when rumpled up, why so slowly when opened.

Y – (a girl of three years and a half old) seeing her sister taken care of and nursed when she had chilblains, said, that she wished to have chilblains.

Z – (a girl between two and three), when her mother was putting on her bonnet, and when she was going out to walk, looked at the cat, and said with a plaintive voice, 'Poor Pussey! You have no bonnet, Pussey!'

X – (5 years old) asked why she was as tall as the trees when she was far from them.

Z – (four years old) went to church, and when she was there said, 'Do those mens do everything better than we; because they talk so loud, and I think they read'. It was a country church, and people sang; but the child said, 'She thought they didn't sing, but roared, because they were shut up in that place, and didn't like it.'

L – (a boy between 3 and 4 years) was standing before a grate with coals in it, which were not lighted; his mother said to him, 'What is the use of coals?'

L – 'To put in your grate.'

Mother – 'Why are they out there?'

L – 'To make fire'

Mother – 'How do they make fire?'

L – 'Fire is brought to them.'

Mother – 'How is fire brought to them?'

L – a little while afterwards, asked leave to light a candle, and when a

bit of paper was given to him for that purpose said, 'But, mother, may I take some light out of your fire to put to it?'
This boy had more exact ideas of property than Prometheus had.
('Notes, Containing Conversations and Anecdotes of Children',
An Appendix to *Practical Education*, Vol. III (London:
J. Johnston, 2nd edition, 1801 [1798]), pp. 321–323)

2.12   *Autobiography of Mrs Fletcher, of Edinburgh, with selections from her letters and other family memorials* (1874)

I have said little yet of my younger children, whose characters were by degrees becoming more and more developed. If I had any system in education, it was to lay as little restraint as was consistent with their good on the wishes and pursuits of my children. They equally shared my sympathy and confidence. I had no pleasures which they did not share, no amusements in which they did not take a part. I thought that in making them happy I should make them good; but I think I erred in encouraging amusements of too exciting a character, such as private theatricals and recitations. In dear Grace they had perhaps a tendency to increase an excessive sensibility and enthusiasm of character, which, while it made her a most attractive and delightful human being to everyone who could appreciate her refined taste and varied talents, would, had she lived, have made her too susceptible to the disappointments of life. I think I did not help my children sufficiently to strengthen their minds by self-discipline; and though I endeavoured to teach them the religion of the Bible, still I think their religious home teaching was too vague and unsystematical to impress habits of self-restraint and self-government from the fear of offending God constantly on their minds. To girls educated at home this is not an unsafe religious education, but to sons, educated as all men are by the world, it is not strict enough to enable them to avoid the seduction of the passions, and the evils of bad example, to which they are so soon exposed. It was on principle, as well as from a feeling of deep gratitude towards the kindest of aunts, that I consented that my three dear girls – Grace, Margaret and Mary – should take it each in turn to spend their winter half-year with my good uncle and aunt at Tadcaster. They all loved home intensely, and it was no small sacrifice for them to remain in a small dull country town with two old people, without variety, and with no society, or such as they considered worse than none; but such was their sense of duty, and such their desire to repay the debt of gratitude their mother owed to this good aunt, that they never complained, when their turn came round, to give up their happy home, and all the pleasures and delights of an Edinburgh society, which they could so fully and richly enjoy, but went cheerfully into their exile; and but frequent letters to and from home, cultivated an ease and liveliness of letter writing which exercised both mind and heart. This was not the only use of these Tadcaster winters, – it abstracted them from the constant whirl of amusement in which other girls of their age were engaged, it proved a seasonable aid to reflection, and enabled them to live contentedly without excitement, for never did an expression of discontent escape from any of them under these circumstances. Fortunately they had no ready access to books of mere amusement, and were thus thrown on solid reading such as Miss Hill's library, aunt Dawson's book shelves, and the York library offered . . .

(Carlisle: C. Thurnham and Sons, 1874, pp. 106–108)

2.13   Harriet Martineau, *Autobiography* (1877)

I am, in truth, very thankful for not having married at all. I have never since been tempted, nor have suffered anything at all in relation to that matter which is held to be all-important to woman, – love and marriage. Nothing, I mean, beyond occasional annoyance, presently disposed of. Every literary woman, no doubt, has plenty of importunity of that sort to deal with; but freedom of mind and coolness of manner dispose of it very easily: and since the time I have been speaking of,* my mind has been free from all idea of love-affairs. My subsequent literary life in London was clear from all difficulty and embarrassment, – no doubt because I was evidently too busy, too full of interests of other kinds to feel any awkwardness, – to say nothing of my being then thirty years of age; an age at which, if ever, a woman is certainly qualified to take care of herself. I can easily conceive how I might have been tempted, – how some deep springs in my nature might have been touched, then as earlier; but, as a matter of fact, they never were; and I consider the immunity a great blessing, under the liabilities of a moral condition such as mine was in the olden time. If I had a husband dependent on me for his happiness, the responsibility would have made me wretched. I had not faith enough in myself to endure avoidable responsibility. If my husband had *not* depended on me for his happiness, I should have been jealous. So also with children. The care would have so overpowered the joy, – the love would have so exceeded the ordinary chances of life, – the fear on my part would have so impaired the freedom on theirs, that I rejoice not to have been involved in a relation for which I was, or believed myself unfit. The veneration in which I hold domestic life has always shown me that that life was not for those whose self-respect had been early broken down, or had never grown. Happily, the majority are free from this disability. Those who suffer under it had better be as I, – as my observation of married, as well as single life assures me. When I see that conjugal love i.e., in the extremely rare cases in which it is seen in its perfection, I feel that there is a power of attachment in me that has never been touched. When I am among little children, it frightens me to think what my idolatry of my own children would have been. But, through it all, I have ever been thankful to be alone. My strong will, combined with anxiety of conscience, makes me fit only to live alone; and my taste and liking are for living alone. The older I have grown, the more serious and irremediable have seemed to me the evils and disadvantages of married life, as it exists among us at this time; and I am provided with what it is the bane of single life in ordinary cases to want, – substantial, laborious and serious occupation. My business in life has been to think and learn, and to speak out with absolute freedom what I have thought and learned. The freedom is itself a positive and never-failing enjoyment to me, after the bondage of my early life. My work and I have been fitted to each other, as is proved by the success of my work and my own happiness in it. The simplicity and independence of this vocation first suited my infirm and ill-developed nature, and then sufficed for my needs, together with family ties and domestic duties, such as I have been blessed with, and as every woman's heart requires. Thus, I am not only entirely satisfied with my lot, but think it the very best for me, – under my constitution and circumstances: and I long ago came to conclusion that, without meddling with the case of the wives and mothers, I am probably the happiest single woman in England. Who could have believed, in that awful year 1826, that such would be my conclusion a quarter of a century afterwards!

* In 1826 Martineau received a marriage proposal, which she ini-

tially accepted, but then her suitor became insane and died. His family treated her harshly, believing her to have been engaged to another, and that this was the source of his problems.

(London: Smith, Elder & Co, 1877, pp. 131–133)

2.14 The diaries of Anne Lister (1819)

Thursday 18 November (Manchester)

... Not much conversation before getting into bed. C– made no objection to her coming to Manchester when he heard she was to meet me, tho' before he did not wish her to go farther than Wilmslow, he hurried them off before seven in the morning that she might have more time to be with me, & on this account, would give her till eight o'clock to be at home tomorrow. ... Asked her how often they were connected &, guessing, found it might be at the rate of about twenty times a year. Got into bed. She seemed to want a kiss. It was more than I did. The tears rushed to my eyes. I felt I know not what & she perceived that I was much agitated. She bade me not or she would begin too & I knew not how she should suffer. She guessed not what passed within me. They were not tears of adoration. I felt that she was another man's wife. I shuddered at the thought & at the conviction that no soffistry [sic] could gloss over the criminality of our connection. It seemed not that the like had occurred to her. (I said, just before we got up, 'Well, come. Whatever C– has done to me, I am even with him. However, he little thinks what we have been about. What would he do if he knew?' 'Do? He would divorce me.' 'Yes,' said I, 'it would be a sad business for us both, but we are even with him, at any rate.' 'Indeed', said M–, laughing, 'indeed we are.' Shewed no sign of scruples ... What is M–'s match but legal prostitution? And, alas, what is her connection with me? Has she more passion than refinement? More plausibility than virtue? Give me a little romance. It is the greatest purifier of our affections & often an excellent guard against liberties.) From the kiss she gave me it seemed as if she loved me as fondly as ever. By & by, we seemed to drop asleep but, by & by, I perceived she would like another kiss & she whispered, 'Come again a bit, Freddy'. For a little while I pretended sleep. In fact, it was inconvenient. But soon, I got up a second time, again took off, went to her a second time &, in spite of all, she really gave me pleasure, & I told her no one had ever given me kisses like hers.

(From *I Know My Own Heart*, edited by Helena Whitbread
(London: Virago, 1988), pp. 104–105)

2.15   The Ladies of Llangollen, from the diaries of Anne Lister (1822)

Tuesday 23 July (Llangollen)

... She asked if I would walk out. Shewed me the kitchen garden. Walked round the shrubbery with me. She said she owned to their having been 42 years there. They landed first in South Wales, but it did not answer the accounts they had heard of it. Then they travelled in North Wales &, taken with the beauty of this place, took the cottage for 31 years – but it was a false lease & they had a great deal of trouble & expense. It was only 4 years since they had bought the place. Dared say I had a much nicer place at home. Mentioned its situation, great age, long time in the family, etc. She wished to know where to find an account of it. Said it had been their humble endeavour to make the place as old as they could. Spoke like a woman of the world about my liking the place where I was born, etc. Said I was not born there. My father was a younger brother but that I had the expectation of succeeding my uncle. 'Ah, yes', said she, 'you will soon be the master & there will be an end of romance.' 'Never! Never!' Said I. I envied their place & the happiness they had there. Asked if, dared say, they had never quarrelled. 'No!' They had never had a quarrel. Little differences of opinion sometimes, but only about the planting of a tree, and, when they differed in opinion, they took care to let no one see it.

At parting, shook hands with her and she gave me a rose. I said I should keep it for the sake of the place where it grew. She had before said she should be happy sometime to introduce me to Lady Eleanor. I had given my aunt's compliments & inquiries. Said she would have called with me but feared to intrude & was not quite well this evening. She, Miss Ponsonby, gave me a sprig of geranium for my aunt with her compliments & thanks for her inquiries. Lady Eleanor was asleep while I was there. Miss Ponsonby had been reading to her *Adam Blair*, the little book recommended to me by M– at Chester. I had told Miss Ponsonby I had first seen an account of them in *La*

Belle Assemblie a dozen years ago, & had longed to see the place ever since. She said some people had been very impertinent, particularly Dr Mavor, who had in some way displeased (laughed at, or something) the old housekeeper to whose memory they had erected a monument in the church yard & it seems the ladies had a particular objection to Dr M–, but Miss Ponsonby appears to have lost her teeth & occasionally mumbles a little that, as a stranger, I did not always perhaps quite understand her. It seems 2 of the Cromptons & their brother (of Esholt) were lately sketching the place. The ladies sent them chairs – went out to speak to them (for they were retiring, fearing they had offended the ladies) – formed an acquaintance &, wanting to know something about the Derwentwater family, which the Cromptons could get to know, there has been a correspondence. Miss Ponsonby said she has not answered their last letter but meant to do it. Leady Eleanor Butler & Miss Ponsonby seem great pedigree people. Antiquarians, topography, etc. I came away much pleased with Miss Ponsonby & sincerely hoping Lady Eleanor will recover to enjoy a few more years in this world. I know not how it is, I felt low after coming away. A thousand moody reflections occurred, but again, writing has done me good . . . I mean to dry & keep the rose Miss Ponsonby gave me. 'Tis now 10 1/4. Sat talking to my aunt. Came upstairs at 11.10.

Saturday 3 August [Halifax]

. . . Foolscap sheet from M– . . . She seems much interested about Lady Eleanor Butler and Miss Ponsonby and I am agreeably surprised (never dreaming of such a thing) at her observation, 'The account of your visit is the prettiest narrative I have read. You have at once excited & gratified my curiosity. Tell me if you think their regard has always been platonic & if you ever believed pure friendship could be so exalted. If you do, I shall think there are brighter amongst mortals than I ever believed there were . . .' I cannot help thinking that surely it was not platonic. Heaven forgive me, but I look within myself and doubt. I feel the infirmity of our nature & hesitate to pronounce such attachments uncemented by something more tender than friendship. But much, or all, depends upon the story of their former lives, the period passed before they lived together, that feverish dream called youth.

(From *I Know My Own Heart*, edited by Helena Whitbread
(London: Virago, 1988), pp. 203–205, 210)

Chapter Three

Philanthropy and politics to 1860

Women's philanthropic activity has traditionally been seen as the result of their having time on their hands on account of a new confinement to the domestic sphere.[1] More recently, historians have suggested that philanthropy enabled women to participate in their local communities and to contribute to the redrawing of social relations that was happening in the years following the French Revolution. In this sense, philanthropy was closely related to other social and political movements.[2] Recent research on aristocratic women and politics in the eighteenth century has similarly emphasised their extensive participation in a political culture that incorporated salons, dinners, garden parties and teas.[3] Women participated in electioneering, and while their participation declined with each extension of the franchise, important political hostesses remained: Justin McCarthy said in 1870 that '[t]he drawing room often settles the fate of the divisions in the House of Commons'.[4] Women were also prominent in the biggest middle-class political campaigns of the early nineteenth century: the anti-slavery movement and the campaign for the repeal of the Corn Laws. The documents in this chapter concern middle-class women's philanthropic activities and participation in political movements in this period.

3.1 Hannah More, 'A Cure for Melancholy: showing the way to do good with little money' (1794)

Hannah More was a pioneer of philanthropic reform in the 1790s and early 1800s who, with her sister Patty, ran Sunday schools and Friendly societies for women in the Mendip villages. Her *Cheap*

Repository series of tracts (1795–1798) drew upon these experiences to attempt to dissuade working people from sympathising with radical and revolutionary politics. They also sought to reshape community relationships, encouraging middle-class women to exert a positive moral influence over the poor. 'A Cure for Melancholy', written by Hannah More, features Mrs Jones, a widow living in reduced circumstances who heeds a sermon on the good Samaritan and becomes involved in philanthropy with the poor.

3.2 Mrs Sarah Trimmer, *The Oeconomy of Charity; or, an address to ladies concerning Sunday schools . . .* (1787)

Sarah Trimmer (1741–1810) was a philanthropic pioneer of the late eighteenth and early nineteenth centuries. She ran a Sunday school in Brentford, advised mothers on reading material for their children, and wrote didactic literature. In *The Oeconomy of Charity* (1787), Trimmer argues for the importance of women's involvement in education. While she puts her case carefully, negotiating potential hostility, it is easy to see how she and other women experienced 'woman's mission' as empowering, enabling them to adopt an important social role.

3.3 Catherine Cappe, *On the Desireableness and Utility of Ladies Visiting the Female Wards of Hospitals and Lunatic Asylums* (1817)

In the 1810s, women extended their visiting routines from the homes of poor women to include prisons, workhouses and hospitals. Catherine Cappe (1774–1822), a Unitarian, first visited York County Hospital and Lunatic Asylum in 1813 and began regular visiting in 1814–1815. In this excerpt, Cappe represents the necessity for women's access to such institutions in domestic terms.

3.4 Ellen Ranyard, *The Missing Link; or, Bible-women in the Homes of the London Poor* (1859)

Ellen Ranyard's (1810–1879) *The Missing Link; or, Bible-women in the Homes of the London Poor* (1859) details a new innovation in the 1850s and 1860s: the employment of working-class Bible-women who, it was believed, would have more affinity with, and therefore more influence over, poor families. The woman discussed here is Marian B., who had worked in various jobs – cutting fire papers, moulding wax flowers or making bags for silversmiths – and whose childhood had been blighted by a drunken father. She visited poor women in their homes and held tea parties at which she attempted to evangelise them.

3.5 Mrs Jameson, *Sisters of Charity and the Communion of Labour* (1855 and 1856)

Philanthropy furnished women with considerable skills and knowledge, whilst at the same time giving them an acute awareness of their lack of power, prior to their admittance to local government, to make real changes. In these lectures, Anna Brownell Jameson (1794–1860) argued that it was in society's interest for men and women to adopt complementary (and remunerated) public roles. Jameson accepted the notion of separate spheres but believed that while men were helped to become proficient in their work, women were not. Complementing rather than usurping men, women could work in a range of public institutions, as hospital nurses, teachers in reformatory schools and visitors to prisons, penitentiaries, houses of refuge and workhouses.

3.6 Anne Lister's diary, Yorkshire local elections (1835)

Anne Lister, a Tory landowner on the West Riding best known for her diaries, written partly in code, which recorded her lesbian affairs (see chapter 2), was also involved in local elections, as shown by these excerpts from her diary of 1835.

3.7 Eliza Fletcher, *Autobiography* (1874)

This excerpt from Eliza Fletcher's *Autobiography* presents the home as a site of political and enlightened sociability. Fletcher, who demonstrates an admirable lucidity within hours of giving birth to her daughter Elizabeth in October 1794, shared her husband's radical sympathies. The excerpt makes reference to the entertaining rumour circulated by Scottish Tories that she possessed a miniature guillotine at home![5]

3.8 Elizabeth Heyrick, *Appeal to the Hearts and Consciences of British Women* (1828)

The anti-slavery movement saw the most impressive mobilisation of middle-class women in the early nineteenth century. Women had been involved in the anti-slavery campaign of the 1780s and 1790s, but it was during the 1820s, following the lead taken by the formation of the Birmingham Ladies' Anti-slavery Society in 1825, that women in many localities formed their own organisations. With their energetic rounds of neighbourhood visiting, fundraising, tract and pamphlet writing and distribution, and canvassing signatures for petitions, women played a key role in the popularisation of anti-slavery which led to Abolition in 1833. *Appeal to the Hearts and Consciences of British Women* (1828) by Elizabeth Heyrick (1769–1831) is less famous than her influential pamphlet advocating *Immediate, not Gradual Abolition* (1824), but nicely illustrates arguments for women's 'influence'.

3.9 Sheffield Ladies' Association for the Universal Abolition of Slavery, *Ladies' Petition* (April 1838)

This petition was drawn up by the Sheffield Ladies' Association for the Universal Abolition of Slavery in opposition to the continuance of the apprenticeship system. This excerpt argues that the treatment of women slaves and the separation of families made anti-slavery a moral, and not just a political issue, and therefore ripe for women's involvement.

3.10 Frederick Bastiat, 'Cobden et La Ligue' (1845)

The Anti-Corn Law League was founded in February 1839. Women attended lectures, participated in soirees, tea-parties, house-to-house canvassing and petitioning. Their activities were at the centre of the ambitious Manchester and Covent Garden Bazaars of 1842 and 1845. This excerpt from 'Cobden et La Ligue' by the French political economist Frederick Bastiat discusses the compatibility of 'women's mission' with the ladies' anti-corn law activities.

3.1   Hannah More, 'A Cure for Melancholy: Showing the way to do good with little money' (1794)

'Sir', said Mrs Jones, 'I am grown shy of the poor since I have nothing to give them.'

'Nothing! madam?' replied the clergyman: 'do you call your time, your talents, your kind offices, nothing? Doing good does not so much depend on the riches as on the heart and on the will. The servant who improved his two talents was equally commended by the lord with him who had ten; and it was not poverty, but selfish indolence, which drew down so severe a condemnation on him who had only one. It is by our conformity to Christ, that we must prove ourselves Christians. You, madam, are not called upon to work miracles, nor to preach the Gospel, yet you may, in your measure and degree, resemble your Saviour *by going about and doing good* . . .

'You, madam, I will venture to say, might do more good than the richest man in the parish could do by merely giving his money. Instead of sitting here, brooding over your misfortunes, which are past remedy, bestir yourself to find out ways of doing much good with little money; or even without any money at all. You have lately studied economy for yourself; instruct your poor neighbours in that important art. They want it almost as much as they want money. You have influence with the few rich persons in the parish; exert that influence. Betty, my housekeeper, shall assist you in anything in which she can be useful . . .'

The sermon, and this discourse together, made so deep an impression on Mrs Jones, that she formed a new plan of life, and set about it at once, as every body does who is in earnest. Her chief aim was the happiness of her poor neighbours in the next world; but she was also very desirous to promote their present comfort: and, indeed, the kindness she showed to their bodily wants gave her such an access to their houses and hearts, as made them better disposed to receive religious counsel and instruction . . .

Mrs Jones resolved to spend two or three days in a week getting acquainted with the state of the parish, and she took care never to walk out without a few little good books in her pocket to give away. This, though cheap, is a most important act of charity: it has various uses; it furnishes the poor with religious knowledge, which they have so few ways of obtaining; it counteracts the wicked designs of those who have taught us at least one lesson, by their zeal in the dispersion of *wicked* books, – I mean the lesson of vigilance and activity; and it is the best introduction for any useful conversation which the giver of the book may wish to introduce.

(The Works of Hannah More, Vol. 3 (London: T. Cadell,
1830), pp. 273–278)

3.2 Mrs Sarah Trimmer, *The Oeconomy of Charity; or, an address to Ladies concerning Sunday-schools; the establishment of schools of industry under female inspection; and the distribution of voluntary benefactions* (1787)

Can ladies view those noble exertions of the other sex, and not be inspired with emulation to join with equal ardour in the undertaking which has for its object the reformation of so considerable a part of the kingdom; and which, in the end, may lead to a general reform?

What can be a greater act of charity than to contribute to the success of an institution like this? What more suited to the tenderness which is allowed to be natural to our sex? Can a woman, accustomed to the exercise of maternal affection towards her own beloved off-spring, be indifferent to the happiness of poor children, who have no means of learning their duty but what these schools can afford? Can she think of multitudes being devoted to ignorance, vice, and perhaps eternal misery, and not reach forth a ready hand to snatch them from so dreadful a fate? Will she not afford every assistance in her power towards the success of an establishment which is calculated to obviate these evils; to inculcate useful knowledge; adorn the mind with Christian graces; and procure for those, who are doomed to suffer the miseries of this life, eternal happiness in a future state? . . .

The task of early education in all families naturally devolves upon mothers; and those who discharge this duty are consequently par-ticularly qualified to open the understandings of poor children, which frequently are, even in those of twelve and fourteen, as destitute of cultivation as the minds of new-born infants.

Accustomed to instruct their families, women acquire a pleasing and easy method of communicating knowledge, which is more engaging to the young and ignorant than the graver methods generally employed by learned and scientific men. Women are besides acquainted with a variety of particulars that fall peculiarly within their own province, which enable them to advise the bigger girls with respect to decorum of behaviour and propriety of dress – points of very essential consequence to young females of every denomination. It is not sufficient to teach poor girls the obligation of moral duties; those who have never had the advantage of good examples require to be instructed minutely and incidentally how to practise them; and surely women are best qualified to give these instructions, as they must be most intimately acquainted with the recesses of the female heart, and with the arguments that will most effectively excite a virtuous emulation to excel in those virtues which are particularly feminine.

I do not mean to derogate from the merit of those gentlemen who have hitherto performed alone that task in which they had a natural and reasonable claim to female assistance; nor would I appear ungrateful for their good offices, which entitle them to respectful thanks; but women are undoubtedly best able to judge of the faults and mismanagements of their own sex, and of their peculiar wants; which in many instances are unavoidably overlooked by those who are unacquainted with the minutiae of domestic business: and therefore it is to be hoped that the worthy conductors of Sunday-schools will allow us to be helps meet for them, in a subordinate capacity, qualified at least to assist in executing what, to their immortal honour, they have so wisely and humanely planned . . .

But not to matrons only would I confine the interesting, the satisfactory office of visiting Sunday-schools. Could unmarried ladies be prevailed on to give their kind assistance, they would find occasions for exercising those amiable qualities, which are partly lost to the world for want of their forming matrimonial connections. Providence has exempted them from family cares; some of them live in affluence; numbers in easy circumstances; their hours often hang heavy on their hands – how then can they apply their superfluities of time and money to more advantage than in affording instruction and employment to poor children? . . . I am persuaded that, would single ladies condescend to become nursing mothers to the poor of the rising generation, their happiness would be greatly increased.

Young ladies may also, with peculiar propriety, assist in Sunday-schools; and it is particularly incumbent on them to do so, since it is for them chiefly that we are endeavouring to train up to religion and virtue, servants, labourers, and mechanics: the rising generation of poor are instructed by us, that our children may be better served than their parents have been, and that, when they have households of their own, 'they may lie down in peace and take their rest', without the dread of being disturbed by the night robber; and travel the road free from the painful apprehension of being molested by the daring highwayman.

(London: Longman and Robinson, 1787, pp. 19–26)

3.3 Catherine Cappe, *On the Desireableness and Utility of Ladies Visiting the Female Wards of Hospitals and Lunatic Asylums* (1817)

A lady visitor in a hospital or asylum, should be to that institution what the judicious Mistress of a family is to her household, – the careful inspector of the oeconomy, the integrity and the good moral conduct of the housekeeper and other inferior servants in their various departments. Are there not many things relating to cleanliness, proper clothing, and a thousand other less obvious matters of great consequence to the sick, into which a male visitor, from motives of delicacy, cannot inquire, and which, if there are no lady visitors, must be entirely left to the uncontrolled superintendence of the nurse or matron? Would the father, the brother, the son, however kind or intelligent, be equally competent to all the duties of a judicious inspector of a bed of sickness, as a mother, a sister, or a daughter? and do not the same principles apply in the one case as in the other? Surely then we need not add how exceedingly in every point of view a regulation so salutary would increase the general utility, and add to the credit and respectability of these several institutions, at the same time that the benefit would be unspeakable to all those for whose assistance they were originally designed.

If then it be admitted that the regular appointment of female visitors would in its results be so conducive to the general welfare, and favourable to the moral character of others, may we not next inquire what would be the effects of this practice, were it to become general, upon their own?

It is well known that in a greater or less degree, all human beings are the children of habit, and that in proportion as the young are trained to the exercise of kindness and benevolence, taught to consider the happiness of others in common with their own, or exclusively to seek more selfish gratifications, such will be their future character. Is this true of both sexes, or are females an exception to a general law? From whom would the father, the son, or the brother, expect the most judicious, affectionate attention in an hour of sickness or under the infirmities of age? from her who had been early accustomed to fulfil every relative and social duty, to 'visit the fatherless and widow in their affliction', and had learned from experience the soothing charm of affectionate sympathy; or from her whose valuable time had been principally squandered in the acquirement of mere showy accomplishments, or in studiously adorning her person that she might excite more general admiration, might figure with more distinguished éclat in the crowded nightly assembly, and run with increasing celebrity the unmeaning, unceasing round of fashionable dissipation? . . .

But the female patients of these institutions, would they feel no repugnance to the idea of being visited by ladies? Rather on the contrary, would they not consider it as a very great privilege to have the power of communicating to persons of their own sex every afflictive circumstance of their suffering state? May there not be a variety of minute circumstances which may occasion great distress, and may retard, if not wholly prevent, recovery, but which can be communicated only to a female ear? Would it not be an unspeakable comfort to be assured, that every species of unfeeling licentiousness would be repressed, and that if they demeaned themselves with modesty and propriety they might depend upon being countenanced by those friends of suffering humanity whilst they remained in the hospital, and occasionally perhaps, in cases of extreme distress, even beyond that period? Even the nurses, such of them at least as were solicitous to do their duty, would be gainers by having their conduct observed and approved . . .

Are these opposers afraid, that were ladies in general to go on improving in mental and moral acquisitions – afraid, that in consequence of more extensive active benevolence, they should attain to yet more enlarged and accurate views of human life and Christian duty, and consequently being more eminently distinguished for wise conduct and judicious discrimination, that their influence should be proportionately increased? The alarm is well founded, for trivial as may be the pursuits, and imperfect as may be the character of too many in our own age and country, (among the daughters of fashion especially,) yet it must be allowed, notwithstanding, that they take a much higher place already than their degraded, unfortunate contemporaries in Constantinople or Hindostan – and to what is this owing, but to their better education, and to their being allowed to consider themselves as rational and accountable creatures? Who then shall say to how much higher degrees of consideration and respectability they might eventually attain, were their minds still further enlarged, and their consequent modes of life more consistent, rational, and disinterestedly benevolent?

(York: T. Wilson and Sons, 1817, pp. 7–11)

3.4 Ellen Ranyard, *The Missing Link; or, Bible-Women in the Homes of the London Poor* (1859)

A LADY, who had long been engaged in promoting the circulation of the Word of God in country districts, walked one midsummer afternoon, about two years since, with a friend through the streets of St Giles's. The friend was a retired physician, who had known the secrets of the Seven Dials in the days of his early practice. The lady had recently become a resident in London, and the two having been village neighbours, this was a kind of exploratory walk to observe the condition of the London poor. Meantime, the question arose, how far these people, in their countless courts and alleys, would be found to be supplied with the Bible.

This inquiry grew into a determination to ascertain that they were so supplied, and led to a reference to one of the active Missionaries of the district. He was asked if he knew of a poor, good woman who would venture with a bag of Bibles into every room, as a paid agent for the BIBLE SOCIETY, and give a faithful account of her trust.

. . . Some of her earliest visits were paid to courts in which no one professes to get an honest maintenance, and where the children, of Irish parents, who were frequently unmarried, have grown up – half naked and buried in dirt – having no knowledge of, or desire for, a better existence. By 'tossing', by thieving, by passing bad money (for in Whitechapel they can get a shilling that few can tell to be false coinage for 2½d) by every species of vice, they live – sometimes in starving indigence, sometimes in reckless abundance: occasionally beef-steaks and potatoes will be tumbled onto a table with no accompaniment of knife or fork. Their dwellings are like cow-houses – save that cow-houses are sweet in comparison – lighted by but one pane of glass, if that be not broken and stuffed with rags, and a heap of shaving or filthy straw for a bed; some of them buy hare and rabbit skins, and hoarding them till they have enough to sell, create a stench which breeds fever; the hair of the women seems never to have known cap or comb; such clothes as they have appear never to be taken off day or night; they have no yards and no back door; perhaps a pump is found in the little square round which they have been built, but the supply of water is very scanty; and five, six, or seven children will swarm in these closets of rooms in the daytime . . .

The difficulty of finding access to the lower population of St Giles's can only be realised by those who have attempted it. 'Out, out, out', was the perpetual summer answer in room after room. Marian found them 'such an unsettled set of people. They have no regular time for dinner. She supposed they did not often have a dinner. She was glad to perceive any sign that they were going to stay – the little bit of curtain at the window, or the picture hung up on the wall; but in their various avocations as watercress sellers, scavengers, road waterers, crossing-sweepers, etc., they are such a wandering folk.' . . .

These BIBLE VISITS, it will be perceived were paid to a class of persons *below the decent poor*, and to those who compose that leg underlying mass of humanity which never seeks to bring itself within the range of moral or spiritual effort for its own elevation. The one concern of these people – winter and summer, and year after year – is merely to live – and to thousands, the easiest and idlest mode to attain this end is by the vice and in the filth amidst which they were born and bred. . . .

A wish arose that God might in His mercy *multiply female agency like this* a hundredfold for neighbourhoods similar to St Giles's; that He might raise up and train by His providence these native reformers of their own class; and that educated Christian Ladies might find them out, and quietly help them in their work.

No LADY, however self-denying, would have been able, by repeated visits, to seek the eight women above described in the haunts from which they came. Places like St Giles's have their own pride and their own reserve. They need female agency *of their own*, co-operative with all present missionary work, and the right beginning and root of such agency is in the SERVICE OF THE WORD OF GOD.

(*The Missing Link*, Chapter II, 'A Message, and the Messenger', and Chapter III, 'Marian's Tea-Party in St Giles's' (London: James Nisbet and Co, 1859), pp. 11–41)

3.5   Mrs Jameson, *Sisters of Charity and the Communion of Labour* (1855–1856)

The questions as yet unsettled seem to be these:–

Whether a more enlarged sphere of social work may not be allowed to woman in perfect accordance with the truest feminine instincts? Whether there be not a possibility of her sharing practically in the responsibilities of social as well as domestic life? Whether she might not be better prepared to meet and exercise such higher responsibilities? Whether such a communion of labour might not lead to the more humane ordering of many of our public institutions; to a purer standard of morals; and to a better mutual comprehension and a finer harmony between men and women, when thus called upon to work together, and (in combining what is best in the two natures) becoming what God intended them to be, the supplement to each other? . . .

Work in some form or other is the appointed lot of all – divinely appointed; and given as equal the religious responsibilities of the two sexes, might we not, in distributing the work to be done in this world, combine and use in more equal proportion the working faculties of men and women, and so find a remedy for many of those mistakes which have vitiated some of our noblest educational and charitable institutions? Is it not possible that in the apportioning of the work we may have too far sundered what in God's creation never can be sundered without pain and mischief, the masculine and feminine influences? – lost the true balance between the element of power and the element of love? and trusted too much to mere mechanical means for carrying out high religious and moral purposes?

It seems indisputable that the mutual influence of the two sexes – brain upon brain – life upon life – becomes more subtle, and spiritual, and complex, more active and more intense, in proportion as the whole human race is improved and developed. The physiologist knows this well: let the moralist give head to it, lest in becoming more intense, and active, and extended, such influences become at the same time less beneficient, less healthful, and less manageable.

It appears to me that we do wrong to legislate, and educate, and build up institutions without taking cognisance of this law of our being. It appears to me that the domestic affections and the domestic duties – what I have called the 'communion of love and the communion of labour' – must be taken as the basis of all the more complicated social relations, and that the family sympathies must be carried out and developed in all the forms and duties of social existence, before we can have a prosperous, happy, and truly Christian community. Yes! – I have the deepest conviction, founded not merely on my own experience and observation, but on the testimony of some of the wisest and best men among us, that to enlarge the working sphere of woman to the measure of her faculties, to give her a more practical and authorised share in all social arrangements which have for their object the amelioration of evil and suffering, is to elevate her in the social scale; and that whatever renders womanhood respected and respectable in the estimation of the people tends to humanise and refine the people.

It is surely an anomaly that, while women are divided from men in learning and working by certain superstitions of a conventional morality, and in social position by the whole spirit and tendency of our past legislation, their material existence and interests are regarded as identical; – identical however only in this sense – that the material and social interests of women are always supposed to be merged in those of man; while it is never taken for granted that the true interests of man are inseparable from those of the woman: so at the outset we are met by inconsistency and confusion, such as must inevitably disturb the security and integrity of all mutual relations.

Here then I take my stand, not on any hypothesis of expediency, but on what I conceive to be an essential law of life; and I conclude that all our endowments for social good, whatever their specific purpose or denomination – educational, sanitary, charitable, penal – will prosper and fulfil their objects in so far as we carry out this principle of combining in due proportion the masculine and the feminine element, and will fail or become perverted into some form of evil in so far as we neglect or ignore it.

(*Sisters of Charity and the Communion of Labour. Two Lectures on the Social Employment of Women* (London: Longman, Brown, Green, Longmans and Roberts, 1859), pp. 72, 80–82)

3.6 Anne Lister's diary, Yorkshire local elections (1835)

26 July 1832

Mr. Rawson's servant brought me my account for the bank and a note asking me to get John Bottomley's vote for Mr. Wortley [Conservative candidate] – went about the latter immediately – not at home – told his wife to send him to speak to me saying he must give me his vote.

30 July 1832

Then had John Bottomley – sent for him to get his vote for Mr. Wortley – had signed, he said, for Lord Grey and Milton [Whigs] but I told him the latter would not come forward, that he Bottomley was therefore at liberty and must give me his vote which he agreed to do.

11 December 1832

Had John Bottomley having sent for him to tell him to vote for Mr. Wortley tomorrow – had ¼ hours talk – he promised to vote for him tomorrow or Thursday . . . They had all been at him and some said they would not employ him again if he would not vote their way but he told them how I wanted him to vote and seeming to care nothing about it except that he thought he ought to oblige me – It is quite useless to have men as he uninfluenced – he knows nothing and cares nothing about it and is likely best satisfied with the idea of pleasing so badly he knows . . .

12 December 1832

Had Thorp – if I could get him his shop window made and a new roof raised a couple of feet, would vote as I liked all his life – had no vote this time because his landladies pay the taxes.

13 December 1832

Mr. Henry Edwards of Pye West called for a few minutes about John Bottomley's vote – gave him a note as follows: 'John Bottomley. I hear mistakes are made by voters going to the wrong booth – I send this by Mr. Henry Edwards of Pye West and wish you would go with him. A Lister, Shibden Hall, Thursday 13 December 1832.'

31 December 1832

So thoroughly unexpected was the disappointment of Mr. James Wortley's losing his election, I have not yet got up my political spirits – I hardly thought myself capable of such strong political excitement and mortification . . . I am completely sick of public events.

(West Yorkshire Archive Service,
Calderdale: SH: ML/E/14–18)

3.7   Eliza Fletcher, *Autobiography of Mrs Fletcher, of Edinburgh, with selections from her letters and other family memorials* (1874)

Not many days after her birth the newspapers were full of the proceedings on the State trials in London – the trial of Thomas Hardy and John Horne Took, &c., &c., for high treason – and the joyful news reached us that these persecuted men were acquitted by a jury of their countrymen. Mr. Fletcher considered this verdict as the noblest proof of the excellence of the British Constitution. Had the juries of England truckled to the Tory Government of the time, as those of Scotland had unhappily done in the convictions of Muir, Joseph Gerald, Fyshe Palmer, &c., &c., he thought that Great Britain would not have been a country for a freeman to live in, because not one in which a man could fearlessly avow his sentiments on political subjects. This assertion of the right of private judgement in matters of State policy being established by the glorious acquittal of Hardy and Horne Took, put hope and confidence into the hearts of all true and honest reformers.

My husband read at my bedside the very interesting details of these trials, and so highly did I sympathize in his delight that the excitement was followed by a sharp attack of fever, and newspapers, juries' verdicts, and all triumphs of Liberal opinions were for a time interdicted to the lady in the straw, who had a somewhat tedious confinement. I was a good nurse in the true sense of the word, never denying my infant its natural food, night or day, when called for. I never allowed any other occupation or amusement to interfere with this first claim of duty. My child grew and prospered, my home was happy. Political animosity around us was increased by the bitter animosity of the Tory party, but this never cooled the friendship between Miss Ferguson and me, and her gentle spirit was often brave in defending me against the aspersions of political rancour.

[Daughter and editor writes:] It is hardly possible to credit now, save as having been uttered in jest, the things gravely said and as gravely believed at that time in Edinburgh concerning those who were generally held to be on the wrong side in politics. That our mother had provided herself with a small guillotine, and exercised the same in beheading poultry, or perhaps 'rats and mice and such small deer', in order to be expert when 'French principles', and practice in accordance, should prevail in our land was one of these. It reached our father's amazed and amused ears by the question asked him in sad earnest by a kindly old clergyman (when in Edinburgh on the business of the General Assembly), whether it was possible that a lady he so much respected could be so 'awfully misled' . . .

(Carlisle: C. Thurnham and Sons, 1874, pp. 62–63)

3.8 Elizabeth Heyrick, *Appeal to the Hearts and Consciences of British Women* (1828)

A celebrated statesman and poet has pronounced, that 'Woman's noblest station is retreat,' and the sentiment has acquired the authority of an established aphorism. Her duties, for the most part, are doubtless of a quiet, unobtrusive nature; she is happily excluded from the great theatre of public business, from the turmoils of ambition, the strife of debate, and the cares of legislation; she may, nevertheless, exert a powerful influence over public opinion and practice without violating that retiring delicacy which constitutes one of her loveliest ornaments. The peculiar texture of her mind, her strong feelings and quick sensibilities, especially qualify her, not only to sympathise with suffering, but also to plead for the oppressed, and there is no calculating the extent and importance of the moral reformations which might be effected through the combined exertion of her gentle influence and steady resolution. No cruel institutions or ferocious practices could long withstand her avowed and persevering censure. Even Slavery, that broadest scandal to her country's laws – that foulest reproach to her country's religion – that most pregnant cause of superabounding crime and misery, which dooms hundreds of thousands to the lowest extremes of human degradation, of moral and physical wretchedness – could not long survive her zealous and steady opposition.

It required an extent of knowledge, a patience of investigation, a resolution and force of mind peculiar to the stronger sex, to bring the system into broad day-light, to expose to public view all its circumstances of shame and infamy, to detect and confute all the sophistry and falsehood employed to discredit the testimony of facts, to overturn the evidence of truth. It required masculine courage, talent, and virtue to withstand the frowns of power, the oppositions of interest; to open the public eyes to the sin and the shame, the extreme folly and the extreme danger of upholding such a monstrous assemblage of crime; but to revive, extend and deepen those general convictions of its enormity which are subsiding into the most reproachful apathy; to array against it a general system of decisive *practical* discouragement, the zealous co-operation of our enlightened and patriotic countrywomen is indispensably requisite.

... The memorable report of the Jamaica House of Assembly, dated November 23rd, 1804, after describing the abolition of slavery as the most fearful of calamities, proceeds to say – 'an abolition by the legislature is not the sole means by which the West Indies may be ruined.' (In colonial language, the destruction of slavery and the destruction of the West Indies are synonymous.) 'The same object', they proceed, 'may be obtained as completely, although with somewhat less rapidity, BY ENCOURAGING THE CULTIVATION OF SUGAR IN THE EAST INDIES, where the fertility of the soil, the facility of irrigation, the abundance of provision, the cheapness of labour, and the structure of society, given advantages which nature has denied to these islands,' &c. The colonists have further informed us that slavery in the British West Indies mainly depends on *British* consumption of its produce. 'The continent', says one of their ablest advocates, 'can be, and *is* supplied with sugar at a cheaper rate than it can be grown by the British Planter.'

These are important admissions. BY THE SIMPLE SUBSTITUTION OF EAST FOR WEST INDIA SUGAR, THE SLAVE-OWNERS THEMSELVES CONFESS THAT SLAVERY MAY BE ANNIHILATED. To effect its annihilation by this simple means, to whom can we appeal with such propriety as to our enlightened and patriotic countrywomen? In the domestic departments, they are the chief controllers; they, for the most part, provide the articles of family consumption; instead of purchasing that luxury, the cultivation of which constitutes at once the chief profits and oppressions of slavery, they can substitute that which is the genuine produce of free labour, and by so doing become a blessing to existing and unborn millions. By so doing they many confer incalculable benefits on the starving population of Ireland, and greatly improve the condition of our own; for the sugar imported from the East Indies would be paid for by the export of home manufactures, which, among a population in our eastern dominions of eighty millions, would find a wide and profitable market . . .

(Leicester: A. Cockshaw, 1828, pp. 3–6)

3.9 Sheffield Ladies' Association for the Universal Abolition of Slavery, *Ladies' Petition* (1838)

. . . TOWNSWOMEN, – We venture to come forward most earnestly to entreat you, one and all, to affix your names to this Petition in behalf of nearly eight hundred thousand of your enslaved brethren and sisters. Shall these wretched beings endure unparalleled injustice and suffering for two years and a quarter longer, without your making *one* effort for their rescue from the house of bondage? Will you not unhesitatingly join us, and *'open your mouth for the dumb, – judge righteously, and plead the cause of the poor and needy?'*

Be not turned aside by the oft-repeated objection, that it is a *political* question, with which *women* have nothing to do. *Nothing to do with slavery?* Nothing to do in behalf of woman, scorned, polluted, ruined, both for time and eternity! *We* regard this as a cause *peculiarly woman's.* Hear the command of Scripture, 'Remember *them that are in bonds as bound with them.'* Oh! if you *were* bound with them, how would you wish others to feel and act for *you?* If *your* parents, husband, children, were bound with them, could you then turn away from the subject as a *political* question, in which you had no interest? Imagine your *own* mother on the treadmill – your *own* innocent daughter chained to a vile wretch, sweeping the streets, for the alleged crime of *indolence*, your *own* cherished infant left to die unattended. Cannot you bear the *thought*? Then sign this Petition in behalf of your Negro sisters, who are experiencing the sad *reality*.

Fear not, that we should ask you to unite in anything unbecoming of your sex. There can be nothing presumptuous in our assuming the humble place of petitioners. We are happily excluded from the great theatre of public business – from the strife of debate, and the cares of legislation; but this privilege does not exempt us from the duty of exerting ourselves in our own appropriate sphere. We desire not to take part in the final adjustment of the question, but we may endeavour to help it on towards a decision. Let us determine to give our rulers no rest, till we have wearied them by our importunity, into compliance with our request.

Be not discouraged by the voice of ridicule or censure. You will be told that such efforts are useless; that a *ladies'* petition can only excite a contemptuous smile. Remember, *Duty* is ours; *Consequences* are in the hands of Him who can accomplish His designs by the most feeble instrumentality.

Come then, immediately and sign this Petition. It is not the time for ceremony, but for action. Forget not, that while you are deliberating on the propriety of affixing your names, the injured Negro is weeping, bleeding, *dying*. To you, amidst all the blessings of your happy lot, two years and a quarter may seem a short period to look forward to; but what must it appear to those who measure the lapse of time by stripes, starvation, tortures, and unutterable woes? To *them*, every hour is of importance. The case admits not a moment's delay.

By your loyalty to your beloved and youthful Queen; the glory of whose opening reign is tarnished by her still being the *Queen of Slaves*, we entreat you to sign this Petition.

By your love of your country, and your thankfulness for your birthright blessings – by your desire that this imperial isle should stand conspicuous above all nations for its hatred of oppression – by your wish to avert those awful judgements which have ever been the *'heritage of oppressors'*, we entreat you to sign this Petition.

By the bitter sorrows of the Slave – by his groans of agony and despair – by the thrilling cry of anguish from the mother in bonds weeping over her children – by the tears and sufferings of those wretched little ones left to perish, neglected and alone, we entreat you to sign this Petition.

By all the horrors of an insurrection, which is confidently expected in the West Indies, if equal liberty for *all* is not proclaimed on the first of August next – and by the fearful laws which in such a case would perpetuate Slavery to an indefinite period, we entreat you to sign this Petition.

By the natural sympathies implanted in your bosoms – by the solemn requirements of revealed truth – by all that you owe to yourselves, to your fellow creatures, to your God, – we call upon you to sign this Petition.

'Whatsoever ye would that men should do to you, do ye even so to them.'

3.10 Frederick Bastiat, 'Cobden et La Ligue' (1845)

Since Mr. Kohl has spoken of the participation of the English ladies in the work of the League, I hope a few reflections on this subject will not be found out of place. I doubt not that the reader is surprised, and perhaps scandalised, to see woman appearing in these stormy debates. Woman seems to lose her grace by risking herself in this scientific melee, bristling with the barbarous words *tariff*, *salaries*, *profits*, *monopolies*. What is there in common between dry dissertations and that ethereal being, that angel of the soft affections, that poetical and devoted nature, whose destiny it is solely to love and to please, to sympathise and to console?

But, if woman does become alarmed at the dull syllogism and cold statistics, she is gifted with a marvellous sagacity, with a promptitude and certainty of appreciation, which make her detect, at once, on what side a serious enterprise sympathises with the tendencies of her own heart. She has comprehended that the effort of the League is a cause of justice and of reparation towards the suffering classes; she has comprehended that almsgiving is not the only form of charity. We are ready to succour the unfortunate, say they; but that is no reason why the law should make unfortunates. We are willing to feed those who are hungry, to clothe those who are cold, but we applaud efforts which have for their object the removal of the barriers which interpose between clothing and nakedness, between subsistence and starvation.

And, besides, is not the part which the English ladies have taken in the work of the League in perfect harmony with the mission of woman in society? There are fetes, soirees, given to the *free-traders*; – éclat, warmth, and life are communicated by their presence to those great oratorical jousts in which the condition of the masses is discussed; – a magnificent prize is held out to the most eloquent orator, or to the most indefatiguable defender of liberty.

A philosopher has said, 'A people has only one thing to do, in order to develope [*sic*] in its bosom every virtue, every useful energy. It is simply *to honour what is honourable, and to contemn what is contemptible.*' And who is the natural dispenser of shame and glory? Woman; woman, gifted with a tact so unerring for discriminating the morality of the end, the purity of the motive, the convenience of the method; woman, who, a simple spectator of our social struggles, is always in possession of an impartiality too often foreign to our sex; woman, whose sympathy, sordid interest, or cold calculation, never ices over – the sympathy for what is noble and beautiful; woman, in fine, who forbids by a tear, and commands by a smile.

In former times the ladies crowned the conqueror of the tourney. Valour, address, clemency, became popularised by the intoxicating sound of their applause. In those times of trouble and of violence, in which brutal force overrode the feeble and the defenceless, it was a good thing to encourage the union of the generosity which is found in the courage and loyalty of the knight, with the rude manners of the soldier.

What! because times are changed; because the age is advanced; muscular force has given place to moral energy; because injustice and oppression borrow other forms, and strife is removed from the field of battle to the conflict of ideas, shall the mission of woman be terminated? Shall she always be restricted to the rear of the social movement? Shall it be forbidden for her to exercise over new customs her benignant influence, or to foster under her regard the virtues of a more elevated order which modern civilisation has called into existence?

No! this cannot be. There is no point in the upward movement of humanity at which the empire of woman stops forever. As civilisation transforms and elevates itself, this empire must be transformed and elevated with it, not annihilated; – there would then be an inexplicable void in the social harmony, and in the providential order of things. In our days it pertains to woman to decree to moral virtues, to intellectual power, to enlightened philanthropy, those inestimable prizes, those irresistible encouragements, which they formerly reserved for the valour of the warrior alone . . .

(Quoted in Archibald Prentice, *History of the Anti-Corn Law League* (London: W & F. G. Cash, 1853), Vol. I, pp. 171–172)

Chapter Four

Working women and the family wage

For women of the working class, the ideology of 'separate spheres' was even more problematic than it was for middle-class women. Working-class women had to work, often participating in paid employment from their own homes, frequently making money in ways not recognised as 'paid work', such as childminding, baking, taking in lodgers, sewing or washing. Throughout the nineteenth century, they continued to work in agriculture, and were employed in their thousands in manufacturing industries, especially the textile trades in which they were specifically targeted as cheap female labour. Women went into service in increasing numbers and the end of the century saw opportunities in shop-work, teaching and clerical work. Various continuities run through women's work which, in relation to that of men, was generally poorly paid, poorly unionised and less skilled. The sources in this chapter cover different aspects of women's work throughout the long nineteenth century, raising issues concerning: the impact of industrialisation; acceptable work for women and the campaigns to have them removed from some workplaces; the diversity of women's work; and the relationship between industrialisation and family life.

4.1 Mrs Burrows, 'A Childhood in the Fens about 1850–1860'

Women had traditionally undertaken a range of agricultural work: they were employed to weed, hoe and harvest crops such as wheat and rye where the lighter sickle was used, and to gather grain and hay at harvest time. They also worked in market gardens and in hop gardens. This work would supplement their responsibility for the household and kitchen garden or the grazing of cows, pigs and poultry, sometimes of common land. This excerpt emphasises the continued use of children's and women's labour in agriculture in the nineteenth century, the casual nature of their employment and the expectation that they would contribute to the family economy.

4.2 Clementina Black, *Married Women's Work* (1915)

According to Maud F. Davies' report on women's farm work in Worcestershire, women engaged in ground-dressing, hop-tying and hay-making and threshing; they picked hops and fruit, pulled mangold and swede, and sorted potatoes and mended sacks. Their work was of importance for the family economy, and women were valued for their ability to perform such tasks. At the same time, women's work was more focused on 'helping' and was defined as less skilled and therefore was less well-paid. The Reports were a result of investigations by the Women's Industrial Council (1894), of which Clementina Black (1854–1922) was a prominent member, in 1909–1910.

4.3 Anthony Ashley Cooper, Lord Ashley, debate on Hours of Labour in Factories, House of Commons, 15 March 1844

The movement of women into factory work formed the first wave of moral panic concerning women's work in the early nineteenth century. Women in weaving, employed because of the reluctance of male handloom weavers to submit to factory discipline, were among the best paid labouring women in the country. Male workers' arguments for the family wage also coincided with the anxieties of middle- and upper-class campaigners about the consequences of women working outside of the home: such women, they claimed, lacked domestic skills, and the absence of home comforts was turning their husbands to drink. The focus of this excerpt from the speech by philanthropist and reformer Anthony Ashley Cooper, Lord Ashley (1801–1885), is the highly visible 'female subculture' of the mill workers, and in particular their adoption of 'male' behaviour which he believed could only lead to familial dislocation.

4.4 Ada Nield Chew, 'A Living Wage for Factory Girls at Crewe', second letter to the *Crewe Chronicle* (1894)

Many female cotton weavers, such as the mill girls of Lancashire, valued their skill and independence. Continuing restrictions from the Factory and Workshop Acts of 1874 and 1878 further reduced women's work, however, and for the half a million women (plus) working in factories at end of the nineteenth century, their work was unskilled, with little opportunity to train; the paternalism of union leaders saw that they made little progress in the labour movement. This excerpt from Ada Nield Chew's second letter to the *Crewe Chronicle* details the conditions of employment: the piece work, poor wages, long hours, obligatory home work and exhaustion. Ada Nield (1870–1945) was sacked once her identity as the author of the letters became known; she then became a paid worker for the ILP (see chapter 9).

4.5 Alice Foley, *A Bolton Childhood* (1973)

Alice Foley (1891–1974) wrote in her autobiography about escaping the Half-Time Factory System which employed many of her friends from the age of 12, on account of her father's opposition to child labour. On leaving school at 13, however, her family needed her income. After an unsuccessful spell as a shop assistant, followed by a demoralising search for employment, she accepted her mother's suggestion to 'put thi clogs on, a' ger' a job in't mill'. Alice moved from the weaving shed to a job as a 'cloth fettler' and then into the 'preparation department', which she talks about here.

4.6 Employment in the mines: the sub-commissioners (1842)

Women's work in the mines was the subject of great controversy in the early 1840s. The investigators working on behalf of the 1840 Parliamentary Commission of Enquiry into children's employment were so horrified to find women working underground in the mines that they refocused their investigations. After an emotive campaign led by Lord Ashley in the Commons the subsequent Mines and Collieries Act of 1842 banned women, and girls and boys under ten years of age, from underground work. As these excerpts from the reports of the sub-commissioners show, the concern of the investigators was less with the conditions of women's employment than with issues of morality: with women working alongside men in dark conditions and states of undress, and the consequences of their paid employment for their domestic skills.

4.7 Employment in the mines: interviews with women and children (1842)

It is difficult to hear women's voices amidst the public outcry. Many emphasised the hard work of their labour in the mines rather than matters of decency. They emphasised that they were often employed by the male hewer as part of a team which frequently drew on family members, and stressed the difficulties of finding alternative employment. The directive nature of the questioning – towards issues of morality, and away from comments on working conditions – is evident from the responses.[1] The quotations selected are problematic in that they leave out positive appraisals by the women of aspects of their work and lives. In many areas, women flouted the ban after 1842, and many more continued to work above ground.

4.8 Henry Mayhew, Letter XI, *Morning Chronicle* (23 November 1849)

This excerpt from Henry Mayhew's reports of his investigations in 1849–1850 into the horrendous poverty suffered by London's needlewomen makes harrowing reading. Needlework was considered to be an acceptable mode of employment for women: it was a feminine occupation, developing domestic skills and undertaken at home or in sweatshop conditions in small workshops. But the wages were so poor that many women were forced into prostitution to eke a subsistence, and/or to hand over their children to the workhouse.

4.9 Clementina Black, *Sweated Industry and the Minimum Wage* (1907)

It is commonly assumed that women preferred home work because it gave a degree of flexibility and allowed them to care for children. But as work became increasingly 'sweated', it was paid at 'piece' rate and the long hours often required the additional labour of children. The work often involved medical hazards. Clementina Black wrote *Sweated Industry and the Minimum Wage* (1907) as a result of the investigations of the Women's Industrial Council.

4.10 Flora Thompson, *Lark Rise to Candleford* (1939)

Domestic servants formed the second largest occupational group throughout the nineteenth century after agricultural labourers. Service was seen by many as the most suitable employment for women. In addition to training girls to be good housewives, it was believed to transmit bourgeois values. Younger, unmarried women tended to be employed as servants; on marriage they would move into other work, often in the garment or laundry trades. Women's experience of service varied. Some women in larger establishments had opportunities, but many, working as maid-of-all-work in a stiflingly hierarchical middle-class household that could afford two servants at best, frequently suffered from overwork and isolation. This excerpt from Flora Thompson's novel tells of the different gradations within service and the dependency of many a family on the wage of a servant daughter.

4.11 Ruth Slate's diary (1907)

Ruth Slate (1884–1953) and Eva Slawson (1882–1917), whose letters and diaries appear in *Dear Girl* (1987), were clerical workers in London at the turn of the twentieth century. Both women, from lower-middle-class nonconformist families in London, were immersed in the big social and feminist questions of these years and in what was termed the New Theology (the application of the gospel to social issues). As is evident from the diary entry included here, Ruth hated her work at Kearley and Tonge's, a City firm with a bad reputation for over-working its employees. Her complaints reflect the general poor situation of women within the expanding retail and white collar sectors: while relatively well paid and comfortable when compared to her earlier manual work or to domestic service (Eva's previous employment), the new job opportunities suffered from low pay and were segregated along gendered lines (women did low-skilled filing and typing, for example).

4.12 Mrs Layton, 'Memories of Seventy years'

In this excerpt, Mrs Layton tells how she became a very experienced midwife, with no formal training. Obviously much in demand and greatly respected by the doctors, she still was failed in the examination for the new Midwives' Act of 1902. This Act forbade any woman without a certificate to call herself a 'midwife' (in effect from 1905), or to act as a midwife for gain (from 1910).

4.1   Mrs Burrows, 'A Childhood in the Fens about 1850–1860' (1931)

In the very short schooling that I obtained, I learnt neither grammar nor writing. On the day that I was eight years of age, I left school, and began to work fourteen hours a day in the fields, with from forty to fifty other children of whom, even at that early age, I was the eldest. We were followed all day long by an old man carrying a long whip in his hand which he did not forget to use. A great many of the children were only five years of age. You will think that I am exaggerating, but I am *not*; it is as true as the Gospel. Thirty-five years ago is the time I speak of, and the place, Croyland in Lincolnshire, nine miles from Peterborough. I could even now name several of the children who began at the age of five to work in the gangs, and also the name of the ganger.

We always left the town, summer and winter, the moment the old Abbey clock struck six. . . . We had to walk a very long way to our work, never much less than two miles each way, and very often five miles each way. The large farms all lay a good distance from the town, and it was on those farms that we worked. In the winter, by the time we reached our work, it was light enough to begin, and of course we worked until it was dark and then had our long walk home. I never remember to have reached home sooner than six or more often seven, even in winter. In the summer, we did not leave the fields in the evening until the clock had struck six, and then of course we must walk home, and this walk was no easy task for us children who had worked hard all day on the ploughed fields.

In all the four years I worked in the fields, I never worked one hour under cover of a barn, and only once did we have a meal in a house. And I shall never forget that one meal or the woman who gave us it. It was a most terrible day. The cold east wind (I suppose it was an east wind, for surely no wind ever blew colder), the sleet and snow which came every now and then in showers seemed almost to cut us to pieces. We were working upon a large farm that lay half-way between Croyland and Peterborough. Had the snow and sleet come continuously we should have been allowed to come home, but because it only came at intervals, of course we had to stay . . . I have been out in all sorts of weather but never remember a colder day. Well, the morning passed along somehow. The ganger did his best for us by letting us have a run in our turns, but that did not help us very much because we were too numbed with the cold to be able to run much. Dinner-time came, and we were preparing to sit down under a hedge and eat our cold dinner and drink our cold tea, when we saw the shepherd's wife coming towards us, and she said to our ganger, 'Bring these children into my house and let them eat their dinner there.' We went into that very small two-roomed cottage, and when we got into the largest room there was not standing room for us all, but this woman's heart was large, even if her house was small, and so she put her few chairs and table out into the garden, and then we all sat down in a ring upon the floor. She then placed in our midst a very large saucepan of hot boiled potatoes, and bade us help ourselves. Truly, although I have attended scores of grand parties and banquets since that time, not one of them has seemed half as good to me as that meal did . . .

For four years, summer and winter, I worked in these gangs – no holidays of any sort, with the exception of very wet days and Sundays – and at the end of that time it felt like Heaven to me when I was taken to the town of Leeds, and put to work in a factory. Talk about White Slaves, the Fen districts at that time was the place to look for them.

> (Margaret Llewellyn Davies (ed.), *Life As We Have Known It.*
> *By Co-operative Working Women* (London: Virago, 1981
> [Hogarth Press, 1931]), pp. 109–112)

4.2 Clementina Black, *Married Women's Work* (1915)

FIELDWORK. – Within the memory of people still alive women worked habitually in the fields in many parts of England. Now it is only in few and far apart districts that women were to be found who, as part of their daily routine, perform certain duties about the fields and farms of their own neighbourhood.

In the North West of Worcester and the contiguous parts of Herefordshire lies a tract where no great change has taken place in the work of women for the past fifty years, and where the young wife of today living 'under a farmer' takes her share in the work of the farm almost as much as a matter of course as did her grand-mother. . . . The countryside is fruitful and extremely picturesque . . . The houses, too, are picturesque. Old timbered cottages, in the walls of which rough-cast lath-and-plaster has been replaced by mellow red brick generally contain three or four rooms. Within, the rooms are often whitewashed; hams and strings of onions hang from the oak beams of the kitchen ceiling; the great open fireplaces are filled with blazing logs, and behind them run deep baking ovens. The red brick floors are uncovered, the furniture plain and simple, and there is an absence of useless litter that, together with the warm colouring, helps to give an impression of genuine comfort. The comfort, however, is too often rather apparent than real. So damp are the walls that where they have been papered the paper is generally peeling off; the bricks that pave the living room are often broken, and generally so porous that a bucketful of water poured upon them vanishes at once. Needless to say, rheumatism is prevalent, and although the disease is usually attributed to cider drinking, the dampness of these dwelling appears to provide sufficient cause. Many of the men employed by farmers live rent free or nearly rent free in a cottage with a garden or 'pig-run', i.e. orchard, belonging to their employer; but it is a condition of so living – and there is usually no alternative – that the wife shall perform certain services for the farmer, such as tying a certain acreage of hops and helping in the hayfield at the busiest times . . .

About thirty women, known to be workers, were visited, most of whom were wives of labourers. Probably a chief share in the work of the homestead falls upon the wife, who also usually bakes her own bread and walks to the nearest town, some five miles distant, for her weekly marketing. Many women work three or four ten-hour days a week (from eight till six, or till dark) for the farmer, and a few go out to work every day in the week. Public opinion approves of wage earning by married women; and the woman who abstains from working in the fields is taunted – even if she has young children – with being lazy. Various inhabitants of the district assert that the houses and children of the women who go out to work are better kept than those who stay at home; and appearances on the whole confirmed the assertion. The work of women is, nevertheless, tending to decrease, and probably no pressure is put upon the mother of young children, even when living 'under the farmer', to go to work.

A woman who works for a farmer as a condition of occupying his cottage is paid 10d., or in some cases 1/- for her day's work, and is usually allowed one pint of cider if she cares to fetch it, which as a rule she does not. A woman whose work is not contributory to her rent receives 1/- per day. Piece work rates – which vary somewhat – yield different totals of course, according to the skill and speed of different workers. Employers and workers alike declare that the women are not pressed. They can take their children with them to the fields, and one farmer said that if a woman took an hour or two off to go and look after their babies no complaint would be made.

By their own account they frequently stop to rest. In an orchard, one day, where they were 'apple picking' several women were found in a picturesque group warming themselves around a large bonfire they had lighted, and appeared in no hurry to resume their work.

Except farm servants, whose duties are of course, of a different kind, no women are employed regularly the whole year round. Those who desire regular work can have it for five to nine months of the year; and during those months the most energetic often work almost daily, filling the places of others less willing to do so.

(Reprint: London: Virago, 1983 [1915], pp. 230–234)

4.3 Anthony Ashley Cooper, Lord Ashley, debate on Hours of Labour in Factories, House of Commons, 15 March 1844

But listen to another fact, and one deserving of serious attention; that the females not only perform the labour, but occupy the places of men; they are forming various clubs and associations, and gradually acquiring all those privileges which are held to be the proper portion of the male sex. These female clubs are thus described: 'Fifty or sixty females, married and single, form themselves into clubs, ostensibly for protection; but in fact, they meet together to drink, sing, and smoke; they use, it is stated, the lowest, most brutal, and most disgusting language imaginable.' Here is a dialogue which occurred in one of these clubs, from an ear witness: 'A man came into one of these club-rooms, with a child in his arms; "Come lass," said he, addressing one of the women, "come home, for I cannot keep this bairn quiet, and the other I have left crying at home." "I won't go home, idle devil", she replied, "I have thee to keep, and the bairns too, and if I can't get a pint of ale quietly, it is tiresome. This is only the second pint that Bess and me have had between us; thou may sup if thou likes, and sit thee down, but I won't go home yet." ' Whence is it that this singular and unnatural change is taking place? Because that on women are imposed the duty and burthen of supporting their husbands and families, a perversion as it were of nature, which has the inevitable effect of introducing into families disorder, insubordination, and conflict. What is the ground on which the woman says she will pay no attention to her domestic duties, nor give the obedience which is owing to her husband? Because on her devolves the labour which ought to fall to his share, and she throws out the taunt, 'If I have the labour, I will also have the amusement.' Observe carefully, too, the ferocity of character which is exhibited by a great mass of the female population of the manufacturing towns. Recollect the outbreak of 1842, and the share borne in that by the girls and women; and the still more frightful contingencies which may be in store for the future. 'I met', says an informant of mine, 'with a mother of factory workers, who told me that all the churches and chapels were useless places, and so was all the talk about education, since the young and old were unable to attend, either in consequence of the former being imprisoned in the mills so many hours, and being in want of rest the little time they were at home; and the latter being compelled to live out of the small earnings of their children, and cannot get clothing so they never think of going to churches or chapels. She added, "when you get up to London, tell them we'll turn out the next time (meaning the women), and let the soldiers fire upon us if they dare, and depend upon it there will be a break out, and a right one, if that House of Commons don't alter things, for they can alter if they will, by taking mothers and daughters out of the factories, and sending the men and big lads in." ' . . .

[T]his system of things must be abrogated or restrained . . . It disturbs the order of nature, and the rights of the labouring men, by ejecting the males from the workshop, and filling their places by females, who are thus withdrawn from all their domestic duties, and exposed to insufferable toil at half the wages that would be assigned to males, for the support of their families. It affects – nay, more, it absolutely annihilates, all the arrangements and provisions of domestic economy – thrift and management are altogether impossible; had they twice the amount of their present wages, they would be but slightly benefited – everything runs to waste; the house and children are deserted; the wife can do nothing for her husband and family; she can neither cook, wash, nor repair clothes, or take charge of the infants; all must be paid for out of her scanty earnings, and, after all, most imperfectly done. Dirt, discomfort, ignorance, recklessness, are the portion of such households; the wife has no time for learning in her youth, and none for practice in her riper age; the females are most unequal to the duties of the men in the factories; and all things go to rack and ruin, because the men can discharge at home not one of the especial duties that Providence has assigned to the females.

(*Hansard*, 1844, pp. 1096–1097, 1099)

4.4   Ada Nield Chew, 'A Living Wage for Factory Girls at Crewe', *Crewe Chronicle*, 19 May 1894

I must explain before proceeding further that I shall speak of the branch of factory work known as 'finishing' only. I have reason to believe that the other branches [of female employment] are not over-paid, but I shall speak only of what I know to be actual fact. . . .

And now to take an average of a year's wage of the 'average ordinary hand', which was the class I mentioned in my first letter, and being that which is in a majority may be taken as fairly representative. The wages of such a 'hand', sir, will barely average – but by exercise of the imagination – 8 shillings a week. I ought to say, too, that there is a minority, which is also considerable, whose wages will not average above 5 shillings a week. I would impress upon you that this is making the very best of the case, and is over rather than under-stating. What do you think of it, Mr. Editor, for a 'living' wage?

I wish some of those, whoever they may be who mete it out to us, would try to 'live' on it for a few weeks, as the factory girl has to do 52 weeks in a year. To pay board and lodging, to provide herself decent boots and clothes to stand all weathers, to pay an occasional doctor's bill, literature, even a holiday away from the scope of her daily drudging, for which even the factory girl has the audacity to long sometimes – but has quite as often to do without. Not to speak of provision for old age, when eyes have grown too dim to thread the everlasting needle, and to guide the worn fingers over the accustomed task. Yet this is a question which some of us, at least, ought to face, ignore it as we may, and are compelled to do. The census showing such a large preponderance of women over men in this country, it follows that the factory girl must inevitably contribute her quota to the ranks of old maidenism – be she never so willing to have it otherwise.

And now as to the number of hours worked to earn – or rather to get – this magnificent sum. I explained in my first letter that we are subject to fluctuations as to the amount of work supplied us. In other words that we have busy seasons and slack ones. It follows, then, that in busy seasons, to total up to the yearly average I have given, we make good wages – and, of course, work a proportionately long number of hours – and in slack seasons bad wages.

Now, sir, our working day – that is, in the factory – consists of from 9 to 10 hours. Take out of this time (often considerable and unavoidably so) to obtain the work, to obtain the 'trimmings' and materials to do it with, and then to get it 'passed' and booked in to us when done, and then calculate how much – say we are getting 2d an hour – we shall be able to earn in an ordinary working day in the factory. It will be plain that in order to average this wage we have in busy seasons to work longer than the actual time in the factory.

Home-work, then, is the only resource of the poor slave who has the misfortune to adopt 'finishing' as a means of earning a livelihood. I have myself, repeatedly, five nights a week, besides Saturday afternoons, for weeks at a time, regularly taken four hours', at least, work home with me, and have done it. This, too, after a close hard day's work in the factory. In giving my own experience I give that of us all. We are obliged to do it, sir, to earn this living wage! It will be unnecessary to point out how fearfully exhausting and tedious it is to sit boring at the same thing for 14 or 15 hours at a stretch – meal times excepted of course.

But we are not asking for pity, sir, we ask for justice. Surely it would not be more that just to pay us at such a rate, that we could realise a living wage – in the true sense of the words – in a reasonable time, say one present working day of 9 to 10 hours – till the eight-hour day becomes general, and reaches even factory girls. Our work is necessary (presumably) to our employers. Were we not employed others would have to be, and if of the opposite sex, I venture to say, sir, would have to be paid on a very different scale. Why, because we are weak women, without pluck and grit enough to stand up for our rights, would we be ground down to this miserable wage?

(Ada Nield Chew, *The Life and Writings of a Working Woman*, London: Virago 1982, pp. 78–80)

4.5   Alice Foley, *A Bolton Childhood* (1973)

I quickly learned how hateful it was having to get up at five o'clock each morning, especially in winter. As a young child I had often lain in bed anticipating the tap-tap of our knocker-up on the window panes, but now that I, too, had to roll out into the cold darkness I dreaded his approach. Dragging on my clothes and washing at the kitchen slop-stone, then crouching before the fire in a dull stupor, I tried to dry myself on our one damp towel. No wonder that I have hated damp towels and damp salt all my life!

The fire was 'raked' at bedtime and piled high with cinders and ashes; in the morning it emanated a little warmth but looked black and forbidding. In the oven a pit of strong tea was left to brew from midnight and after a mug of this and a slice of bread we tumbled out into the freezing gloom of unlit streets, amid a clatter of clogs as doors opened and shut along the street.

With a shawl pulled tightly round head and shoulders, I trudged off to the mill, praying silently that no one would catch up to me whilst in that morose, uncivilised state of mind. Yet, from this period of inward rebellion, there emerges a gleam of remembered beauty. On certain frosty mornings before the break of dawn I awoke from torpor to the vision of a full moon riding majestically and aloof in the clear heavens with a host of stars and planets poised in channels of vastness. On occasions Venus glittered and glowed in proximity to a slip of a moon and weariness of spirit fell away for a moment in the thrill and contemplation of such serene beauty and mystery.

On reaching the factory yard one groped one's way over rough cobbles and then climbed a still darker stairway into a cold, silent room, smelling closely of oil and cotton. When I had found my frame I sat down on a weft box, leant against a steel pillar and prayed that the engine would never start. But it always did – first with faint creakings, then a crawling movement of shaftings, then a flickering and winking of incandescent lights, until, faster and faster, steam was at full throttle and our working day had begun.

For the first hour we moved and worked mechanically as if in a coma, silently nodding to fellow-workers but rarely speaking. By seven o'clock we thawed out into small human beings capable of observation and a degree of communication. My near partner, an older girl who had a boyfriend, slowly began to talk about their previous evening's outing. Monday was usually regarded as 'ironing' night for girls, but on Tuesdays Teresa and her fiance went to a variety show at the local theatre and I recall how, with a bleak dawn showing faint and chilly through the windows, she recounted in queer snatches, for we were constantly passing up and down the alley piecing broken yarns, the thrill of *The Silver King* or the anguish of *Lady Audley's Secret*. This kept us going until the buzzer sounded at eight o'clock for the breakfast half-hour. Those workers who lived near-by rushed off home, whilst others 'brewed-up' at adjoining cottages, paying twopence per week 'hot water money' and eating their food at the looms or frames.

(Manchester University Extra-Mural Department, 1973, pp. 52–54)

4.6   Children's Employment Commission, *First Report of the Commissioners on the Employment of Children: Mines* (1842)

137. WEST RIDING OF YORKSHIRE: SOUTHERN PART . . . Michael Thomas Sadler, Esq., surgeon, Barnsley: 'I strongly disapprove of females being in pits; the female character is totally destroyed by it; their habits and feelings are altogether different; they can neither discharge the duties of wives nor mothers. I see the greatest differences in the homes of those colliers whose wives do not go into the pits in cleanliness and good management. It is a brutalizing practice for women to be in collieries; the effect on their morals is very bad; it would be advisable to prevent females from going into pits' [J.C. Symons Esq., Evidence, No. 139: p. 261, 1.44]. – Mr Crooks, surgeon, Barnsley: 'What seems most revolting is, that girls are employed in the pits as well as boys; and when they have a little relaxation all congregate together, and no one in particular to overlook them; at these times their morals, I fear, are injured' (ibid. No. 166: p. 267, 1.46). – John Wood Berry, Esq., clerk to the Wakefield Union: 'As to the working girls in pits, I am decidedly of the opinion that it is injurious to their morals' (ibid. No. 198: p. 278, 1.54). – Rev. Oliver Levey Collins, Incumbent of Ossett: 'There is a good deal of drunkenness and sensuality. Bastardy is sadly too common. They look upon it as a misfortune, and not as a crime' (ibid. No. 236: p. 285, 1.17) . . . – The Rev. Richard Earnshaw Roberts, incumbent of St George's, Barnsley: 'I think the practice of working females in mines is highly objectionable, physically, intellectually, morally, and spiritually' (ibid. No. 124: p. 255, 1.61). – John Thornely, Esq., one of her Majesty's justices of the peace for the county of York: 'I consider it to be a most awfully demoralising practice. The youth of both sexes work often in a half-naked state, and the passions are excited before they arrive at puberty. Sexual intercourse decidedly frequently occurs in consequence. Cases of bastardy frequently also occur, and I am decidedly of opinion that women brought up in this way lay aside all modesty, and scarcely know what it is but by name. I sincerely trust that before I die I shall have the satisfaction of seeing it

prevented and entirely done away with (ibid. No. 96: p. 246, 1.45).

138. The Sub-Commissioner says, 'Under no circumstances is any sort of employment in collieries proper for females. The practice is flagrantly disgraceful to a Christian as well as to a civilised country. From the guarded evidence of Mr. Clarke, who states that it is "not suitable work for girls", to the indignant resolution of the collective body of the colliers themselves, that it is a "scandalous practice", I found scarcely an exception to the general reprobation of this revolting abomination' (J.C. Symons, Esq., Report, 119, 227: App. Pt 1, pp. 182, 196).

139. BRADFORD AND LEEDS. – The Sub-Commissioner for this district states that he has made, through various channels, minute and particular inquiries into the effect of the employment of females during Childhood in preventing them from forming the domestic habits usually acquired by women in their station, and in rendering them less fit than those whose early years have not been spent in labour for performing the duties of wives and mothers, and he reports that the 'result of these inquiries is, in every case, to show that the employment of female Children and Young Persons in labour, to the degree which at present prevails, has the effect of preventing them from acquiring the most ordinary and necessary knowledge of domestic management and family economy; that the young females in general, even where presenting the most tidy and respectable personal appearance before marriage, are nearly ignorant of the arts of baking and cooking, and, generally speaking, entirely so of the use of the needle; that when they come to marry, the wife possesses not the knowledge to enable her to give to her husband the common comforts of a home; that the husband, even if previously well disposed, is hence often led to seek at the public-house that cheerfulness and physical comfort which his own fireside does not afford, whence all the evils of drunkenness in many cases grow up; that the Children, quite apart from any evils which the altered conduct of the father may bring upon them, but solely from the bad training of the mother, are brought up in no habits of order and comfort, but are habituated from their youth to all the evils of a disorderly and ill-regulated family, and must give birth to still a worse state of things in a succeeding generation; that under these accumulated evils the wife and the mother is perhaps herself the most acute sufferer from the consequences of her own defective education. Such are the evils which the evidence I have taken appears to establish as the result of the temptations offered by the present high rates of wages for the employment of female labour. From this source a fearful deterioration of

the moral and physical condition of our working population is rapidly taking place' (W.R. Wood, Esq., Report, 56, 57: App. Pt. II., p. H 10).

(*British Parliamentary Papers* (1842), Vol. XV, pp. 32–33)

4.7   Children's Employment Commission, *First Report of the Commissioners on the Employment of Children: Mines* (1842)

Elizabeth Day, aged 17. Examined March 13th; working in Messrs. Hopwood's pit at Barnsley: 'I have been nearly nine years in the pit. I trapped for two years when I first went, and have hurried ever since. I have hurried for my father until a year ago. I have to help to riddle and fill, and sometimes I have to fill by myself. It is very hard work for me at present. I have to hurry by myself. I have hurried by myself going fast on three years. Before then, I had my sister to hurry with me. I have to hurry uphill with the loaded corves, quite as much up as down, but not many have to hurry uphill with the loaded corve. When I riddle I hold the riddle, and have to shake the slack out of it, and then I throw the rest into the corf. We always hurry in trousers as you saw us to-day when you were in the pit. Generally I work naked down the waist like the rest, I had my shift on today when I saw you, because I had had to wait, and was cold; but generally the girls hurry naked down to the waist. It is very hard work for us all. It is harder work than we ought to do a deal. I have been lamed in my ancle [sic], and strained my back; it caused a great lump to rise on my ancle-bone once. The men behave well to us, and never insult or ill-use us, I am sure of that. We go to work between five and six, but we begin to hurry when we get down. We stop an hour to dinner at 12; we generally have bread and a bit of fat for dinner, and some of them a sup of beer; that's all. We have a whole hour for dinner, and we get out from four to five in the evening; so that it will be 11 hours before we get out. We drink the water that runs through the pit. I am not paid wages myself; the man who employs me pays my father; but I don't know how much it is. I have never been at school. I had to begin working when I ought to have been at school. I don't go to Sunday-school. The truth is, we are confined bad enough on week-days, and want to walk about on Sundays; but I go to chapel on Sunday night. I can't read at all. Jesus Christ was Adam's son, and they nailed him on a tree; but I don't rightly understand these things.'

Mary Holmes, age 14 ½. [Meal Hill, Hepworth, Yorkshire coalfield]: 'I have been eight years working in pits. I have always hurried. I have never thrust much. I always hurry as you saw me, with a belt round my waist and the chain through my legs. I hurry so in the board-gates. I always wear lads' clothes. The trousers don't get torn at all. It tires me middling; my back doesn't ache at all, nor my legs. I like being in pit, and don't want to do naught else. I never tried to do anything else. Sometimes I get cold by its being so wet. The wet covers my ankles. I am sure nobody has told me what to say. I go to Sunday-school. I read in Spelling-book. I don't know all my letters. I don't know who Christ was; I haven't heard much about him. They thrash me sometimes in the pit; its not the getters, it's the hurriers that does it; they don't hurt me much. There are 13 children in my family – four are boys; they are all in the same pit with me. I have no other sister working now in the pit. I have a shilling for hurrying two dozen – that is 16 corves. This is my regular stint . . . I don't know how long I shall stop in the pit. I have two sisters married, and one is at service; they all hurried before. I am sure I would rather be in the pit, where I am thrashed sometimes, and work in the wet, than do anything else.'

Isabel Hogg, 53 years old, was a coal-bearer [in East Scotland]: 'Been married 37 years; it was the practice to marry early, when the coals were all carried on women's back, men needed us; from the great sore labour false births are frequent and very dangerous.

I have four daughters married, and all work below till they bear their bairns – one is very badly now from working while pregnant, which brought on a miscarriage from which she is not expected to recover.

Collier-people suffer much more than others – my guid man died nine years since with bad breath; he lingered some years and was entirely off work 11 years before he died.

You must tell the Queen Victoria that we are guid loyal subjects; women people here don't mind work, but they object to horse-work; and that she should have the blessings of all the Scotch coal-women if she would get them out of the pits, *and send* them to other labour.'

[Mrs Hogg is one of the most respectable coal-wives in Peniston, her rooms are well furnished, and the house is the cleanest I have seen in East Lothian].

(*British Parliamentary Papers*, 1842, Vol. XVI, pp. 244, 295, 460)

4.8   Henry Mayhew, Letter XI to *The Morning Chronicle* (23 November 1849)

The next speaker was the most eloquent of all. I never before listened to such a gush of words and emotion, and perhaps never shall again. She spoke without the least effort, in one continued strain, for upwards of half an hour, crying half hysterically herself, while those around her sobbed in sympathy: –

'Between ten and eleven years ago I was left a widow with two young children, and far advanced in pregnancy with another. I had no means of getting a living, and therefore I thought I would take up slop-work. I got work at slop-shirts – what they call secondhand. I had no security, and therefore could not get the work myself from the warehouse. Two months before I was confined, I seemed to do middling well. I could manage three or four shirts – what they call "rowers" – at 3d. each, by sitting closely at work from five or six in the morning till about nine or ten at night; but, of course, when I was confined I was unable to do anything. As soon as I was able to sit up I undertook slop shirts again; but my child being sickly, I was not able to earn so much as before. Perhaps I could earn 9d. a day by hard work, when I get 3d. each shirt; but sometimes I only get 2½d., and I have been obliged to do them at 1½d. each, and, with my child sickly, could only earn 4d., or at most 6d. a day. At other times I hadn't work. On the average I calculate that I have earnt 9d. a day when the prices were better; 1s. 9d. a week went for rent; and as to living, I don't call it that; I was so reduced with it, and my child being so bad, it couldn't be considered a living. I was obliged to live on potatoes and salt; and for nine weeks together I lived on potatoes, and never knew what it was to have a half-quartern loaf, for the loaf was 9d. then. By that means my health was declining, and I wasn't able to do hard work. My child's health, too, was declining, and I was obliged to pawn the sheets off my bed and my blankets to procure a shilling. At last I found it impossible to pay my rent. I owed 7s. arrears, and my landlady plagued me much to pay her. She advised me to raffle away a large chest that I had. I did so, and gained 12s., and then paid her the 7s. I owed her; but I became so reduced again, that I was obliged to get an order to get into the "house". I didn't wish to go in, but I wanted relief, and knew I couldn't get it without doing so. I felt it a hard trial to have my children taken from my bosom: we had never been parted before, and I can't help remembering what were my feelings then as a mother who always loved her children. I thought rather than we should be parted that I would make-away with myself. . . . And never shall I forget that Saturday afternoon, as I travelled along Gravel-lane to the "house", with feelings that it was impossible for me to enter, for I thought "How can I bear to have my dear children taken away from me – they have never been taken away from me before!" I reflected, "What can I do but go there?" So I mustered courage at all events to get to the gate; and, oh, it is impossible to describe what my feelings were as I passed through! I was admitted to a room where they were toasting the bread for the mistress's tea. A little girl was there, and she said, "Look at these dear little children. I will give them a bit of the toast." The children took it, and thought it very nice, but they little thought that we were so soon to be parted. The first was seven years old, the second, three, and the infant was in my arms. A mother's feelings are better felt than described. The children were taken and separated, and then, oh, my God! what I felt no tongue can tell.' [Here the woman's emotions overcame her, and she could not proceed with her narrative for weeping. At length, recovering herself, she continued]: – 'I was in hopes of getting my children back within a week or two, but my business could not be settled so soon. My babe took the measles; they went inwardly, and it took a deep decline. I knew it was very bad, and asked leave to go and see him. The mistress was very kind, and gave me leave. I found my child very bad, and the infant in my arms seemed declining every day. My feelings then were such as I can't tell you. I thought, "Oh, if I could only get out and have my children with myself, how much better it would be!" I hurried them to settle my business for me; it originated in a dispute between St George's and Wapping about our parish, my husband being at the sugar-house at work. At last the dispute was settled, but the one child died, whilst the other – the youngest – was dying . . .

4.9 Clementina Black, *Sweated Industry and the Minimum Wage* (1907)

The investigators of the Women's Industrial Council visited personally nearly four hundred workers. Perhaps the very poorest trade investigated was match-box making, which, for the last fifteen years at least, has occupied some hundreds of workers in East London alone. The women fetch out from the factory or the middlewoman's, strips of notched wood, packets of coloured paper and sandpaper, and printed wrappers; they carry back large but light bundles of boxes, tied up in packets of two dozen. Inside their rooms, the boxes, made and unmade and half-made, cover the floor and fill up the lack of furniture. I have seen a room containing only an old bedstead in the very last stage of dirt and dilapidation, a table, and two deal boxes for seats. The floor and the window-sill were rosy with magenta match-boxes, while everything else including the boards of the floor, the woodwork of the room and the coverings of the bed, was of the dark grey of ingrained dust and dirt. At first sight it is a pretty enough spectacle to see a match-box made; one motion of the hands bends into shape the notched frame of the case, another surrounds it with the ready-pasted strip of printed wrapper, which, by long practice, is fitted instantly without a wrinkle, then the sandpaper or the phosphorus-paper, pasted ready beforehand, is applied and pressed on so that it sticks fast. A pretty high average of neatness and finish is demanded by most employers, and readers who will pass their match-boxes in review will seldom find a wrinkle or a loose corner of paper. The finished case is thrown upon the floor; the long narrow strip which is to form the frame of the drawer is laid upon the bright strip of ready-pasted paper, then bent together and joined by an overlapping bit of the paper; the edges of paper below are bent flat, the ready-cut bottom is dropped in and pressed down, and before the fingers are withdrawn they fold over the upper edges of the paper inside the top. Now the drawer, too, is cast on the floor to dry. All this, besides the preliminary pasting of wrapper, coloured paper and sandpaper, had to be done 144 times for 2¼d.; and even this is not all, for every drawer and case have to be fitted together and the packets tied up with hemp. Nor is the work done then, for paste has to be made before it can be used, and boxes, when they are ready, have to be carried to the factory. Let any reader, however deft, however nimble-fingered, consider how many hundred times a day he or she could manage to perform all these minute operations. But practice gives speed, especially when stimulated by the risk of starvation.

The conditions of life secured in return for the continuous and monotonous toil are such as might well make death appear preferable. The poor dwelling – already probably overcrowded – is yet further crowded with matchboxes, a couple of gross of which, in separated pieces, occupy a considerable space. If the weather be at all damp, as English weather often is, even in summer, there must be a fire kept up, or the paste will not dry; and fire, paste, and hemp must all be paid for out of the worker's pocket. From her working time, too, or deducted from that of her child messenger, must be deducted the time lost in fetching and carrying back work, and, too often, in being kept waiting for it before it is given out.

(London: Duckworth & Co., 1907, pp. 3–7)

4.10   Flora Thompson, *Lark Rise to Candleford* (1939)

. . . When the place was found, the girl set out alone on what was usually her first train journey, with her yellow tin trunk tied up with thick cord, her bunch of flowers and brown paper parcel bursting with left-overs.

The tin trunk would be sent on to the railway station by the carrier and the mother would walk the three miles to the station with her daughter. They would leave Lark Rise, perhaps before it was quite light on a winter morning, the girl in her best, would-be fashionable clothes and the mother carrying the baby of the family, rolled in its shawl. Neighbours would come to their garden gates to see them off and call after them 'Pleasant journey! Hope you'll have a good place!', or 'Mind you be a good gal, now, an' does just as you be told!' . . .

Laura once saw the departure of such a couple, the mother enveloped in a large plaid shawl, with her baby's face looking out from its folds, and the girl in a bright blue, poplin frock which had been bought at the second-hand clothes shop in the town – a frock made in the extreme fashion of three years before, but by that time ridiculously obsolete. Laura's mother, forseeing the impression it would make at the journey's end, shook her head and clicked her tongue and said, 'Why ever couldn't they spend the money on a bit of good navy serge!' But they, poor innocents, were delighted with it.

They went off cheerfully, even proudly; but, some hours later, Laura met the mother returning alone. She was limping, for the sole of one of her old boots had parted company with the upper, an eighteen-months-old child must have hung heavily on her arm. When asked if Aggie had gone off all right, she nodded, but could not answer; her heart was too full. After all, she was just a mother who had sent her young daughter into the unknown and was tormented with doubts and fears for her.

. . .

The girls who 'went into the kitchen' began as scullerymaids, washing up stacks of dishes, cleaning saucepans and dish covers, preparing vegetables, and doing the kitchen scrubbing and other rough work. After a year or two of this, they became under kitchen-maids and worked up gradually until they were second-in-command to the cook. When they reached that point, they did much of the actual cooking under supervision; sometimes they did it without any, for there were stories of cooks who never put hand to a dish, but having taught the kitchen-maid, left all the cooking to her, excepting some spectacular dish for a dinner party. This pleased the ambitious kitchen-maid, for she was gaining experience and would soon be a professional cook herself; then, if she attained the summit of her ambition, cook-housekeeper.

Some girls preferred house to kitchen work, and they would be found a place in some mansion as third or fourth house-maid and work upward. Troops of men and maid-servants were kept in large town and country houses in those days.

The maids on the lower rungs of the ladder seldom saw their employers. If they happened to meet one or other of them about the house, her ladyship would ask kindly how they were getting on and how their parents were; or his lordship would smile and make some mild joke if he happened to be in a good humour. The upper servants were their real mistresses, and they treated beginners as a sergeant treated recruits, drilling them well in their duties by dint of much scolding; but the girl who was anxious to learn and did not mind hard work or hard words and could keep a respectful tongue in her head had nothing to fear from them. . . .

As soon as a mother had even one daughter in service, the strain upon herself slackened a little. Not only was there one mouth less to feed, one pair of feet less to be shod, and a tiny space left free in the cramped sleeping quarters; but, every month, when the girl received her wages, a shilling or more would be sent to 'our Mum', and, as the wages increased, the mother's portion grew larger. In addition to presents, some of the older girls undertook to pay their parents' rent; others to give them a ton of coal for the winter; and all sent Christmas and birthday presents and parcels of left-off clothing.

(Reprint: Penguin, 1981 [1939]), pp. 162–165)

4.11   Ruth Slate's diary (1907)

Thursday, 2 May 1907

I have just returned from the City Temple! A longing to see Mr Campbell again possessed me, so I have done without lunch for once, in order to hear part of his sermon. But perhaps a trouble which is weighing heavily on my mind just now – a problem to which I can find no solution – prevented me giving him my whole attention. I have written very little, or nothing, in my diary, about business, but a climax has come, and the course of my life may be altered by it. I have not written previously, because I knew if I started I should want to say so much, moreover it would be difficult to express the disgust and indignation I daily feel. The whole system is so abominable, and so unjust – its influence so crushing – that I wonder it does not bring about revolt; but the crushing, I suppose, prevents that. The most terrible instances of the effect this slave-driving process has, is the case of the Brentwood manager, who threw himself under a train and was decapitated; and of another, who went mad. The firm is universally spoken of as a firm of 'sweaters', and the experience proves the name truly given.

Numbers and numbers of office staff, male and female, have been trying to get the small increase in salary which in most cases, including my own, has been long overdue. Yesterday we were told it is in vain to ask and that if we are not satisfied we had better look for something else. It is only the thought of the home folk which has kept me there so long, and prevents me leaving on Saturday, but I have finally determined to do as they suggest and 'look out for something else'. . . .

But the bitterest drop in my cup, I know, is the knowledge that whereas I might have been fitting myself for some higher order of work, I have drifted along, absorbed in my trouble over Wal, or day-dreaming. I know myself to be ignorant and incompetent, and the knowledge *is very bitter*. What shall I now turn to?

(*Dear Girl. The Diaries and Letters of Two Working Women 1897–1914*, edited by Tierl Thompson (London: The Women's Press, 1987), pp. 102–103)

4.12   Mrs Layton, 'Memories of Seventy Years' (1931)

When my husband was promoted to the position of under-guard, we had to leave Brondesbury and come to Cricklewood to live. Then it was I gave up washing and took up nursing. My husband's wages had now risen to £1 3s. a week, and he had an allotment. I got a nice little flat for 7/- a week, so that I did not live a life of drudgery, but had to do something to help. The chance of nursing came through one of the members of our Management Committee, who advised his master to come for me when his wife was ill, saying 'She is not a nurse but I am sure she will do, and be kind to your wife.' I did what I could and satisfied both patient and doctor, who recommended me to others of his patients. My first maternity case came to me in an unexpected manner. One of our Guild members was expecting her confinement and could not find a nurse. So at last I got a crippled girl I knew to stay in my house while I went to the Guild member's house, and acted as maternity nurse for a fortnight. I did not intend to take up maternity nursing, but after I had started, other Guild members came to me to attend them. I began to like the work, and the doctors were so satisfied with me that I determined to keep on. Then several doctors advised me to go in for midwifery, but I could not go into hospital for training. The fees were a bar to me. I found that the cheapest training I could get would cost anything from £30 to £50, and then I should have to be away from home for three months. This was quite impossible for my husband's health needed all the care I could bestow on it to keep him anything like fit for work part of his time. I had no money, only as I earned it week by week, and it was impossible to save. So I had to content myself with being a maternity nurse. I read and asked questions of the doctors and in this way knew a great deal about the theory of midwifery, and I was gaining experience in the practical part. There were three doctors who were very good to me and were willing to lend me books or to teach me anything. I was taught to deliver with forceps, which midwives are not taught in hospitals. I went to several post-mortems with a doctor. One was the case of a young girl who was pregnant and had poisoned herself. The doctor opened the womb and let me see the dear little baby lying so snugly in its mother, and gave me a lot of information that was real knowledge to me, showing me things in the human body which were both interesting and instructive.

Quite a large number of young married people came to live in Cricklewood, and I had sometimes as many as a hundred cases in a year. The doctors left so much to me, and did so little for their fees, that people asked me to take their cases without a doctor. I did not care to do so at first, so I asked a doctor (who, when he thought my husband had not many days to live, had promised him to help me) if he thought I should be right to take cases without a doctor. He told me I was quite all right, but that if at any time I came across a case that I was not sure was quite straightforward, he would come to my assistance. I was very pleased with his offer and did many cases on my own responsibility, and both patients and doctors were satisfied, but I was not. I was called a midwife, but I felt I should have liked a hospital training, and as I earned more money I began to save to get the training I longed for. I scraped and saved, twisted and turned clothes about, even went as far as to turn an overcoat for my husband. I managed to save £30, and got the necessary papers which had to be signed by a doctor. When I went to him, he positively refused to sign it. He said it would be a wicked waste of money, that I knew more than the hospital would teach me, that I could not be spared from the neighbourhood for three months, and advised me to give up the idea. . . .

(Margaret Llewellyn Davies (ed.), *Life As We Have Known It, By Co-operative Working Women* (London: Virago, 1982 [1931]), pp. 42–45)

Chapter Five

Working-class domestic life

While working-class women frequently undertook some form of paid work, they were primarily responsible for looking after their own homes and raising their children. Most women married and the possibilities of maintaining an independent life as a single woman were slim. Working-class women who married in their teens or twenties could expect ten pregnancies, and therefore to spend up to 15 years of their lives either pregnant or nursing.[1] The sources included here do not provide a balanced representation of different periods throughout the long nineteenth century. While some deal with the earlier period, most focus on the turn of the twentieth century, when social investigators and commentators, many of them women, and a considerable number among them members of the socialist movement, wrote extensively on working-class women's domestic lives and their experiences as mothers. The accessibility of women's writing in this period owes much to a series of books reprinted by the women's publishing house, Virago, during the first wave of women's history writing in the late 1970s to early 1980s. The chapter tries to reflect this interest in women's lives and focuses on writings by working-class women themselves, by people sympathetic to their experiences, as well as including some analyses from a perspective critical of women's domestic skills. The sources in this chapter explore the centrality of home and family life to women's lives, looking at: domestic labour and the notion of 'respectability'; women as household managers; the importance of neighbourhood and kinship networks; motherhood and maternal health; and the debate about the 'health of the race', in which working-class women (and especially mothers) became the targets of social policy in the late nineteenth and early twentieth centuries.

5.1 Elizabeth Gaskell, *Mary Barton* (1848)

Elizabeth Gaskell's *Mary Barton*, set in Manchester, details some of the hard choices facing poor women, who frequently went without food in order to feed their children, knew that working long hours themselves meant they had to neglect their families, and needed to send their children out to work, but acknowledged that the work was too hard for them. The two excerpts from chapter 10 tell of the self-deprivations of John Barton's mother and, in Jane Wilson's commentary, the lack of domestic skills of women who had been sent out to work from an early age.

5.2 Janet Hamilton, 'Aul' Scotlan' ' (1865)

The importance of domestic comfort to mid-Victorian respectability is suggested by Janet Hamilton's 'Aul' Scotlan' '. The poem addresses the manners and morals of the working classes and advocates the values of the pious Protestant family exemplified by the author's own childhood, in which her father led family prayer, her mother questioned children on the church sermon, and both parents contributed to the family income and took care of the house and children. Hamilton, born in Lanarkshire in 1795, where her parents were agricultural labourers and her father later established a shoe-making business, kept the house and spun yarn from being a young girl; she was taught to work at the tambouring frame by her mother. After marrying her father's apprentice, Janet had ten children. Although she had been taught to read by her mother and had composed poems since her teens, Hamilton only learned to write in her fifties, when she began to contribute to Cassell's *Working Man's Friend*, a prime promoter of working-class literature. For the reader unfamiliar with this Scottish dialect, this poem might take a few readings; a short glossary has been provided.[2]

5.3 Alice Foley, *A Bolton Childhood* (1973)

Alice Foley's autobiography tells how as a young girl in the late nineteenth century she was given some responsibilities for the upkeep of the home. Her duties were not only chores but, as she reveals here, included the pleasurable task of collecting library books for the family and reading aloud to her (non-reading) mother.

5.4 Margaret Loane, *From Their Point of View* (1908)

In this excerpt from *From Their Point of View* (1908), Margaret Loane discusses the reliance of many working-class women on the all-important kinship networks and neighbours. Loane, a District Nurse and social commentator who wrote a number of books on the culture of the poor, takes issue with Lady Florence Bell who, in *At the Works* (1907), criticised the perceived dependence of the poor upon charity. Women lent one another food, helped out with fetching water, doing laundry or shopping, and gave assistance at the time of childbirth or family illness. Elderly women in the family looked after the children of working mothers, for which they were often paid.

5.5 Kathleen Woodward, *Jipping Street* (1928)

As household managers, women were responsible for paying the rent and feeding and clothing a family on a low income, and they developed various strategies for survival. Kathleen Woodward's *Jipping Street* captures the drudgery of working-class mothers' daily lives. Woodward's mother, a most unmaternal mother of six, was responsible for bringing in an income for the family after her husband became ill, as well as maintaining the home.

5.6 Elizabeth Andrews, *A Woman's Work is Never Done* (1948)

Elizabeth Andrews' autobiography is aptly titled *A Woman's Work is Never Done*. In this excerpt, she recalls her childhood in a Rhondda mining community, where as a young girl she helped with domestic chores and with mending pit clothes. The second half of the nineteenth century had seen massive migration to the Rhondda valleys, mainly from within Wales and neighbouring English counties. Women's lives were determined entirely by their husband's work, as baths and meals were dictated by shifts. Women also washed, cleaned, cooked and cared for children, in poor housing with inadequate facilities. Many women also took in lodgers; Dot Jones cites the example of 42-year-old Elizabeth Morgan, who, according to the 1881 Census was looking after her husband, two mining sons and three younger children, as well as taking in four miners as lodgers. The women paid a price, with a high mortality rate, relative to both their men and the national average.[3]

5.7 'Food: Chief Articles of Diet', *Round About a Pound a Week* (1913)

A record of the daily lives of poor women in Lambeth from 1909–1913, this book starts from the premise that poor nutrition and the general conditions of poverty, rather than women's ignorance and neglect, were responsible for the high infant mortality rates and poor health in working-class families. The investigators, members of the Fabian Women's Group, were keen to teach the general public about the resourcefulness of women who were good cooks and able managers, but whose families were scarcely able to survive on their woefully inadequate incomes. The Fabian Women's Group supported the 'state endowment of motherhood' that was later to be enshrined in family allowances. The dietary and budgetary details included here, like most in the book, relate to a family living on what would be considered at the time to be a 'reasonable' wage; others were much less well off. That women put their children's hunger before their own, surviving largely on diets of bread, margarine and tea, and saved meat and any 'relish' for the man, confirmed the findings of R. Seebohm Rowntree's *Poverty: A Study of Town Life* (1901).

5.8 *Maternity: Letters from Working Women* (1915)

Margaret Llewellyn Davies' edited collection of women's letters to the Women's Co-operative Guild makes for harrowing reading. While infant mortality declined after 1911, maternal mortality remained high, and was second to tuberculosis as cause of death among married women from 1911–1930.[4] As illustrated by this letter, extensive childbearing had grave implications for women's health. Medical care was largely unavailable or unaffordable, and most women laboured at home with no pain relief. Women were hardly given a chance to recover from childbirth because of unrelenting domestic labour, poverty and poor nutrition. The National Insurance Act of 1911 saw the beginnings of a change, with the provision of a Maternity Benefit Scheme to women whose husbands paid their contributions. *Maternity* was part of the Guild's campaign for maternity allowances and healthcare.

5.9 Hannah Mitchell, *The Hard Way Up,* on motherhood in the 1890s

Hannah Mitchell (1871–1956), later a suffragette and Labour Party campaigner in Lancashire, was supported by her husband in her decision to limit her family. Her experience of the difficult birth of her son in the late 1890s, and her memories of her mother's life of drudgery in poverty in the Peak District, fixed her resolve to have no more children. The later decades of the nineteenth century saw a decline in family size, beginning among the middle classes. A shared focus of husband and wife on domestic issues was a crucial factor in family limitation in the working class prior to the First World War.

5.10 Sir George Newman, *Infant Mortality: A Social Problem* (1906)

The late nineteenth century saw widespread anxiety about the health of the nation's children. Fuelled by the perceived threat to British imperial supremacy by German and American industrial growth and competition, and brought into sharp focus both by Booth and Rowntree's surveys and by reports of the numbers of men deemed unfit for service in the Boer War, Britain's declining birth rate and high infant mortality rates came under scrutiny. Children were seen as a national asset, motherhood became a national duty and issues that had previously been women's concerns, such as infant health and hygiene and breastfeeding, came to be seen as matters of national interest. Sir George Newman, CMO to the Board of Education, who undertook a study of infant mortality in Finsbury at the turn of the twentieth century, acknowledged regional differences and the role of poverty and housing conditions in infant mortality. His conclusions chimed in with the view that it was the inadequacy of working-class women as mothers, rather than poverty, that was to blame for the state of the nation's children.

5.1 Elizabeth Gaskell, *Mary Barton, A Tale of Manchester Life* (1848)

... Deeper and deeper still sank the poor; it showed how much lingering suffering it takes to kill men, that so few (in comparison) died during those times. But remember! we only miss those who do men's work in their humble sphere; the aged, the feeble, the children, when they die, are hardly noted by the world; and yet to many hearts, their deaths make a blank which long years will never fill up. Remember, too, that though it may take much suffering to kill the able-bodied and effective members of society, it does *not* take much to reduce them to worn, listless, diseased creatures, who thenceforward crawl through life with moody hearts and pain-stricken bodies.

The people had thought the poverty of the preceding years hard to bear, and had found its yoke heavy; but this year added sorely to its weight. Former times had chastised them with whips, but this chastised them with scorpions. ...

'He was such a good husband,' said she, in a less excited tone, to Mary, as she looked up with tear-streaming eyes from behind her apron. 'No one can tell what I've lost in him, for no one knew his worth like me.'

Mary's listening sympathy softened her, and she went on to unburden her heavy laden heart.

'Eh, dear, dear! No one knows what I've lost. When my poor boys went, I thought the Almighty had crushed me to th' ground, but I never thought o' losing George; I did na think I could ha' borne to ha' lived without him. And yet I'm here, and he's – .' A fresh burst of crying interrupted her speech.

'Mary,' – beginning to speak again, – 'did you ever hear what a poor creature I were when he married me? And he such a handsome fellow! Jem's nothing to what his father were at his age.'...

'If you'll believe me, Mary, there never was such a born goose at housekeeping as I were; and yet he married me! I had been in a factory sin' five years old a'most, and I knew nought about cleaning or cooking, let alone washing and such-like work. The day after we were married, he went to his work after breakfast, and says he, "Jenny, we'll ha' th' cold beef, and potatoes, and that's a dinner for a prince." I were anxious to make him comfortable, God knows how anxious. And yet I'd no notion how to cook a potato. I know'd they were boiled, and I know'd their skins were taken off, and that were all. So I tidied my house in a rough kind o' way, then I looked at that very clock up yonder,' pointing at one that hung against the wall, 'and I seed it were nine o'clock, so, thinks I, th' potatoes shall be well boiled at any rate, and I gets 'em on th' fire in a jiffy (that's to say, as soon as I could peel 'em, which were a tough job at first), and then I fell to unpacking my boxes! and at twenty minutes past twelve, he comes home, and I had the beef ready on th' table, and I went to take the potatoes out o' th' pot; but oh! Mary th' water had boiled away, and they were all a nasty brown mess, as smelt through all the house. He said nought, and were very gentle; but, oh, Mary, I cried so that afternoon. I shall ne'er forget it; no, never. I made many a blunder at after, but none that fretted me like that.'

'Father does not like girls to work in factories,' said Mary.

'No, I know he does not; and reason good. They oughtn't to go at after they're married, that I'm very clear about. I could reckon up' (counting with her fingers), 'ay, nine men I know, as has been driven to th' public-house by having wives as worked in factories; good folk, too, as though there was no harm in putting their little ones out to nurse, and letting their house go all dirty, and their fires all out; and that was a place as was tempting for a husband to stay in, was it? He soon finds out gin-shops, where all is clean and bright, and where th' fire blazes cheerily, and gives a man a welcome as it were.'

Alice, who was standing near for the convenience of hearing, had caught much of this speech, and it was evident the subject had previously been discussed by the women, for she chimed in.

'I wish our Jem could speak a word to th' queen about factory work for married women. Eh! but he comes it strong when once yo get him to speak about it. Wife o' his'n will never work away fra' home.'

(Reprint: Harmondsworth: Penguin 1994, chapter 10, pp. 105–106, 111–113)

5.2   Janet Hamilton, 'Aul' Scotlan'' (1865)

The world's sair altert. In my day,
Afore my hair grew thin and grey,
A wife had thocht it sin and shame
If that she brang nae siller hame.
The warkman's wage was geyan sma',
And sae the wife tuk pirns to ca',

Or wrocht at the tambourin' tent,
To eke the wage an' help the rent.
In hairst she keep it up her rig,
An' left the wee bairns wi' the big;
An' wi' the fee bocht claes and shoon,
An' keepit aye their heids abune.
The bits o' lassocks, blate and douce,
Were learnt to work and red the hoose;
A stripit toush, an' plaidin' coat,
Maist feck o' a' the duds they got.
A towmond ye micht ta'en to seek,
Nor seen a pipe in callan's cheek,
Or heard an aith. They kept the neuk
Ilk nicht whan faither tuk the beuk,
An' ran at biddin, wrocht their wark,
An' gat their schulin' efter dark.
There's been an unco grit ado,
An' muckle cry an' little woo,
Aboot what big fock ca' the masses –
Whilk means, ye ken, the workin' classes;
To gie them lear, and learn the weemin
The airts o' cookery and cleanin'.
   An' noo, ye Scottish wives and mothers,
This speaks to you abune a' ithers –
Ye maun be geyan sair to blame,
An' weel I wat I think great shame,
That ony man should need to tell ye
To clean your hoose, and tent your belly
Wi' weel-made-ready halesume meat,
An' to be careful an' discreet.
A' this is very gude an' needfu',
But, oh! ye should be unco heedfu'
To airt yer bairns to a' that's richt,
An' frae a' ill to warn and fricht;
An' aye be shure ye gie a sample
O' what ye bid in your example.
Your wark's afore ye, never swither –
Be juist a true, gude Christian mother! (311)

Glossary:

   Sair – sore
   abune – above

blate and douce – shy and serious
towmond – twelvemonth
callan – a lad, a boy
neuk – nook
beuk – book
unco – great, strange
muckle – large, much
fock – folk

(In Janet Hamilton, *Poems, Essays and Sketches: Comprising the Principle Pieces for her Complete Works* (Originally published in 1865. Reprint: Glasgow: James Maclehose, 1880), pp. 116–118)

5.3   Alice Foley, *A Bolton Childhood* (1973)

On reaching an appropriate age we younger children were allocated small duties about the house and I remember with deep pleasure my first initiation into the care of our family aspidistra which, at that time, occupied a place of honour on top of the sewing machine. Each Friday morning the ritual was observed, first to place the giant plant-pot overhead in water in the kitchen sink. Even today I can hear the eager bubbling and gurgling of those thirsty roots sucking in the refreshing draught. Then the single leaves were carefully sponged with a wash-leather, cracked portions and faded tips nipped off to make room for the younger shoots, and all finally polished with a spot of milk. Under these ministrations our aspidistra flourished prodigiously, and though in after years this household favourite of the poor became despised and rejected, for me, in those formative decades, it was a much-loved green oasis in a flower-less home.

Later I graduated to the care of our cobbled yard and the 'necessary house' situated near the back-gate. We knew it as 'the petty' and when it became my responsibility much labour was devoted to its transformation. The wooden seat was scrubbed to faultless whiteness and the floor vigorously 'donkey-stoned'. The white-washed walls were adorned with picture almanacs and scraps of verses, whilst within handy reach of the occupant I hung a neat pile of 'bum papers' culled from father's old racing handicaps. When mother inspected the work she remarked 'Eh, child, tha's made a grand job, but tha'll never get lads out of it' and, sure enough, I frequently had to go down the yard bawling, 'Mam wants to know if you're staying in there all day; yo'r tea's going cold.'

We were a reading family and, in process of time, I became the chief book-borrower. This entailed carrying a bag of heavy books on Monday evenings for exchange at the branch library some distance away. In those days there was no access to open shelves and the selection of books was quite a business. First came the job of probing through massive catalogues for author and book number, followed by reference to an in-and-out card index – green in, black out, which often entailed a tedious repetition. After the selection I usually crept upstairs to the reading-room, trying to still the clatter of clogs on the stone steps, but on settling down with a picture magazine, up came an irate caretaker, and I was shunted out like an unwanted animal.

When I reached home the borrowed books were dished out to brothers and sisters and, within a few minutes, all were engrossed in the opening chapters. I remember one such occasion when mother startled the family by suddenly jumping up and exclaiming 'Well, I met as weel goo eaut, for this place is nowt but a deaf an dumb schoo'.' Somewhat embarrassed by this outburst, I offered to read aloud some pages of my book, which happened to be *Alice in Wonderland* and, to my surprise, mother entered quite briskly into the activities of the rabbit hole. From that time onwards I became mother's official reader and almost every day when I returned from school she would say coaxingly: 'Let's have a chapthur.' When I stumbled over big or unknown words, she would say encouragingly 'o, ca' it Manchester' and so it was until both spelling and reading ability improved.

(Manchester University Extra-Mural Department, 1973, pp. 24–26)

5.4   Margaret Loane, *From Their Point of View* (1908)

In a recent book, *At the Works*, the writer seems to be of the opinion that a family is necessarily limited to one household, and that every married woman who cannot afford paid service for herself and her infant children has nothing to depend upon when incapacitated by illness but the charity of the upper classes. I have known towns where family life embraced six or more households, and services of all kinds were constantly and freely interchanged. Was it washing-day at Aunt Susan's? Very well, the children repaired to Aunt Mary at dinner-time with no further explanation than 'Mother's busy, and we're so hungry.' Was Uncle Tom convalescing, 'and that arritable the boys darsn't come a-nigh him'? Then grandmother would have them, 'and welcome'. Even in towns such as described by Lady Bell friendships are soon formed that are scarcely less fruitful in kindness than blood relationships. Even the most undesirable neighbour, whose house half the women in the street have vowed – with good reason – never to enter again, has no lack of help when the hour of stress arrives. In fact, the only persons I have ever found lonely or deserted are the too rigidly exclusive and 'stand-offish'. They, indeed, may 'perish in their pride' while kindly neighbours hold urgency meetings not ten yards away, each trying to induce the other to 'put herself forward,' and none among them having sufficient courage to break down invisible barriers.

One of the incidental advantages of early marriages is that the grandparents are still comparatively young and strong; not only do they need no help from their children, but can give them a great deal of valuable assistance. Within an hour I was speaking to two very poor women. One said regretfully, 'I couldn't never do as much for my children as I should of liked, 'specially in the way of taking of them out o' doors. You see, my mother died not long after I was married. She was over forty when I was born, so it was much the same tale with her; but then she on'y had me and my two brothers, so it didn't seem to matter so much. And then father was a much handier man in the house than what my husband is.' The other, resentful of some chance criticism, said angrily, 'It's all very well for Mrs. Cripps to talk of what she does. She's got a mother to help her, and a sister, and her old father will mind her little boys by the hour when he's down at the allotments.'

(London: Edward Arnold, 1908, pp. 33–34, 35–36)

5.5   Kathleen Woodward, *Jipping Street* (1928)

You must see my mother as she most familiarly comes back to me: from out of the wash-house in Jipping Street, for ever full of damp, choking, soapy steam from the copper, which settles on the broken window panes and in a moment becomes a thousand little rivulets falling drunkenly down the surface of the windows, and hangs in tiny tremulous drops on the ledges which I can watch as I wait to turn the wringer. I wait, and watch the steam on the window, and listen to mother.

Out of the steam comes mother's face – pinkish purple, sweating, her black hair putting forth lank wisps that hang over her forehead and cling to the nape of her neck. The hairpins in her hair rust in the damp and steam.

'Christ!' she gasps, and wipes the sweat from her face, and for a few moments rests her hands on the side of the wash-tub – hands unnaturally crinkled and bleached from the stinging soda water.

'Wash, wash, wash; it's like washing your guts away. Stand, stand, stand; I want six pairs of feet; and then I'd have to stand on my head to give them a rest . . .'

I eagerly looked forward to those nights when we left the wash-house at nine to take home the finished washing and collect more washing.

Down Jipping Street we went, round the hospital bend, over the interminable London Bridge carrying the bundle of washing in turn – the clean-smelling, soapy clean washing – the insufferable day behind us.

When we got to Mrs. Moody's in Thames Street we wedged our feet in the front door lest it be shut in our faces without the washing money, and our emotions were divided between the agonising uncertainty of Mrs. Moody's finances and the inexpressible relief of the day behind us.

On our way home we stopped at the 'World On Its Toes', where mother had a glass of beer, and life took on a different look in the warm smell of fresh beer and sawdust; the gaslights turned full on, and everybody being friendly, at ease, and telling secrets to each other, and confidences. Nellie the barmaid would be pinked up and shrill, her unmanageable bosom protruding grossly over the bar counter; and we could sit on the form in the public bar for as long as mother could possibly take to drink her glass of beer; and from where I sat I could look at the sponge cakes under a glass vase on the bar shelf, cakes that you could eat until you again felt hungry – only, no one could afford so many sponge cakes.

After the long day, with the background of the 'World On Its Toes', mother's face often comes back to me, and she sighs with a sort of contentment, and sips her beer, and there are six or seven hours between her and the scrubbing brush to-morrow.

(London: Longmans, Green and Co, 1928, pp. 11–14)

5.6 Elizabeth Andrews, *A Woman's Work is Never Done: being the recollections of a childhood and upbringing amongst the South Wales miners and a lifetime of service to the Labour movement in Wales* (1948)

I was born on December 15th, 1882, at Hirwaun, Breconshire, nr. Aberdare, one of a family of eleven children – four boys and seven girls. I was the third child. One baby sister died when a few weeks old, and one brother died in his teenage; the other nine reached maturity and all married.

. . . I commenced school when I was about four years old and I remember taking my two pennies every Monday to pay for it. Small children under five paid 2d. or 1/- for a family. I loved school from an early age . . .

I had a great desire to become a teacher. My ambition was favoured by my Headmistress, and I was often sent to help in the Infant School when I was in the upper standards. I had to leave school at twelve owing to our large family and the coming ninth baby. My baby sister died and I had the chance to return to school for another year. My school career ended at thirteen when I had passed the seventh standard.

Two years after leaving school I attended the first evening classes held in the village. At the end of the session I carried away two first prizes for the best essay and for the best pie! The Inspector was very interested in my essay and asked the Headmistress to try and get my parents to agree for me to return to school to be trained as a teacher. But my parents could not afford the trainfare to travel to Aberdare for higher education. They also needed my help at home with three miners at work and six children attending school. The washing, ironing, cooking and mending were endless and the hard times, low wages and strikes made it very difficult for us all. Babies arrived every two years and being the eldest girl, I had to be little mother. There was little chance of play after school hours unless I had a baby in my arms. Prams were rare those days in working-class homes; babies were nursed in shawls. My two elder brothers were part-time in school and part-time in the pit . . .

We always had Sunday-best frocks that were passed down to the younger ones when we had outgrown them. Luckily for us Mother was a good needlewoman and a good cook. She would sew until the early hours of the morning to keep us tidy. She bought a sewing machine to help her, and I learnt to sew at a very early age.

My father mended our boots and the family had to help with an allotment, so that we grew most of our vegetables. We also rented a perch of land from a local farmer to grow enough potatoes for the winter. These were stored in mounds of earth in the back garden. The cooking, washing, bathing and the drying of pit clothes had to be done in the kitchen; the fire had to be kept in all night in an open grate.

When I was very young I had to help to mend the pit clothes. This was hard work. The needle and thread had to be waxed for nearly every stitch before I could get it into the moleskin. This job often kept us at it until the early hours of the morning because of the long hours the miners worked.

Our only relaxation was on Sunday where we all turned out to Chapel and Sunday School. It was a pleasure to see the miners and their families in their Sunday best. The blue scars on their hands and faces were the only mark they carried of their trade.

I marvel at the way our parents managed to rear decent families in the latter part of the last century, and the beginning of this century, especially during periods of strikes. I remember one strike lasting six months, the only income being a small strike pay from the Miner's Federation. But the women stood loyally by their men-folk in their struggle for higher pay, shorter hours and better conditions. The Masters tried to starve them into submission.

(Glamorgan : Cymric Democrat Publishing Society, 1948?, pp. 1–3)

5.7 'Food: Chief Articles of Diet', *Round About a Pound a Week* (1913)

Meat is bought for the men, and the chief expenditure is made in preparation for Sunday's dinner, when the man is at home. It is eaten cold by him the next day. The children get a pound of pieces stewed for them during the week, and with plenty of potatoes they make great show of the gravy.

Bread, however, is their chief food. It is cheap; they like it; it comes into the house ready cooked; it is always at hand, and needs no plate or spoon. Spread with a scraping of butter, jam, or margarine, according to the length of the purse of the mother, they never tire of it as long as they are in their ordinary state of health. They receive it into their hands, and can please themselves as to where and how they eat it. It makes the sole article in the menu for two meals in the day. Dinner may consist of anything, from the joint on Sunday to boiled rice on Friday. Potatoes will play a great part, as a rule, at dinner, but breakfast and tea will be bread.

Potatoes are not an expensive item in the 20s. budget. They may cost 1s. 3d. a week in a family of ten persons, and 4d. a week in a family of three. But they are an invariable item. Greens may go, butter may go, meat may diminish almost to the vanishing point, before potatoes are affected. When potatoes do not appear for dinner, their place will be taken by suet pudding, which will mean that there is no gravy or dripping to eat with them. Treacle, or – as the shop round the corner calls it – 'golden syrup', will probably be eaten with the pudding, and the two together will form a midday meal for the mother and children in a working man's family. All these are good – bread, potatoes, suet pudding; but children need other food as well.

First and foremost children need milk. All children need milk, not only infants in arms. When a mother weans her child, she ought to be able to give it plenty of milk or food made with milk. . . . The reason why the infants do not get milk is the reason why they do not get good housing or comfortable clothing – it is too expensive. Milk costs the same, 4d. a quart, in Lambeth that it costs in Mayfair. . . .

As things are, once weaned, the child of a labouring man gets its share of the family diet. It gets its share of the 4d. tin of separated milk, its share of gravy and potatoes, a sip of the cocoa on which 3d. or 4d. a week may be spent for the use of everyone, and, if its father be particularly partial to it, a mouthful of fat bacon once or twice a week, spared from the not too generous 'relish to his tea'. Besides these extras it gets bread.

Women in the poorer working-class districts nurse their babies, as a rule, far longer than they should. It is not unusual for a mother to say that she always nurses until they are a year old. In many cases where a better-off mother would recognize that she is unable to satisfy her child's hunger, and would wean it at once, the poor mother goes hopelessly on because it is cheaper to nurse. It is less trouble to nurse, and it is held among them to be a safeguard against pregnancy. For these three reasons it is difficult to persuade a Lambeth woman to wean her child . . .

The articles of diet other than bread, meat, potatoes (with occasional suet puddings and tinned milk), are fish, of which a shilling's worth may be bought a week, and of which quite half will go to provide the bread-winner with 'relishes', while the other half may be eaten by the mother and children; bacon, which will be entirely consumed by the man; and an occasional egg. The tiny amounts of tea, dripping, butter, jam, sugar, and greens, may be regarded rather in the light of condiments than of food.

The diet where there are several children is obviously chosen for it cheapness, and is of the filling, stodgy kind. There is not enough of anything but bread. There is no variety. Nothing is considered but money.

> (Reprint: Maud Pember Reeves, *Round About a Pound a Week* (London: Virago, 1979 [Hogarth Press, 1913]), pp. 97–103)

5.8   *Maternity: Letters from Working Women* (1915)

I was married at twenty-eight in utter ignorance of the things that most vitally affect a wife and mother. My mother, a dear, pious soul, thought ignorance was innocence, and the only thing I remember her saying on the subject of childbirth was, 'God never sends a babe without bread to feed it.' Dame Experience long ago knocked the bottom out of that argument for me. My husband was a man earning 32s. a week – a conscientious, good man, but utterly undomesticated. A year after our marriage the first baby was born, naturally and with little pain or trouble. I had every care, and motherhood stirred the depths of my nature. The rapture of a babe in arms drawing nourishment from me crowned me with glory and sanctity and honour. . . . Fifteen months later a second baby came – a dear little girl, and again I was in a fairly good condition physically and financially, but had incurred heavy doctor's bills and attendance bills, due to my incapacity for work owing to eczema. Both the children were delicate, and dietary expenses ran high. Believing that true thrift is wise expenditure, we spent our all trying to build up for them sound, healthy bodies, and was ill-prepared financially and physically to meet the birth of a third baby sixteen months later. Motherhood ceased to be a crown of glory, and became a fearsome thing to be shunned and feared. The only way to meet our increased expenditure was by dropping an endowment policy, and losing all our little, hard-earned savings. I confess without shame that when well-meaning friends said: 'You cannot afford another baby; take this drug,' I took their strong concoctions to purge me of the little life that might be mine. They failed, as such things generally do, and the third baby came. Many a time I have sat in daddy's big chair, a baby two and a half years old at my back, one sixteen months and one one month on my knees, and cried for very weariness and hopelessness. I fed them all as long as I could, but I was too harassed, domestic duties too heavy, and the income too limited to furnish me with a rich nourishing milk . . .

Two years later a fourth baby came. Varicose veins developed. I thought they were a necessary complement to childbirth. He was a giant of a boy and heavy to carry, and I just dragged about the housework, washing and cleaning until the time of his birth; but I looked forward to that nine days in bed longingly; to be still and rest was a luxury of luxuries. Economics became a greater strain than ever now that I had four children to care for. Dimly conscious of the evils of sweating, instead of buying cheap ready-made clothes, I fashioned their little garments and became a sweated worker myself. The utter monotony of life, the lack of tone and culture, the drudgery and gradual lowering of the standard of living consequent upon the rising cost of living, and increased responsibilities, was converting me into a soulless drudge and nagging scold. I felt the comradeship between myself and husband was breaking up. He could not enter into my domestic, I would not enter into his intellectual pursuits, and again I had to fight or go under. I could give no time to mental culture or reading and I bought Stead's penny editions of literary masters, and used to put them on a shelf in front of me on washing-day, [and] fastened back their pages with a clothes peg. . . .

Three years later a fifth baby came. I was ill and tired, but my husband fell ill a month prior to his birth, and I was up day and night. Our doctor was, and is, one of the kindest men I have ever met. I said: 'Doctor, I cannot afford you for myself, but will you come if I need?' 'I hope you won't need me, but I'll come.' I dare not let my husband in his precarious condition hear a cry of pain from me, and travail pain cannot always be stifled; and here again the doctor helped me by giving me a sleeping draught to administer him as soon as I felt the pangs of childbirth. Hence he slept in one room while I travailed in the other, and brought forth the loveliest boy that ever gladdened a mother's heart. So here I am a woman of forty-one years, blessed with a lovely family of healthy children, faced with a big deficit, varicose veins, and an occasional loss of the use of my hands. I want nice things, but I must pay that debt I owe. I would like nice clothes (I've had three new dresses in fourteen years), but I must not have them yet. I'd like to develop mentally, but I must stifle that part of my nature until I have made good the ills of the past, and I am doing it slowly and surely, and my heart grows lighter, and will grow lighter still when I know that the burden is lifted from the mothers of our race.

Wages 32s. to 40s.; five children, one miscarriage.
(Reprint: Margaret Llewellyn Davies (ed.), *Maternity: Letters from Working Women* (London: Virago, 1978 [1915]), pp. 44–48)

5.9 *The Hard Way Up. Autobiography of Hannah Mitchell, Suffragette and Rebel (1968)*

When I realized that I was to become a mother, fresh problems presented themselves, and I cannot say that the prospect gave me any pleasure at first. Living on our small income was hard enough for two ...

I had been able to buy a few necessaries each week with my own savings, but I foresaw that the coming of a baby would mean giving up my own work, for a few months anyhow. At first I felt desperate, and wept many bitter tears, but by and by, as I recovered from the nausea of the first few weeks, I began to feel more hopeful. I remembered my sister-in-law who now had four children, and still only eighteen shillings a week to keep them on.

'What other women did, I could surely do', I told myself grimly.

I must work harder at my dressmaking [to earn money], let the housework go for a few months, and try to save a little money for the event. But goodbye to all hopes of study and self-improvement: there would be no time even to read, or for fresh air and walks in the country. ....

I spent long hours at the sewing machine, and found myself, two months before the baby was due, with three whole golden sovereigns saved. I spent these on muslin, calico and flannel, for a modest layette which I made myself. Then having cleaned the house thoroughly, put up clean curtains and polished my scanty furniture, I waited the event.

I feared the ordeal, but tried to keep my fears to myself, remembering that other women got over it, not once only, but many times. My husband was sympathetic, but like most men had the comfortable idea that women do not feel pain as much as men. I think they have a subconscious feeling that childbirth cannot be so very painful or their mothers would not have faced it so often – Poor dead and gone mothers, who often bore ten or twelve children. How they must have suffered. My heart aches at the thought of it.

At last my own time came. One Friday, having done my weekend cleaning and baked a batch of bread during the day, I hoped for a good night's rest, but I scarcely had retired before my labour began. My baby was not born until the following evening, after twenty-four hours of intense suffering which an ignorant attendant did little to alleviate, assuring me at intervals that I should be much worse yet. At last a kindly neighbour, herself the mother of three children, coming in to see how things were shaping, took matters into her own hands. She sent my husband for the doctor, charging him to insist on immediate attendance, and bustled me into bed. But my strength was gone, and I could do no more to help myself, so my baby was brought into the world with instruments, and without an anaesthetic.

This operation was sheer barbarism and ought to be regarded as 'wiful cruelty' and dealt with accordingly. Since then, even in an easy and natural labour, I have often seen a kindly doctor give a little relief to an exhausted woman to ease her suffering.

'A woman in her travail hath sorrow because her hour has come, but as soon as she is delivered of the child, she remembereth no more the anguish for joy that a man is born into the world.' So the Scriptures, but in my case they were wrong. 'She remembereth for ever the anguish' would be a more accurate rendering. My joy was clouded by the fear that I could not give my baby the opportunities in life which I had missed so much, and my convalescence was retarded by worry about the future. Only one thing emerged clearly from such bitter thinking at that time, the fixed resolve to bring no more babies into the world. I felt it impossible to face again either the personal suffering, or the task of bringing a second child up in poverty.

Fortunately, my husband had the courage of his Socialist convictions on this point, and was no more anxious than myself to repeat the experience . . .
(Reprint: edited by Geoffrey Mitchell (London: Virago 1977 [1968]),
pp. 99–102)

5.10 Sir George Newman, *Infant Mortality: A Social Problem* (1906)

IX PREVENTATIVE METHODS: (I) THE MOTHER

This book will have been written in vain if it does not lay the emphasis of this problem upon the vital importance to the nation of its motherhood. Wherever we turn, and to whatever issue, in this question of infant mortality, we are faced with one all-pervading primary need – the need of a high standard of physical motherhood. Infant mortality in the early weeks of life is evidently due in large measure to the physical conditions of the mother, leading to prematurity and debility of the infant; and in the later months of the first year infant mortality appears to be due to unsatisfactory feeding of the infant. But from either point of view it becomes clear that the problem of infant mortality is not one of sanitation alone, or housing, or indeed of poverty as such, but is mainly a question of motherhood. No doubt external conditions as those named are influencing maternity, but they are, in the main, affecting the mother, and not the child. They exert their influence upon the infant indirectly through the mother. Improved sanitation, better housing, cheap and good food, domestic education, a healthy life of body and mind – these are conditions which lead to efficient motherhood from the point of view of child-bearing. They exert but an indirect effect on the child itself, who depends for its life in the first twelve months, not upon the State or the municipality, nor yet upon this or that system of creche or milk-feeding, but upon the health, the intelligence, the devotion and maternal instinct of the mother. And if we would solve the great problem of infant mortality, it would appear that we must first obtain a higher standard of physical motherhood. . . .

'Nothing seems to be wanting,' writes the Medical Officer of Burnley, 'but a department to teach the burgesses common sense, mothers how to feed a child till its teeth come, and how to nurse it when it is poorly.' (Report on Health of Burnley, 1904, p. 4). Few facts receive more unanimous support from those in intimate touch with this question than the ignorance and carelessness of mothers in respect of infant management. Such ignorance shows itself not only in bad methods of artificial feeding, but in the exposure of the child to all sorts of injurious influences, and to uncleanly management and negligence. Death in infancy is probably more due to such ignorance and negligence than to almost any other cause, as becomes evident when we remember that epidemic diarrhoea, convulsions, debility, and atrophy, which are among the most common causes of death, are brought about in large measure owing to improper feeding or ill-timed weaning; bronchitis and pneumonia are due not infrequently to careless exposure (indoor or outdoor);* and death from measles and whooping-cough is largely caused by mismanagement of nursing. To remedy this condition of things three different measures need to be carried out: (a) instruction of mothers, (b) the appointment of lady health visitors, and (c) the education of girls in domestic hygiene.

*[footnote: In a London market street on a raw, cold, foggy night in November (1904), between the hours of 9 and 10, I have counted 67 infants in arms. A month later 66 were counted by another observer in the same street at the same time of night. Report on Health of Finsbury, 1904, p. 263]

(London: Methuen, 1906, pp. 257–258, 262)

Chapter Six

Community, politics and religion

Women were active in working-class and radical politics in the first half of the nineteenth century, although their participation took a different form from that of men. They participated in collective and community protests, formed Reform Unions and were involved in large numbers in the big movements of the 1820s and 1830s: Owenism, the Ten Hours' Movement, the Anti-Poor Law Movement and Chartism. Within radical culture generally there was considerable discussion about the proper roles of men and women. Women often drew upon the Bible to support their protest. Even where not linked to radical political activity, religious belief and practice could give women an authoritative role in their communities. The sources in this chapter look at the issue of women's roles and authority in working-class communities, particularly in relation to collective protest, radical culture and religion.

6.1 Charles Redwood, *The Vale of Glamorgan* (1839)

Women played an important role in the collective community protests of the eighteenth century, including the bread riot, the 'St. Monday' holiday, anti-enclosure protests and the 'skimmington' or 'rough-musicking', known in Wales as the 'ceffyl pren'.[1] Here, transgressors of community norms were humiliated by being paraded on a wooden horse on a pole. Charles Redwood's account in *The Vale of Glamorgan* (1839) describes the use of the Coolstrin court against a hen-pecked husband and his 'vixen' wife. The men of the village decided that action needed to be taken in support of a tailor named Rissin who, while he could make breeches for anyone in Wales, was unable to wear them at home as Nest, his wife, 'a notorious vixen, and very strapping', would not let her husband have a drink in peace in the local pub. Gronow Punter, the cobbler, elected to the position of judge, claimed this was 'slavery to petticoat government, and a disgrace to manhood.'[2] While this excerpt focuses on a female transgressor, by the middle of the nineteenth century, wife beaters and (male) adulterers were often the target of such action, with women playing a role either as purveyors of information through gossip networks, sometimes delivering verbal abuse or carrying the wooden structure and acting as spokespeople.

6.2 William Thompson and Anna Wheeler, *Appeal, of one half of the Human Race, Women, . . .* (1825)

Owenism is recognised as being especially focused on gender issues and the 'woman question'. The movement encompassed reformers from different social backgrounds and included trade unionism, education, community building and women's rights within its political vision. An inspirational text for many Owenites was the *Appeal* (1825), by William Thompson (1775–1833) and Anna Wheeler (1785–1850?). Both from upper-class Irish backgrounds, Thompson was greatly influenced by the works of Robert Owen, William Godwin and Mary Wollstonecraft. Wheeler, who had married a violent alcoholic at the age of fifteen, leaving him after twelve years and eventually finding her way to London with her two daughters, was also acquainted with Owen. The *Appeal* was a refutation of James Mill's article *On Government* (1819), which supported the continued exclusion of women from the franchise on the premise that they were represented by their husbands and fathers. Thompson and Wheeler argued that all women as well as men should have the vote. They argued that the oppression of women was institutionalised through government, the law, the Church and the family, and perpetuated by the many men who were 'despots in the home'. Marriage was a form of slavery: the state sanctioned rape in marriage and the double standard which ensured men were not socially reprimanded for adultery, but women lost their reputation. Thompson and Wheeler emphasised the conjugal ideal, the companionate marriage, where both partners were involved in work, decision-making, childcare and household duties.

6.3 Letter to *The Pioneer,* 'To the Females of the Working Class' (1834)

This letter from 'A Bondswoman' in Birmingham is believed to have been written by Frances Morrison, wife of James Morrison, the editor of the Owenite trade union paper *The Pioneer*, who helped her husband run a small newspaper shop as well as bringing up their four daughters. Addressing questions raised in an earlier letter from 'A London Mechanic's Wife' about the low value accorded to women's work, the author argues that it was not just the employers who treated women badly, but working men who refused to join in union to protect them, and who often felt threatened by political and educated wives. Both letters were composed at the time of the 1833–34 silk strike in Derby which involved many women workers. As Catherine Hall has noted, men's industrial superiority was ensured by male unionists who combined calls for shorter hours with demands for the exclusion of women.[3]

6.4 Shrove Tuesday in Derby, *The Pioneer* (1834)

Owenism had a cultural dimension, expressed in educational activities, meetings and festivals. The Derby silk weavers' march, reported in *The Pioneer* in 1834, can be seen as a critique of popular culture. The march occurred on Shrove Tuesday, the day usually given over to street football, which in Derby was a particularly rowdy event which the authorities had tried to ban. The strikers sought to replace it with a respectable radical cultural event. Women dressed in white in order to symbolise their virtue and respectability.

6.5 *The Book of Murder!* (1839)

Attempts to implement the New Poor Law, which began in the North in 1837, were met with massive resistance. Economic depression meant that unemployment and occasional employment were frequent, and men, who might be busy for a week or two then laid off, were under constant threat of their families being interned in the dreaded 'Bastille'. Women formed their own anti-poor law organisations, held weekly meetings, engaged in publicity and propaganda, and were sometimes involved in direct-action. They emphasised the immorality of the workhouse, particularly the practice of separating husbands, wives and children, and drew on the Scriptures to give moral weight to their campaign. The famous piece of anti-Poor Law propaganda, *The Book of Murder!*, was published in 1838. It allegedly came from two pamphlets, which were thought to be the work of the Poor Law Commissioners or their Malthusian supporters. The excerpt included here focuses on the wrongs done to single mothers and their infants under the New Poor Law. Not only was an unwed mother imprisoned in the workhouse, but her 'seducer', the child's father, was not required to provide any support. Infanticide is discussed as an understandable response by desperate women, who found it hard to find work after giving birth, as fears of immorality impeded attempts to place them in service, and who would have limited means of supporting themselves and a child.

6.6 Address to the *Northern Star* from the Chartist Women of Newcastle (1839)

In 1838–1839, there were over 100 Female Charter Associations or Female Radical Associations, which met in pubs, homes and in town and village Rooms or Socialist Halls. Chartist women were involved in a range of activities, including sewing banners and caps of liberty; running schools and Sunday schools; organising Chartist social events, including tea parties, soirees, concerts and dances; participating in demonstrations, church occupations and strikes and riots; and, in their hundreds of thousands, signing the Chartist petitions of 1839 and 1842. They also wrote to the Chartist newspaper, the *Northern Star*, the proprietor of which, Fergus O'Connor, was fervently against women's enfranchisement, maintaining that 'it would lead to family dissensions'.[4] The authors of this Address argue that they cannot be good wives and mothers because government policy (unemployment, wage levels, the Poor Law, etc.) had made their homes 'destitute of comfort'. The extent to which the emphasis on their domestic role was a strategy adopted by Chartist men and women has been debated by historians.[5]

6.7 George Eliot, *Adam Bede* (1859)

The role of women was one of the conflicts which beset Methodism in the 1790s and early 1800s, as the Methodist leadership exerted pressure on women not to preach. In 1803, a group led by Hugh Bourne in Staffordshire broke away from the parent body to form the Primitive Methodists. The 'Prims' had among their number over 200 women preachers, many of whom travelled on preaching tours far and wide.[6] Dinah Morris, in George Eliot's *Adam Bede*, was modelled on the Primitive Methodist preacher (and relative of Eliot), Betsy Tomlinson, who itinerated on the Staffordshire and Derbyshire Methodist circuits at the turn of the nineteenth century. In this excerpt, Eliot describes Dinah's femininity and her belief in the relevance of God to the poor.

6.8 *Hymns Selected for the use of the Female Revivalists* (1824)

Religious belonging offered women a form of public expression and a community, enabling the defence of the neighbourly and familial traditions of the labouring poor against the ravages of industrialisation. These women were not deferent, but challenged many middle-class ideals, using the Bible, especially Old Testament stories of people freeing themselves from bondage, to support their reproof against employers and reformers. Working-class women in particular drew on the tradition of important female figures in the Bible, and took the title of Mothers in Israel in order to take a prominent role in their communities, in the campaigns against the new Poor Law, in the Ten Hours' Movement and in Chartism. The Female Revivalists, led by Ann Carr, were based in Leeds, and such sentiments are very much in evidence in their *Hymns*.

6.9 Revd Francis Close, *A Sermon, Addressed to the Female Chartists of Cheltenham* (1839)

Many early trade unionists and Chartists were members of Methodist sects and working-class radicalism in the 1830s and 1840s was suffused with Christian morality. In order to state their objection to the complicity of the church in the oppression of the poor, Chartist men and women adopted a strategy of church occupations and protests during the height of the campaign in the late 1830s. It was in response to one such occupation in Cheltenham that the Revd Close composed his *Sermon*. Close invokes the Scriptures to read a 'theological riot act' against women engaging in politics (and indeed venturing beyond the home).[7] He saw undomesticated women as symbols of social disorder, reminiscent of the 'unnatural' women of the French Revolution.

6.10 Marianne Farningham, *A Working Woman's Life: an Autobiography* (1907)

The most common form of religious involvement for girls and women was as Sunday school teachers. In her autobiography, Marianne Farningham (1834–1909) describes the place of Sunday school teaching and chapel attendance in her social and cultural life. In this excerpt, Farningham describes her desire to join the Baptist Church and her decision to become an assistant at Durdham Down School in Bristol in 1857.

6.11 Rosina Davies, *The Story of My Life* (1942)

For Rosina Davies (1863–1949), a teenage evangelist from the Rhondda, membership of the Salvation Army enabled her involvement in missionary work in Wales and England and in America in the late nineteenth and early twentieth centuries. In this extract from her autobiography she describes her reception as the Welsh 'girl Evangelist'.

6.1   Charles Redwood, *The Vale of Glamorgan: Scenes and Tales Among the Welsh* (1839)

'But now', said old Gronow, in conclusion, 'the upshot of all this is, that it is my judgement *we must hold a riding upon Nest and Rissin*, that these hectoring wenches may see what a pretty figure they cut, and learn what it is we think of them; and that all men may be put in mind to keep the reigns tight, and not part with the breeches, nor ever knock under to hen-pecking.'

Here there was a loud huzza, and the Court broke up in a manner sufficiently uproarious. Some were even for carrying Gronow Punter on their shoulders through the village, for his exemplary conduct as judge. But the old man declined that honour; so they began to lay their hands together about arranging for the important day of their procession.

When that day came, the whole village was in commotion. From an early hour the children clustered in groups, and looked and talked as though something great impended. Every now and then you might see the men pass hastily to and from about their dwellings, and at some doors they hung out like bees before a swarm. Presently those who were to act a part in the procession made their appearance, and drew a concourse after them to the churchyard; and as soon as they had all collected, they began to form the order of their train.

The front was taken by old Gronow Punter, who still wore the large triangular horse's bone upon his head, and the 'robe' about his shoulders. He was followed by two of the solemn officers with long white wands; and a couple of rustics bearing pitchforks succeeded them. Next came band of musicians, consisting of one who beat a frying-pan upon a gridiron, and others with poker, tongs, and shovel, and kettles beat upon with various instruments, so as to make up a chorus of kitchen-music, in addition to a fife and drum. After these were two standard-bearers; one with a petticoat at the top of a pole, and the other bearing breeches in the same manner, only reversed, with the upside down. These proceeded to two who impersonated Rissin and Nest – the heroine brandishing a ladle, and the poor cully carrying a broom. A great rabble-rout brought up the rear.

As soon as Grownow Punter and the officers of his court began to move on, with a solemn dignity of demeanour, the band of kettles, frying-pans, gridirons, horns, fife and drum, struck up and the whole procession followed with a shout. The standard-bearers now flouted the breeches and the petticoat; the virago began to firk her cully; and all the train let loose their antic gestures and grimaces.

In this manner they proceeded to take a large circuit through the vale, and excited no small commotion in the little villages. The men everywhere received them with shouts and merriment, and sometimes even with bell-ringing; but the women kept within doors, and only mocked at them through the windows.

But when at length they returned to their own village, the women there had collected to scoff at them, and poured out a din of hoots and yells, that could not be drowned even by the Coolstrin band of kitchen-music, and the triumphant shouts of the riding, as it passed the little tailor's cottage. Here everything was now fastened up and still, and without sign of inmate, except a dirty, fretful-looking cat, which stared at them through the broken window.

The pole on which the petticoat flourished was now fixed opposite the house, and the emblem of woman's sway pelted at with mud, stones, addle eggs, and dirt, until it dropped in tatters to the ground, amid a wild uproar of shouts and hoots, the clangor of the horn, the hollow dub of the drum, the whiffle of the fife, and the jangling of frying-pans, gridirons, and kettles of all sizes. Upon this the pole with the breeches was elevated on the roof; and as soon as the standard of masculine government waved above the house, all their din was redoubled at seeing the snivelling face of the little tailor chuckling in the window, behind the staring cat.

(London: Saunders and Otley, 1839, pp. 290–295)

6.2 William Thompson and Anna Wheeler, *Appeal of one Half of the Human Race, Women, Against the Pretensions of the Other Half, Men, to Retain them in Political, and thence in Civil and Domestic, Slavery* (1825)

The despotism of man over woman in marriage, by personal force maintained, as by law established, is then rendered gentle by the dependence of man on woman for the gratification of his amorous propensities! How long shall such insulting falsehoods be substituted for reasons on which depend the happiness of one half of the human race? The dependence of man on the smiles of woman, is always *voluntary* on the part of the man, and is limited to the short-lived moment previous to possession. The dependence of woman on the smiles of man is eternal, may be voluntary for a moment before the *contract*, but is unrelentingly *forced* during the whole remainder of life . . .

But that is not all: another and more glaring falsehood is assumed and reasoned on as fact, in the pretext of modifying man's despotism in marriage by his sexual dependence on woman. Not only is a *natural* dependence for the gratification of man's love in marriage assumed, but a legal dependence, a legal obligation, is feigned. A legal, is added to the natural, sexual dependence! It is assumed that the laws bind men to the gratification of the wives whom they take. The laws made by man absolve him from all such dependence. Against absolute desertion, starvation, or violence threatening life, alone, the laws protect women in marriage; just as the West-India and United States slave-codes guarantee the slaves. Such is man's dependence! Woman can demand no enjoyment from man as a matter of right; she must beg it, like any of her children, or like any slave, as a favour. If refused, she must submit, contented or not contented. Once married, a woman must submit to the *commands* of her master . . . If woman does not comply with his caprices, man is justified by vile law and viler opinion, to compel obedience. If man refuse any request of woman, the legal, the moral, and the physical power of compelling obedience are equally wanting. Man disdains to beg for what he can command. Such voluntary compliance, the gracious result of the understanding and the affections, improving and exalting the happiness equally of the giver and receiver, is spurned by the ignorant, short-sighted, selfishness of man. He must be obeyed, and for execrable pleasure of commanding, he loses – and were he alone concerned, justly loses, – the delights of the sweetest human social intercourse, that of esteem and confidence between equals, heightened by the glow of sexual attachment. Man, by law, superstition, and opinion, commands: woman, in marriage, by law, superstition, and opinion, obeys. Woman must cast nature, or feign to cast it, from her breast. She is not permitted to appear to feel, or desire. The whole of what is called her education training her to be the obedient instrument of man's sensual gratification, she is not permitted even to wish for any gratification for herself. She must have no desires: she must always yield, must submit as a matter of duty, not repose upon her equal for the sake of happiness: she must blush to own that she enjoys his generous caresses, were such by chance ever given. . . .

To secure what seem to his ignorance the advantages of superiority of strength, he makes the mind of his victim as feeble as nature, but particularly as artificial circumstances, have rendered her body, by excluding from her, and reserving to himself, all sources of knowledge and skill; by vesting in himself all power to create, all right to possess and control, property; by excluding her from all those offices, actions, and incidents, which afford opportunities for exercising the judgement, and calling into life all the higher and most useful intellectual powers; and lastly, by making her swear, when about to enter on life and assist in producing and rearing a family, to renounce the exercise of that reason of which his vile practices have deprived her, to surrender the control over her voluntary actions, to be in all things, going out and coming in, in the minutest incidents of life, *obedient* to his will, be it wise or capricious. Black slaves are not insulted with the requisition to swear or vow obedience to their masters: the compulsion of the slave-code is sufficient without unnecessary childish insult. For white slaves – parcelled out amongst men (as if to compensate them for their own cowardly submission almost everywhere to the chains of political power), the uninquiring instruments first of their voluptuousness, and, when that is sated, of their caprice of command – was and is reserved this gratuitous degradation of swearing to be slaves, of kissing the rod of domestic despotism, and of devoting themselves to its worship . . .

(Reprint: London: Virago, 1983 [1825], pp. 62–66)

6.3 'To the Females of the Working Class', *The Pioneer* (Feb. 1834)

Sir,

I have been anxiously looking, for this week or two past, for some friend to respond to the letter of the mechanic's wife, in London. It is time the working females of England began to demand their long-suppressed rights. Let us, in the first place, endeavour to throw off the trammels that have so long enshackled our minds, and get knowledge, when all are making their way to the temple of truth and justice. Let not woman – patient, suffering, long neglected woman – stay behind on the road to improvement. Not but I know the time will come, ere long, when men will see the necessity of educating their wives, in all matters that concern themselves, equally as all men see the necessity of their knowing how our government acts as regards them. May be the time is not distant when the superiority of educated females will be acknowledged over those that are kept in blind and stupid ignorance. No wonder at the present state of affairs, when the mothers of the most able, most useful of England's sons, have been denied the acquisition of truth of every kind. The mother is the first to sow the seed of instruction in the youthful mind; and if the seed is bad, what can we expect from the fruits? Sisters, bonds-women, arise! And let us unite to gain our rights. Let us unite and teach the oppressors, our employers, their duty.

In manufacturing towns, look at the value that is set on woman's labour, whether it be skilful, whether it be laborious, so that woman can do it. The contemptible expression is, it is made by woman, and therefore cheap. Why, I ask, should woman's labour be thus under-valued? Why should the time and the ingenuity of the sex, that could be so usefully employed otherwise, be monopolized by cruel and greedy oppressors, being in the likeness of man, and calling them-selves masters? Sisters, let us submit to it no longer; let us once get to the knowledge of our wrongs, and our cause is won; once entered on the path to improvement, the flowers that are strewed on the road will invite us to travel on. Then we will cast the foul aspersions that have been heaped on our sex into oblivion. The itch for scandal, tattling, and other vices, which we are said to possess, placed in the scale of truth, with affection, sincerity, perseverance, ingenuity, and many other virtues; these, properly cultivated, will ever outweigh the vices that have been forced into our naturally noble minds. Then will woman do justice to the fair form nature has given her. Men, in general, tremble at the idea of a reading wife, being taught to believe it an evil by designing tyrants. Woman's rights, like man's, have been withheld from motives purely political, by deep concerted plans of early oppressors. The sage priests of olden time well knew, if woman's penetrative and inquisitive mind was allowed its liberty, their well-laid schemes of bigotry and superstition would soon have come to light. But, to return to our immediate interest: let our class generally unite; let us make a beginning in Birmingham; there are great numbers of females employed in this town. If our first efforts are feeble, let us fear not; a change must come, and that speedily. The women of Derby have entered the bonds of union; let us, in compliment to these noble but oppressed women, plant the standard of female union in Birmingham. Women of Birmingham, your children's, your own, your country's interests demand it. Be slaves no longer, but unite and assert your just rights! With the anxious hope that we may soon establish a union that will be a shield from oppression of every kind,

I subscribe myself, fellow countrywomen,
An earnest assistant in our cause,

A Bondswoman
Birmingham, Feb. 2, 1834

6.4 Shrove Tuesday in Derby, *The Pioneer* (Feb. 1834)

. . . The operatives in union having resolved to walk in procession through the town, on Shrove-Tuesday, to Duffield, a delightful little village, four miles on the Buxton road, matters we so arranged that the operatives of all classes in union, between five and six hundred women, and upwards of thirteen hundred men, met opposite the Infirmary, on the London road, and commenced their march about one o'clock, in the following order:–

MACE BEARER.
Two leaders, with purple scarfs, rosettes, and union-jacks.
First motto, 'Let Prudence be our Guide'.
Musical Band.
Two hundred women, with crimson silk bands,
and knots over their shoulders.
Second union-jack flag. Third flag, motto, 'Union is Strength,
Knowledge is Power.'
. . .
Women four abreast, with white silk bands &c.
Fifth flag, motto, 'Brotherly-love is Virtue.'
Twist hands, or lace-makers, three abreast.
Sixth flag, union jack, and Derby arms.
Joiners and carpenters, three abreast.
Seventh flag, union club
Shoemakers, three abreast.

Eighth flag, motto, 'Union is Strength, Knowledge is Power'.
Plasterers, three abreast.
Ninth flag, union jack.
Wood sawyers, three abreast.
Tenth flag, lion sleeping with the lamb.
Motto, 'Be not weary in well doing'.
Tailors, three abreast.

Eleventh flag, motto, 'The public mind is mighty, and must prevail.'
Broad silk-weavers, ditto, ditto.
Twelfth and thirteenth flags.
Labourers, ditto, ditto. . . .
Fifteenth flag, motto, 'Just laws and equal rights'.
Sixteenth flag, motto, 'Liberty and unity.'
Smallware weavers, ditto, ditto.
Seventeenth flag, representing a weaver at work in a loom.
Motto, 'Increase of trade; Weave truth with trust.'

Eighteenth superb flag, the bird of Jove snapping asunder
the chains of Tyranny.
Twisters, three abreast.
Nineteenth flag, union jack, twentieth ditto.
Twenty-first flag, motto, 'Pledge of better times.'
Silk throwsters, ditto, ditto.
Twenty-second flag, motto, 'Let unity prevail.'
Bricklayers, ditto, ditto
Twenty-third extremely rich flag, motto, 'Let us support our trade,
and keep out others that would it invade.'
Stone-masons, ditto, ditto.

When the procession had nearly reached Duffield, they were met on the road by four musical bands, and the whole of the trades that were in union at Duffield, Belper, and other hamlets, amounting to between one and two hundred. The praiseworthy host and hostess of the White Lion had been indefatigable in providing for their numerous expectant visitors. In a four-acre field, opposite their house, they had made a large fire in the centre, with blocks of wood and a load of coals; a marquee was erected, and seats fixed for the accommodation of the female part of the procession. The surrounding hills were thronged with people to gaze at this prospect, that augured of better times to come. The numbers of people that followed, and came to see the procession, made it rather difficult for them to be supplied with refreshments, but, upon the whole, considering the little notice that was given, it gave pretty general satisfaction. The people that were collected together in this field, and Mr Vicars, from Belper, a most worthy individual, and a strong advocate for the interest of the working classes, addressed them very appropriately upon the occasion of their meeting together at Duffield. The Unionists then returned to Derby, the females singing on the way, and through the streets of Derby, hymns and popular songs.

The procession was renewed on the Wednesday, and they proceeded to Spondon, a pleasant little village three or four miles on the Nottingham road, in the same order as the day before; the females were conducted to a field where seats and refreshments were provided for them; the men went forward to Ockbrook, a little further, to regale themselves, and returned to Derby a little after six o'clock in the evening, the band playing through the streets into the market-place, where the women sang – 'Praise God, from whom all blessings flow', &c. And this truly novel and pleasing sight was concluded with all the order, friendship, and goodwill which ever distinguished true Unionists, by repeating a short pious ejaculation.

The men and women in union were truly respectable, and they have gained an accession of friends by their orderly and peaceable conduct during the two days' procession; several of the tyrants could not help having a corner peep as the procession passed their dwellings. And many remarks of good feeling were expressed by respectable people as the procession moved along, such as – 'What sort of man can that be, who has the heart to starve such females as these?' And several others expressed their astonishment that, after ten week's privation, the women could look so clean and respectable. Yours in union,

A PLANE DRIVER.

6.5 *The Book of Murder! A Vade-Mecum for the Commissioners and Guardians of the New Poor Law throughout Great Britain and Ireland, Being an exact reprint of The Infamous Essay on the Possibility of Limiting Populousness, by Marcus, one of the three. With a Refutation of the Malthusian Doctrine (1839)*

The Murder-Book denies that the children of the poor have any right to live; and the new poor law was brought forward with the declaration that the adult poor have no right to demand support, and consequently it is denied to them that they have any right to live! The Murder-Book proposes that the poor shall be supervised and coerced; and the new poor law provides that they shall not only be supervised and coerced, but imprisoned, half or wholly starved – separated the husband from the wife (no more infants to be allowed them – mark the coincidence!) the wife from the husband, the parents from the children! The Murder-Book proposes that population shall be kept down by murdering infants by wholesale. The new poor law absolves the fathers of illegitimate children from the responsibility of feeding and nourishing their own offspring, or of assuaging the suffering and sorrow of the unhappy mothers, whom the fathers have seduced. The father of the illegitimate child, therefore, is already authorized by law to murder his own infant, if that shall occur by his withholding from it necessary nourriture and support. Gracious and almighty and just and merciful God! ... The new poor law, therefore, is the evident, palpable, and undeniable precursor of the Murder-Book. It is the first-born of the philosophical and political school from which the Murder-Book has proceeded. ... And, the additional facts are these – that not only did the framers of the new poor law and its more active supporters (we charge not with the guilty knowledge, all who merely voted for it), not only did these framers and active supporters devise and foresee that the distracted mothers of illegitimate children might be driven to infanticide, – to the murder of their helpless infants, – because they well knew it is impossible for many of such mothers to support the children; but what has since followed? Two young women were convicted at the last year's assizes of the murder of their illegitimate children; and though found guilty and sentenced to death, their sentence was commuted to imprisonment and transportation. And though child-murder was expected and *intended*, it is becoming more and more frequent, the efforts to detect the perpetrators have been relaxed! Formerly, rewards were offered for the discovery of the murderers. That practice has been abandoned! As examples, in two of the workhouses of London itself, in the last week of January, 1839, two Coroner's Inquests found, upon view of the bodies of two dead infants, verdicts of Wilful Murder against some person or persons unknown: – and yet, the parochial authorities have offered no reward for the discovery and apprehensions of the murderers!!! – We suspect not the so called *Guardians* of the Poor of a Criminal Intention; – but, have they not been silently influenced? At all events is there not a manifest *Conspiracy*? We appeal to the great tribunal of Public Opinion for its verdict; and we already hear the *united* and mighty sound of twenty millions of voices pronounce – GUILTY!

(London: William Dugdale, 1839, pp. 5–6)

6.6 Address to the *Northern Star* from the Chartist women of Newcastle (9 February 1839)

Fellow countrywomen, we have been told that the province of woman is her home, and that the field of politics should be left to men; this we deny; the nature of things renders it impossible, and the conduct of those who gave the advice is at variance with the principles they assert. Is it not true that the interests of our fathers, husbands, and brothers, ought to be ours? If they are oppressed and impoverished, do we not share those evils with them? We have read the records of the past, and our hearts have responded to the historian's praise of those women, who struggled against tyranny, and urged their countrymen to be free or die.

Acting from those feelings when told of the oppression exercised upon the enslaved negroes in our colonies, we raised our voices in denunciation of our tyrants, and never rested until the dealers in human blood were compelled to abandon their hell-born traffic; but we have learned by bitter experience that slavery is not confined to colour or clime, and that even in England cruel oppression reigns – we are compelled by our love of God and hatred of wrong to join our countrywomen in their demand for liberty and justice.

We have seen that because the husband's earnings could not support his family, the wife has been compelled to leave her home neglected, and, with her infant children, work at a soul and body degrading toil. We have seen the father dragged from his home by a ruffian press gang, compelled to fight against those that never injured him, paid only 34s per month, while he ought to have had £6, his wife and children left to starve or subsist on the scanty fair doled out by hired charity. We have seen the poor robbed of their inheritance and a law enacted to treat poverty as a crime, to deny misery consolation, to take from the unfortunate their freedom, and to drive the poor from their homes and their fatherland, to separate those who God has joined together, and tear the children from their parent's care – this law was passed by men and supported by men, who avow the doctrine that the poor have no right to live, and that an all wise and beneficent Creator has left the wants of his children unprovided for.

For years we have struggled to maintain our homes in comfort, such as our hearts told us should greet our husbands after their fatiguing labours. Year after year has passed away, and even now our wishes have no prospect of being realised, our husbands are over-wrought, our houses half furnished, our families ill fed, and our children uneducated – the fear of want hangs over our heads . . .

We have searched and found that the cause of these evils is the Government of the country being in the hands of a few of the upper and middle classes, while the working men who form the millions, the strength and the wealth of the country, are left without the pale of the Constitution, their wishes never consulted, and their interests sacrificed by the ruling Factions, who have created useless officers and enormous salaries for their own aggrandisement – burthened the country with a debt of 18 hundred millions sterling annually, and an enormous taxation of 54 millions sterling annually, which ought not to be more than 8 millions; for these evils there is no remedy but the just measure of allowing every citizen of the United Kingdom, the right of voting in the election of the members of Parliament, who have to make the laws that he has to be governed by, and grant the taxes he has to pay; or, in other words, to pass the Peoples' Charter into a law and emancipate the white slaves of England. This is what the workingmen of England, Ireland and Scotland are struggling for, and we have bonded ourselves together in union to assist them; and we call on our fellow countrywomen to join us.

We tell the wealthy, the high and mighty ones of the land, our kindred shall be free. We tell the lordly dames we love our husbands as well as they love theirs, that our homes shall no longer be destitute of comfort, that in sickness, want and old age, we will not be separated from them, that our children are near and dear to us and shall not be torn from us.

We harbour no evil wishes against anyone, and ask for nought but justice; therefore we call on all persons to assist us in this work, but especially those shopkeepers which the Reform Bill enfranchised. We call on them to remember it was the unrepresented workingmen that procured them their rights . . . they ought to remember that our pennies make their pounds, and that we cannot in justice spend the hard earnings of our husbands with those that are opposed to their rights and interests.

Fellow countrywomen, we entreat you to join us to help the cause of freedom, justice, honesty and truth, to drive poverty and ignorance from our land, and establish happy homes, true religion, righteous government, and good laws.

6.7   George Eliot, *Adam Bede* (1859)

He knew but two types of Methodist – the ecstatic and the bilious. But Dinah walked as simply as if she were going to market, and seemed as unconscious of her outward appearance as a little boy: there was no blush, no tremulousness, which said 'I know you think me a pretty woman, too young to preach'; no casting up or down of the eyelids, no compression of the lips, no attitude of the arms, that said, 'But you must think of me as a saint.' She held no book in her ungloved hands, but let them hang down lightly crossed before her, as she stood and turned her grey eyes upon the people. There was no keenness in the eyes; they seemed rather to be shedding love than making observations; they had the liquid look which tells that the mind is full of what it has to give out, rather than impressed by external objects. . . .

'Dear friends', she said, in a clear but not loud voice, 'let us pray for a blessing.' She closed her eyes, and hanging her head down a little, continued in the same moderate tone, as if speaking to someone quite near her:-

'Saviour of sinners! When a poor woman, laden with sins, went out to the well to draw water, she found Thee sitting at the well. She knew Thee not; she had not sought Thee; her mind was dark; her life was unholy. But Thou didst speak to her. Thou didst teach her, Thou didst show her that her life lay open before Thee, and yet Thou wast ready to give her that blessing which she never sought. Jesus! Thou art in the midst of us, and Thou knowest all men: if there is any here like that poor woman – if their minds are dark, their lives unholy – if they have come out not seeking Thee, not desiring to be taught; deal with them according to the free mercy which Thou didst show to her. Speak to them, Lord, open their ears to my message; bring their sins to their minds, and make them thirst for that salvation which Thou art ready to give' . . .

'Dear friends', she began raising her voice a little, 'you have all of you been to church, and I think you must have heard the clergyman read these words: "The spirit of the Lord is upon me, because he hath anointed me to preach the gospel to the poor." Jesus Christ spoke those words – he said he came *to preach the gospel to the poor*: I don't know whether you ever thought about those words much; but I will tell you when I remember first hearing them. It was on just such a sort of evening as this, when I was a little girl, and my aunt, as brought me up, took me to hear a good man preach out of doors, just as we are here. I remember his face well: he was a very old man, and had very long white hair; his voice was very soft and beautiful, not like any voice I had ever heard before . . . That man of God was Mr Wesley, who spent his life in doing what our blessed Lord did – preaching the Gospel to the poor . . .

'Why, you and me, dear friends, are poor. We have been brought up in poor cottages, and have been reared on oat-cake and lived coarse; and we haven't been to school much, or read books, and we don't know much about anything but what happens just round us. We are just the sort of people that want to hear good news. For when anybody's well off, they don't much mind about hearing news from distant parts; but if a poor man or woman's in trouble and has hard work to make out a living, he likes to have a letter to tell him he's got a friend as will help him . . .

'But perhaps doubts come into your mind like this: Can God take much notice of us poor people? Perhaps he only made the world for the great and the wise and the rich. It doesn't cost him much to give us our little handful of victual and bit of clothing; but how do we know he cares for us any more than we care for the worms and things in the garden, so as we rear our carrots and onions? Will God take care of us when we die? And has he any comfort for us when we are lame and sick and helpless? Perhaps, too, he is angry with us; else why does the blight come, and the bad harvests, and the fever, and all sorts of pain and trouble? For our life is full of trouble, and if God sends us good, he seems to send bad too. How is it? How is it?

'Ah! Dear friends, we are in sad want of good news about God . . .'

(Reprint: Penguin 1988 [1859], pp. 66–70)

6.8   *Hymns Selected for the use of the Female Revivalists* (1824)

'Fear not, O land: be glad and rejoice: for the Lord will do great things . . . And your sons and your daughters shall prophesy.' Joel.

Hymn 321 by Martha Williams

> HAPPY *Magdalen*, to whom
> Christ the Lord vouchsaf'd t'appear?

Newly risen from the tomb,
Would he first be seen by her?
Her by seven devils possest,
Till his word the fiends expell'd;
Quench'd the hell within her breast,
All her sins and sickness heal'd.

Yes, to her the Master came,
First his welcome voice she hears,
Jesus calls her by her name,
He the weeping sinner cheers;
Let her the dear task repeat,
While her eyes again run o'er;
Let her wash his bleeding feet,
Kiss them, and with joy adore.

Who can now presume to fear,
Who despair his Lord to see?
Jesus, wilt thou not appear,
Shew thyself alive to me?
Yes, my God, I dare not doubt,
Thou shalt all my sins remove;
Thou hast cast a legion out,
thou wilt perfect me in love.

Surely thou hast call'd me now,
Now I hear the voice divine!
At thy wounded feet I bow,
Wounded for whose sins but mine?
I have nail'd him to the tree,
I have sent him to the grave;
But the Lord is risen for me,
Hold of him but faith I have.

Hymn 331 by Martha Williams

O Women! whither travel ye?
Where are ye bent to go?
Poor Pilgrims, and despis'd are we,
Who happiness wou'd know.

Where did you lately sojourn? Tell,
Simply relate your case:
We sojurn'd in the world, by hell,
'Till we were call'd by Grace.

What is your stock, and what your birth?
Strangers, ye seem to be:
Our Stock is Christ, (scarce known on earth,)
Our birth is heavenly.

Then are you near of kin to us,
Our Father is the Lamb:
He us begat, we bear his cross,
We wear his own new Name.

Brethren rejoice! our Saviour bless,
For these his Daughters are:
Sisters, be glad! ye heirs of Peace,
Our Father's Sons are here.

We greet you, heaven-born maids, and own
With greatest joy our kin:
We you salute, whom God will crown
Kings over death and sin.

We're pleas'd to see you Zion-ward,
Your narrow way pursue:
We thank our dearest Lamb, the Lord,
And say the same by you.

Join then, O Damsels highly lov'd!
To bless our Saviour's Hand:
Amen, dear Brethren, 'till we're mov'd
To dwell in our own land.

(Dewsbury: J. Willan, 1824)

6.9 Revd Francis Close, *A Sermon, Addressed to the Female Chartists of Cheltenham, Sunday, August 25th, 1839, on the Occasion of their Attending the Parish Church in a Body* (1839)

. . . [I]f it be true, as I think I have proved both from scripture and from fact, that Christianity has mitigated the curse of woman and elevated her to a place where she was not placed before, and given her an influence in the nation altogether new, it surely follows, Christian Sisters, *that your obligations have increased proportionably*; and that you are bound by the ties of gratitude and love to that Saviour who has taken you to himself and chosen you as his own, to use the influence he has given you for the Glory of God, and for the promotion of peace, virtue and integrity, and everything that is good and useful among men. Did you ever reflect that your means of use-fulness are almost incalculable? Did you ever consider that in what-ever situation of life you may be placed, you have an influence for which you are responsible to God and man? See the mother of a young family to whom God has entrusted perhaps three, five, or eight, little children, precious, immortal souls, with whom God has blessed and graced her household? Tell me Christian mothers, if you can calculate the moral, civil, national and religious influence which you possess through these children? . . . The results are wholly incalculable. Or think of the important duties of women who are wives. If a woman be a wise and Christian woman, what a blessed influence may she exercise over her husband, what good may she not accomplish, for herself, for her children, for her family, and for her country! Many a rash act has been prevented, by the kind and affectionate entreaties of a loving wife! Often has the intemperate resolution been abandoned through the kind and judicious expostu-lations of a sensible and affectionate woman! As the scripture said, 'a virtuous woman is a crown of glory to her husband', the choicest gift of God to man! 'For a prudent wife is from the Lord!' Nor is the influence of a sister over a brother to be forgotten; this also is a hallowed and blessed affection. I have known young men at college wholly restrained from vice simply by this influence; . . . O Christian sisters! Christian wives! use the influence which God has given you for the happiness of your own families, for the peace of your own bosoms, for the good of your fellow creatures, and for the glory of the great God! Sure I am that if you zealously exerted yourselves the whole mass of our population would soon be leavened with virtue, peace and holiness!

But on the other hand, what a vast instrument of mischief and misery, may one ungodly woman be! Truly female influence is for *woe* as well as for *weal*! . . . In the humbler class of life such a mother of a family equally neglects her children, leaving them in the lanes and streets of the city, while she seeks her pleasure elsewhere; perhaps in meetings for political discussion; or perhaps in scenes of abandonment and vice! What a curse are such women to the country! Their children must grow up revolutionists, for they have been taught revolution at home! They never will submit themselves to wholesome restraint for they have not been taught subordination in infancy! A bad mother of a family is far more mischievous in the country than a bad father, because the infant children are entrusted to her; and the impressions of infancy are those which remain to the latest moments of life. Insomuch that someone has said, 'we do what our mothers make us!' There seems also to be no medium with women. If they are bad, they are bad indeed! Profligate and intriguing women are the pests and curse of any society; they are the most suitable instruments for propagating on every side discord, scandal, calumny, backbiting, and every species of moral and social evil; and the page of history teaches us that the destinies of nations, have oft times been changed, the wisest schemes have been frustrated, and misery and destruction occasioned by the baneful influence perhaps of a single woman! During the French Revolution, when the barriers of society were overthrown, and the restraints of Christianity were withdrawn, when the women of Republican France became lost to feelings of delicacy and decorum, the excesses they committed are appalling to contemplate: they became more ferocious fiends than even the men themselves; plunged more deeply into crime; glutted themselves with blood; and danced like maniacs amidst the most fearful scenes of the reign of Terror! Surely female influence upon Society can barely be exaggerated, whether it be for weal or for woe! Nor can the moral obligations of every woman, in every circle of life, and in every grade of society be too strongly enforced.

(London: Hamilton, Adams & Co., 1839, pp. 12–14)

6.10   Marianne Farningham, *A Working Woman's Life: an Autobiography* (1907)

I must have been born a Baptist. Not a doubt assailed me as to the proper persons to receive baptism, nor the mode in which it was to be given. 'The disciples first believed, then were baptised, then were added to the Church.' . . . The picture of myself as I sat there, a child among the elders, often recurs to me. I was small for my age [she was 14]. I remember that I wore a lilac print dress, and it was, I think, the first dress I had worn with long sleeves. I was very much in earnest. I longed with a great longing that this little company would accept me as a member, and receive me into their midst, and allow me to be baptized, and take the Lord's Supper with them. I felt that I was very unworthy, young, and poor, and of no account, but my one plea and qualification was that I was full of love to Jesus and His people. It was because with all my youthful fervour I wanted to follow my Lord and obey His commands, that I asked to be baptized. I was very nervous and frightened, but presently the minister asked me to retire for a few minutes, while they consulted about me. I went out into the chapel ground among the trees, for the moments of suspense that followed. I scarcely dared to hope that their decision would be favourable; but it was my father who called me back, and there was a happy look on his face as he kissed me.

'Marianne', said Mr Reynolds, 'we are all very much interested in what you have told us, and the friends have decided to receive you into Church fellowship after baptism.'

It was almost more than I could bear, and I had to choke back my tears.

Most of our social life centred in the chapel. On my return from Bristol, when I offered my services to the superintendent to take a class in the school, he told me that the girls of the Bible class, being without a teacher, had asked that I should take it. I was fairly nonplussed by this suggestion, and said that I could not do it, for I was no older than the other girls, and certainly knew no more than they. He said that I could study the lesson during the week, and he hoped I would try. The girls themselves came to see me, and declared that they would not leave until they had persuaded me. So I yielded, and promised to do my best. We had a good many very happy Sunday afternoons. We were a class without a teacher, but everybody contributed something, and whether or not we learned much, we carried away from that corner pew many pleasant memories. I have still in my possession, and indeed not many days pass without my using it, a copy of Cruden's Concordance with which the girls presented me, and with my name written in it by Mr. Henry Rogers, the superintendent of the Sunday School. It has been worth its weight in gold to me. Its inscription bears the date December 17 1857.

What glorious times we had, attending every service for which the chapel was opened! Our Sunday walks to and from were delightful. I always felt we were like the glad tribes going up to Jerusalem. There would be a long line of us, ten or a dozen young people of both sexes, marching along and singing as we went, so that the mile between the two villages seemed as nothing. We would sing 'All hail the power of Jesus' Name', to Miss Lane, or 'Sweet is the work, my God, my King', to Montgomery, a capital tune to march to, though there was one better still which we always sang when the moon shone or the stars were unusually bright, 'The spacious firmament on high'. I never hear this sung now without wanting to keep time with my feet, as I did in those good old days. I often wonder whether the village chapels can be as much to those who worship in them to-day as they were to us.

(London: James Clarke, 1907, pp. 55–57, 69–70)

6.11   Rosina Davies (Evangelist), *The Story of My Life* (1942)

Later on there was a change of Officers, and Captain and Mrs. Richardson came to Treherbert, and soon wanted to open a new Station over the mountains in the Maesteg Valley, and asked my parents, as they could not sing much, if they would allow me to come and help them begin the new station. To my joy, they allowed me to go, just for two or three days.

We found rooms: I had a most comfortable place, with a Miss Davies, a maiden lady living alone, in a cosy little cottage in John Street. She was spotlessly clean, and a beautiful Christian, and we grew fond of each other. She took such care of me. The Richardsons were purely English, and did not even understand a word of Welsh, but they were earnest Christians, so I sang in Welsh and witnessed for Christ in Welsh, Maesteg then being a real Welsh place. When we began to sing the people came. The crowd increased night after night, until at last one minister called upon me and asked what accounted for the crowd coming to meetings that were carried on in an unusual way. I told him if he would pray, they would come and hear him also. 'I preach and I have something to say, but how is it that these rough men listen to you, and change their lives?' I again said, 'Perhaps you do not pray in the right way'. Of course I had no argument, so he went away and said that curiosity might bring them if he wore a woman's dress. Even he became less prejudiced when he saw the changes in the lives of men, and the different atmosphere in the churches. Soon the chapels were at our disposal and requests came for meetings to be held down in the town. I was now called 'The Little Welsh Girl' and the crowds followed and picked up the songs, and converts joined the different churches. Dear mother came to seek me, and take me home. To her surprise, I was in Tabor which was over-crowded with people. Someone found out she was my mother, and with difficulty got her in. She heard my voice on the gallery singing 'Come to Jesus Just Now', – in Welsh of course, and a number of converts following me down to the big seat. She was rather alarmed and begged me to come home. I told her, I must be about 'My Father's business', so she reluctantly returned home without me, and some of the leaders of the Churches, when she came again to fetch me, implored her not to take me away. For the third time, both my parents were distressed, because of my age, and my need of more school and education. The third time I had to decided 'now' or 'never'. General Booth wanted me to go to London or somewhere to make me an officer. The whole place was roused at this, and a Committee was formed of Ministers and laymen, representing the churches of denominations. A girl Evangelist in Wales was a phenomenon; for women to take part in any public capacity was unthinkable, and that sentiment continued among ministers and laymen for a long time, with some exceptions; the women mothered me, even the wives of the ministers who objected. . . .

All doors were open to me in Maesteg, as it was central for my Mission work. General Booth wished to make me a permanent worker, which would mean my leaving Maesteg and probably Wales. The Salvation Army, or rather God through their instrumentality, had awakened the churches and the Rhondda was a changed valley. My dear parents were now more resigned to my absence from home, and many of the leading men of the churches in Treherbert came over the mountains to Maesteg, to share in the great times we were having there . . .

(Llandyssul: Gomerian Press, 1942, pp. 30–33)

Chapter Seven

Women in diaspora
Irish, Jewish, Black and Asian women in Britain

The major nineteenth-century diasporas saw people coming to Britain to escape economic hardship or persecution. Travelling from Ireland, Eastern Europe, the Caribbean and, to a lesser degree, India and China, migrant peoples contributed in myriad ways to the making of Britain: through their participation in the labour force and political movements, and contribution to the cultural life of the nineteenth century. Experiences of migration and of empire are also part of the British story, therefore, and are addressed in this and the following chapter. Placing these documents together in a chapter on diaspora enables exploration of specific questions: historiographical issues concerning ethnicity and history; the impact on gender roles of immigration; the importance of autobiography and, as with the case of Irish women's history, the absence of autobiographical material.[1]

7.1 James Phillips Kay, *The Moral and Physical Condition of the Working Classes of Manchester* (1832)

The most readily accessible sources about the Irish in nineteenth century Britain come from the pens of concerned English social commentators, keen to express their anxieties about the domestic conditions of Irish migrants. As James Phillips Kay notes, the Irish in Manchester – as elsewhere – settled in areas where there was demand for unskilled labour and relatively cheap housing, often in an 'Irish colony' on the edge of a town, close to industrial districts. Kay (later Kay-Shuttleworth), a doctor who had become acquainted with

Manchester's poorest areas at the time of the cholera epidemic of 1832, recorded encounters with impoverished and dirt-ridden homes and courts. Such conditions were explained in terms of the moral degradation of the Irish poor rather than as a result of material poverty. Such hostility was a compound of anti-Catholic sentiment, horror at Irish domestic habits, a great fear of the Irish worker under-cutting wages and pulling down the condition of work for all men, and in some cases, an anxiety about the proclivity towards radical politics of many Irish men. The Irish were seen as a great threat to order and to the 'social body' in English towns.

7.2 Henry Mayhew, *London Labour and the London Poor* (1861–1862)

Henry Mayhew (1812–1887) was a journalist and social investigator who had been a founder of the satiricial weekly, *Punch*. In 1849, he began his interviews of the London poor for the *Morning Chronicle*. These were eventually published as the four-volume *London Labour and the London Poor* (1861). His interviews were conducted in an ethnographic style and have been described as the best oral history of the period. Among the women interviewed by Mayhew were Irish coster-mongers, who had migrated to East London in the late 1840s. Mayhew described the poverty of the area and of individual homes; compared to Kay, he was relatively generous in his understanding of the causes of such hardship.

7.3 Tom Barclay, *Memoirs and Medleys: The Autobiography of a Bottlewasher* (1934)

While there is an abundance of material about the Irish as a social problem in nineteenth-century England and Scotland, memoirs by Irish migrants, and especially by women, are few and far between. Tom Barclay's *Memoirs and Medleys* (1934) is a fair substitute, however. Barclay, born in Leicester to Irish migrant parents, tells of poverty and a loving family life, of working out complicated issues of loyalty and identity, and of striving for an education. He exposes the key role played by his mother in ensuring her children's knowledge of Irish culture and politics. Like many other Irish women, Mrs Barclay contributed to the family economy, cared for her children, socialised them into the beliefs of the Catholic church and, speaking the Irish language at home, taught them the myths, ballads and traditions of Irish culture.

7.4 Patrick MacGill, *Children of the Dead End* (1914)

Children of the Dead End provides a particularly vivid account of (Irish and Scottish) women working as potato harvesters in Scotland in the early years of the twentieth century. MacGill (1889–1963), the eldest of eleven children in a Donegal family, left school at twelve years of age and, after a short period of employment as a labourer, joined a gang of 'tattie howkers', young boys and girls led by an older male 'ganger', and travelled to Scotland to harvest the potato crop. MacGill stayed in Scotland to work as a navvie on the railways. In 1908, virtually self-taught, he published 'Gleanings from a navvie's scrapbook', the first of many novels and poems, and by 1911 was working as a journalist for the London Daily Express. *Children of the Dead End* (1914), which sold extremely well, is based on his experiences as a 'tattie howker', and provides a social commentary on a range of subjects, including labouring conditions for migrants in Scotland, prostitution and – his particular interest (shared with late nineteenth-century reformers and social investigators) – issues of gender and morality.

7.5 Grace Aguilar, *The Women of Israel* (1845)

The dominant image of the hard-working Jewish housewife and devoted mother, tends to obscure the reality of Jewish women's lives in Britain. It was an image to which women contributed, however, including the mid-nineteenth-century Anglo-Jewish novelist, Grace Aguilar (1816–1847). Many of Aguilar's novels, written mainly in the 1830s but published after her death in 1847, were concerned with Jewish and domestic themes. She depicted the lives of the respectable middle classes (even though she herself worked as a school teacher in London's East End), and through her writing supported claims for the extension of civil and political rights. In this excerpt from *The Woman of Israel* (1845), Aguilar contests (contemporary evangelical) claims that Christianity enabled women to live at the apex of civilised life, arguing instead that women's status as spiritual and domestic beings had its origins in Jewish faith and culture.

7.6 Constance Rothschild Battersea, *Reminiscences* (1922)

Lady Battersea's *Reminiscences* describe her philanthropic visits on behalf of the Jewish Ladies' Benevolent Loan Society in the last quarter of the nineteenth century to poor Jewish women in London's East End. Battersea (1843–1901) was from an established and extremely wealthy Anglo-Jewish family, while the women she visited were among the 100,000 Ashkenazi immigrants, many of them impoverished, who came to Britain after 1880 to escape poverty and persecution in Russia and Austro-Hungary. Battersea's account displays some humility, acknowledging the seriousness with which women approached their responsibilities for overseeing preparation for the Sabbath and for festivals, managing the socialisation of children and undertaking the enormously demanding task of keeping a kosher household. Lara Marks has argued that women's domestic skills saved many Jewish women from the criticism levelled at poor British women during the 1890s to early 1900s.[2] As Eileen Yeo has suggested, however, social class is of crucial importance when trying to understand the relationship between philanthropists and poorer Jewish women. While protective and concerned, middle-class and upper-class philanthropists also sought to mould respectability and acculturate the new arrivals into the cultural practices of English Jews,[3] and were concerned to shield from public view the economic activity of women as well as evidence of poor living conditions. They judged the cultural and political climate: less than exemplary household management would, alongside the 'Maiden Tribute' scandal, speculation about the identity of 'Jack the Ripper' and the publicity surrounding sweatshop labour, fuel the hostility that was soon to see the passage of the 1905 Alien's Act.[4]

7.7 Lily Montagu, *My Club and I: the Story of the West Central Jewish Club* (1941)

In this excerpt from *My Club and I*, Lily Montagu describes the work and general conditions of life of many Jewish girls in late nineteenth-century London. Montagu (1873–1963), from a well-to-do Ortho-dox Anglo-Jewish family, established her club in 1893 in Dean Street, London WC1. She later became a key figure in the development of liberal Judaism as a founder of the Liberal Jewish Synagogue in

London and the World Union for Progressive Judaism in 1926.[5] The Club, which began as a Sabbath class for girls, provided education, a drama class and discussions of moral issues, and sought to instil self-discipline and a sense of responsibility to counteract the corrupting effects encouraged by workshop employment. As this excerpt shows, Montagu supported the campaigns of the Women's Industrial Council to improve the conditions of employment of young women. Although she talks of the political apathy of many of her girls and their families, we know from other sources that many Jewish women had been involved in political movements in their country of origin. The Women's Trade Union League, the leadership of which included Louise Lady Goldsmid, Emily Routledge and May Abraham, helped to organise the East End Jewish Tailoresses Union (1888), Society of Tailors and Tailoresses in Leeds (1888), and the Cigarette Makers' Union (1888), all of which involved many Jewish working women.

7.8 *Nocturnal Revels* (1779)

It is estimated that the late eighteenth century saw a considerable Black population in Britain: Peter Fryer has suggested that up to 10,000 people of African descent lived in London at this time (when the population of London was about half a million).[6] As Joan Grant suggests, it is likely that there were several black communities in London, which may have been very separate from one another. Black servants to white West Indians and Indian ayahs (nannies) to wealthy British families would have lived in affluent areas in London. There were also those black people who lived among the white poor in St Giles, Seven Dials and Holborn, who were likely to have married white British spouses, and whose presence can be seen in the prints of Cruickshank and Hogarth.[7] It is likely that black men greatly out-numbered black women, though many women came to England as slaves, a number of them deserting their masters and mistresses to live within the free black community, where they worked as servants, barmaids and sometimes prostitutes. 'Black Harriet' of this excerpt was an ex-slave from Jamaica who came to London with her master and after his death worked as a prostitute for an upper-class clientele in the 1770s. This account gives some detail about her background in Jamaica, though, as Grant notes, we should bear in mind that it was written to titillate a male audience. Harriet's was ultimately a sad story: after losing a lot of money she was twice imprisoned before dying of TB in 1779.

7.9 The History of Mary Prince, a West Indian Slave, Related by Herself (1831)

The History of Mary Prince is the most well-known story of a woman's experience of slavery and her bid for freedom. Mary Prince (1788?–1833) had been born in Turks Island and had for 40 years worked in domestic slavery, coming to England from Antigua in 1828 with her owners, the Woods. Mr and Mrs Wood were unpleasant employers, subjecting Mary to overwork, paying no heed to her rheumatic disabilities, sometimes abusing her and refusing to allow her to purchase her freedom. While in London, Mary took the dramatic step of leaving them. In so doing she risked great hardship and, unable to return to the West Indies as a free woman, was permamently separated from her husband, Daniel James, a free (black) man whom she had married in Antigua. She was eventually taken in by the secretary of the Anti-Slavery Society, Thomas Pringle, to work in his household as a servant, and her story was related to, and written down by, Susannah Strickland and other abolitionist women. The excerpt included here comes from Prince's harrowing account of her mother's preparation of herself and her sisters for their unexpected and separate sales. The breaking of family bonds and the ill-treatment of girls and women were key themes in women's contribution to the anti-slavery movement in this period. These were subjects that could be discussed openly, unlike the sexual abuse suffered by Mary, or that she had lived with a white Captain for some years prior to her marriage; it was important that she came across as a modest, Christian woman. The History was nonetheless controversial, leading Pringle into two libel actions as a result of the pro-slavery lobby's attempts to discredit her account.

7.10 The Wonderful Adventures of Mrs Seacole in Many Lands (1857)

The excerpt from *The Wonderful Adventures of Mrs Seacole* concerns Mary Seacole (1805–1881), who was celebrated in her day for her compassionate work with British soldiers at Sebastopol during the Crimean War. Seacole, raised in Jamaica and of African and Scottish ancestry, worked as a 'doctress', as her mother had done before her. Her initial bid to travel to Sebastopol as part of the military support was rejected, she believed on the basis of her 'somewhat duskier skin'. Instead, Mary Seacole travelled independently, and became extremely popular with ordinary soldiers. In this excerpt, she describes her care for the men. The verse comes from a poem published in *Punch* in 1856 as part of a campaign to support Seacole after she returned to England facing financial difficulties. Although her death in 1881 saw a public celebration of her life, Mary Seacole then disappeared from history until the later twentieth-century endeavours in women's and Black history.

7.11 Joseph Salter, *The Asiatic in England: Sketches of Sixteen years' Work among Orientals* (1873)

Joseph Salter worked for the London City Mission as 'missionary to the Orientals and Africans' in East London. He helped establish an Ayahs' Home in Aldgate for the support (and conversion) of Indian 'ayahs', or nannies, women who had come to England as employees of East India Company personnel and had left their employ or been dismissed and who struggled to survive in London. Salter also ran the 'Asiatic Rest', a 'Strangers' Home' mainly accommodating Indian and Chinese lascars (seamen) and to which he invited ayahs for afternoons of tea and proselytising. In this excerpt, he describes the 'dens of vice' run by Indian and Chinese men, and refers to the English, Chinese and Indian women who had lived and worked with them and who had been rescued from a life of vice.

7.12 *The Letters and Correspondence of Pandita Ramabai* (1884–5)

Pandita Ramabai (1858–1922), a social reformer who studied at Cheltenham College in the 1880s, was a converted Christian who struggled with the wishes of her patrons that she should return to India to become a missionary. In these excerpts, Ramabai discusses her conflicts with English Christians. She suggests that they wilfully misunderstood her questioning attitude to faith and were suspicious of her reluctance to reject as 'bad' all things to do with Indian culture and religious belief.

7.1 James Phillips Kay, *The Moral and Physical Condition of the Working Classes of Manchester in 1832* (1832)

The township of Manchester chiefly consists of dense masses of houses, inhabited by the population engaged in the great manufactories of the cotton trade. Some of the central divisions are occupied by warehouses and shops, and a few streets by the dwellings of some of the more wealthy inhabitants; but the opulent merchants chiefly reside in the country, and even the superior servants of their establishments inhabit the suburban townships. Manchester, properly so called, is chiefly inhabited by shopkeepers and the labouring classes. Those districts where the poor dwell are of very recent origin. The rapid growth of the cotton-manufacture has attracted hither operatives from every part of the kingdom, and Ireland has poured forth the most destitute of her hordes to supply the constantly increasing demand for labour. This immigration has been, in one important respect, a serious evil. The Irish have taught the labouring classes of this country a pernicious lesson. The system of cottier farming, the demoralisation and barbarism of the people, and the general use of the potato as the chief article of food, have encouraged the growth of population in Ireland more rapidly than the available means of subsistence have been increased. Debased alike by ignorance and pauperism, they have discovered, with the savage, what is the minimum of the means of life, upon which existence may be prolonged. The paucity of the amount of means and comforts necessary for the mere support of life, is not known by a more civilised population, and this secret has been taught the labourers of this country by the Irish. As competition and the restrictions and burdens of trade diminished the profits of capital, and consequently reduced the price of labour, the contagious example of ignorance and a barbarous disregard of forethought and economy, exhibited by the Irish, spread. The colonisation of savage tribes has ever been attended with effects on civilisation as fatal as those which have marked the progress of the sand flood over the fertile plains of Egypt. Instructed in the fatal secret of subsisting on what is barely necessary to life, – yielding partly to necessity, and partly to example, – the labouring classes have ceased to entertain a laudable pride in furnishing their houses, and in multiplying the decent comforts which minister to happiness. What is superfluous to the mere exigencies of nature is too often expended at the tavern; and for the provision of old age and infirmity, they too frequently trust either to charity, to the support of their children, or to the protection of the poor laws ...

Some idea of the want of cleanliness prevalent in their habitations, may be obtained from the report of the number of houses requiring white-washing; but this column fails to indicate their gross neglect of order, and absolute filth. Much less can we obtain satisfactory statistical results concerning the want of furniture, especially of bedding, and of food, clothing, and fuel. In these respects the habitations of the Irish are most destitute. They can scarcely be said to be furnished. They contain one or two chairs, a mean table, the most scanty culinary apparatus, and one or two beds, loathsome with filth. A whole family is often accommodated on a single bed, and sometimes a heap of filthy straw and a covering of old sacking hide them in one undistinguished heap, debased alike by penury, want of economy, and dissolute habits. Frequently, the Inspectors found two or more families crowded into one small house, containing only two apartments, one in which they slept, and another in which they ate; and often more than one family lived in a damp cellar, containing only one room, in whose pestilential atmosphere from twelve to sixteen persons were crowded. To these fertile sources of disease were sometimes added the keeping of pigs and other animals in the house, with other nuisances of the most revolting character.

(James Kay-Shuttleworth, *Four Periods of Public Education
as Reviewed in 1832, 1839, 1846, 1862* (London:
The Harvester Press, 1978 [1862]), pp. 5–7)

7.2   Henry Mayhew, *London Labour and the London Poor* (1861–1862)

The homes of the street-Irish

In almost all of the poorer districts of London are to be found 'nests of Irish' – as they are called – or courts inhabited solely by the Irish costermongers. These people form separate colonies, rarely visiting or mingling with the English costers. . . .

Perhaps there is no quarter of London where the habits and habitations of the Irish can be better seen and studied than in Rosemary-lane, and the little courts and alleys that spring from it on each side. Some of these courts have other courts branching off from them, so that the locality is a perfect labyrinth of 'blind alleys;' and when once in the heart of the maze it is difficult to find the path that leads to the main-road. As you walk down 'the lane,' and peep through the narrow openings between the houses, the place seems like a huge peep-show, with dark holes of gateways to look through, while the court within appears bright with the daylight; and down it are seen rough-headed urchins running with their feet bare through the puddles, and bonnetless girls, huddled in shawls, lolling against the door-posts. . . .

I visited one of the paved yards round which the Irish live, and found that it had been turned into a complete drying-ground, with shirts, gowns, and petticoats of every description and colour. The buildings at the end were completely hidden by 'the things,' and the air felt damp and chilly, and smelt of soap-suds. The gutter was filled with dirty grey water emptied from the wash-tubs, and on the top were the thick bubbles floating about under the breath of the boys 'playing at boats' with them. . . .

After looking at the low foreheads and long bulging upper lips of some of the group, it was pleasant to gaze upon the pretty faces of the one or two girls that lolled against the wall. Their black hair, smoothed with grease, and shining almost as if 'japanned,' and their large grey eyes with the thick dark fringe of lash, seemed out of place among the hard features of their companions. It was only by looking at the short petticoats and large feet you could assure yourself that they belonged to the same class.

In all the houses that I entered were traces of household care and neatness that I had little expected to have seen. The cupboard fastened in the corner of the room, and stocked with mugs and cups, the mantelpiece with its images, and the walls covered with showy-coloured prints of saints and martyrs, gave an air of comfort that strangely disagreed with the reports of the cabins in 'ould Ireland.' As the doors to the houses were nearly all of them kept open, I could, even whilst walking along, gain some notion of the furniture of the homes. . . . In another room, I found a home so small and full of furniture, that it was almost a curiosity for domestic management. The bed, with its chintz curtains looped up, filled one end of the apartment, but the mattress of it served as a long bench for the visitors to sit on. The table was so large that it divided the room in two, and if there was one picture there must have been thirty – all of 'holy men,' with yellow glories round their heads. The window-ledge was dressed out with crockery, and in a tumbler were placed the beads. The old dame herself was as curious as her room. Her shawl was fastened over her large frilled cap. She had a little 'button' of a nose, with the nostrils entering her face like bullet holes. She wore over her gown an old pilot coat, well-stained with fish slime, and her petticoats being short, she had very much the appearance of a Dutch fisherman or stage smuggler . . .

The one thing that struck me during my visit to this neighbourhood, was the apparent listlessness and lazy appearance of the people. The boys at play were the only beings who seemed to have any life in their actions. The women in their plaid shawls strolled along the pavements, stopping each friend for a chat, or joining some circle, and leaning against the wall as though utterly deficient in energy. The men smoked, with their hands in their pockets, listening to the old crones talking, and only now and then grunting out a reply when a question was directly put to them. And yet it is curious that these people, who here seemed as inactive as negroes, will perform the severest bodily labour, undertaking tasks that the English are almost unfitted for.

(London, 1861–1862, Vol. 1, pp. 110–112)

7.3   Tom Barclay, *Memoirs and Medleys: The Autobiography of a Bottlewasher* (1934)

Whenever an English man or woman did anything disreputable, my mother was wont to remark 'Ah well, sure, what better could one expect from the breed of King Harry?' The Sassenach was regarded by us with a mixture of contempt and hatred. God had made him it is true and Jesus Christ had died to save him, but we clean forgot that, and only saw him embodied in Calvin and Cranmer, the lustful King Henry VIII, Queen Bess the Persecutor, the Orangeman's idol, William of Orange, 'the bloody Cromwell'. There were though a few good Englishmen no doubt, like Alfred the Great, Sir Thomas Moore, and William Cobbett who wrote the history of the Protestant Reformation. My father was a Limerick man, and we were often hearing eulogies of the hero Patrick Sarsfield, and women of Limerick who fought and repelled the English during the siege of that city. How we gloated over the way the Irish Brigade defeated the English at Fontenoy! But what filthy little wretches we children were, and how could it be otherwise? Not Papuans nor Basutos nor Fijians could I think be more degraded. And this was the middle of the nineteenth century. O great and glorious empire! . . .

What sort of existence was it where a mother giving suck had to be hours away from home trying to earn something? When the kids of the yard were not molesting us, I as eldest was nurse, and often have I put my tongue into baby's mouth to be sucked in lieu of 'titty' to stop her cries. The cries used to cease for a minute, and then were resumed as the tongue gave no satisfaction. Poor cooped-up vermin-infested brats! But I am suffering much more now probably in simply remembering our state than I actually suffered then. . . .

There is a proverb that the grey mare is often the best horse: mother was the grey mare of our family: untiring energy, unfailing health and hope and faith, and never a new dress, never a holiday, never any leisure or amusement, never I fear even a generous meal of victuals. All work and no play, but still not dull. I'm sure we never had a complete bath in all our childhood's years, unless such a thing is indispensable to the newly-born. Mother did all that was possible, but she had neither time nor means to boil our rags of shirts and sheets when washing. We had no wash-tub nor dolly-pegs, not to speak of wringing and mangling machines: there could have been no room for such in a room only nine feet by nine, even had we possessed them, eh, Mother? So we went unwashed, and pediculus thrived greatly in his two principal species, *capitis* and *vestimenti*, and God's beautiful image was preyed upon daily and nightly. No fault of Mother's.

She was not permitted, even had she the money and leisure, to indulge in beer and dominoes of an evening like my father: her consolation was an old Irish lamentation or love song and the contemplation of the sufferings of 'Our Blessed Lord' and his virgin mother. We males can revert to paganism and forget for an hour or two in revel and song the Man of Sorrows – the poor gibbeted God: where now, while we are carousing, are Gethsemane and Calvary? We are lapped in the Elysium of ale and skittles and cards. We are no Christians tonight, we, but Bacchanals. The woman – the mother is at the same time and hour kneeling at the feet of the Blessed Virgin, or scheming and troubling how she shall pay next week's shop and rent. We get credit till Saturday from the little grocer's shop at the corner, but we must pay each Saturday or have to go hungry all next week . . .

Mother taught me to spell and read. She was held to be quite exceptional among her countrywomen in that she could read Dr Gallacher's sermons in Irish. This Gallacher was the bishop of Raphoe in Donegal. How she who read English with difficulty could read these sermons, though in Roman characters, with their

transliteration nearly as bad as Welsh, is something I do not understand: but read them she could, and often have I seen the tears come
into her eyes over the sermon on the passion of Our Lord. This she
used to read on a Good Friday. 'Glory to God, but you're the one!'
neighbours used to exclaim. It did them good to hear a blessed
sermon read in the first language they ever spoke. I don't know was
her maiden name MacLin or Maglyn, for I never saw it written; her
mother's people were O'Reilly's. She was well acquainted with the
old legends of Oisin, and Fin, and Cuchullan, and the Gobawn Sayr,
and could sing and recite a goodly number of old Irish songs and
poems. The old bardic legends must have been transmitted from
generation to generation for centuries: they were crooned and told
round the turf fire of a winter's night.

(Leicester, 1934, pp. 6–7, 9–10, 23–24)

7.4   Patrick MacGill, *Children of the Dead End. The Autobiography of a Navvy* (1914)

The potato merchant met us on Greenock quay next morning, and
here Micky's Jim marshalled his squad, which consisted in all of
twenty-one persons. Seventeen of these came from Ireland, and the
remainder were picked up from the back-streets of Greenock and
Glasgow. With the exception of two, all the Irish women were
very young, none of them being over nineteen years of age, but the
two extra women needed for the squad were withered and wrinkled
harridans picked from the city slums. These women met us on the
quay.

'D'ye see them?' Micky's Jim whispered to me. 'They cannot make
a living on the streets, so they have to come and work with us. What
d'ye think of them?'

'I don't like the look of them', I said.

The potato merchant hurried us off to Buteshire the moment we
arrived, and we started work on a farm at midday. The way we had
to work was this. Nine of the older men dug the potatoes from the
ground with short three-pronged graips. The women followed
behind, crawling on their knees and dragging two baskets apiece
along with them. Into these baskets they lifted the potatoes thrown
out by the men. . . .

All day long, on their hands and knees, they dragged through the slush and rubble of the field. The baskets which they hauled after them were cased in clay to the depth of several inches, and sometimes when emptied of potatoes a basket weighed over two stone. The strain on the women's arms must have been terrible. But they never complained. Pools of water gathered in the hollows of the dress that covered the calves of their legs. Sometimes they rose and shook the water from their clothes, then went down on their knees again. The Glasgow women sang an obscene song, 'just by way o' passing the time', one of them explained, and Micky's Jim joined in the chorus. Two little ruts, not at all like the furrows left by a coulter of a skidding plough, lay behind the women in the black earth. These were made by their knees.

We left off work at six o'clock in the evening, and turned in to look up our quarters for the night. . . .

One of the strange women was called Gourock Ellen, which goes to show that she had a certain fame in the town of that name. The day's drag had hacked and gashed her knees so that they looked like minced flesh in a butcher's shop window. She showed her bare knees, and was not in the least ashamed. I turned my head away hurriedly, not that the sight of the wounds frightened me, but I felt that I was doing something wrong in gazing at the bare leg of a woman. I looked at Norah Ryan, and the both of us blushed as if we had been guilty of some shameful action. Gourock Ellen saw us, and began to sing a little song aloud:

> 'When I was a wee thing and lived wi' my granny,
> Oh! it's many a caution my granny gi'ed me,
> She said: "Now be wise and beware o' the boys,
> And don't let the petticoats over your knee." '

When she finished her verse she winked knowingly at Micky's Jim, and, strange to say, Jim winked back . . .

In the byre there was no screen between the women and the men. The modesty of the young girls, when the hour for retiring came around, was unable to bear this. The strange women did not care in the least.

The Irish girls sat by their bedsides and made no sign of undressing. I slid into bed quietly with my trousers still on; most of the men stripped with evident unconcern, nakedly and shamelessly.

'The dark is a good curtain if the women want to take off their clothes,' said Micky's Jim, as he extinguished the only candle in the place. He re-lit a match the next moment, and there was a hurried scampering under the blankets in the stalls on the other side of the passage.

'That's a mortal sin, Micky's Jim, that ye're doin' ', said Norah Ryan, and the two strange women laughed loudly as if very much amused at persons who were more modest than themselves.

'Who are ye lyin' with, Norah Ryan? Is it Gourock Ellen?' asked my bedmate.

'It is', came the answer.

'D'ye hear that, Dermod – a nun and a harridan in one bed?' said Jim under his breath to me.

Outside the raindrops were sounding on the roof like whip-lash. Jim spoke again in a drowsy voice.

'We're keepin' some poor cows from their warm beds to-night', he said.

(London: Herbert Jenkins, 1914, pp. 74–79)

7.5   Grace Aguilar, *The Women of Israel, or, Characters and Sketches from the Holy Scriptures of Jewish History* (1845)

We must refer once more, though unwillingly, to the Nazarenes' assertion, that their religion was the first, and is the only one which provides for women. '*For woman never would, and never could have risen to her present station in the social system, had it not been for the dignity, with which Christianity invested those qualities, peculiarly her own,*' etc [Quote is from *Woman's Mission*, p. 140]. We can quite understand and sympathise in the Christian woman's love for her own faith, and heartfelt eloquence in the privileges it assures her. We can quite understand – when she compares her lot with that of the Heathen and Mahomedan, and remembers, that had it not been for the wider spread of Christianity, her fate would still have been the same – the glow of mind and heart, which must infuse her whole being, and naturally be reflected in her writings; but then, in her eloquent appeal to her young country-women to remember what they owe to Christianity, let her not be so unjust as to count the Jewish religion amongst those in which woman, in her clinging and truly feminine character, is uncared for and unvalued. The moral laws to which she owes her privileges came from US, and US alone. Who were the apostles and preachers? Who went about, giving the

Heathen a knowledge of Israel's God, though they disregarded the ceremonial law? Who but HEBREWS, whose whole minds and hearts were imbued, *not* with new doctrines, but with the Hebrew moral law, which they disseminated in their wanderings, in such simple language as was best fitted for the long-darkened understandings of the Heathen whom they addressed? Jesus himself was a Jew . . .

[T]he ordinances and commands of our holy faith interfere much less with woman's retired path of domestic pursuits and pleasures, than with the more public and more ambitious career of man. Her duty is to make home happy; her mission, to *influence* man, alike in the relative duties of mother to her son, wife to her husband, sister to her brother, and, in her own person, to upraise the holy cause of a religion, which, from its pure spirituality and long concealment, is, by the multitude misunderstood, vilified, and charged with such false accusations as only *acts* can remove. Something more is needed for the elevation of our faith, than even making it known through books (though that may accomplish much). We must prove the superiority of our guiding law, by the superiority of our own conduct, as women of Israel, in our own houses.

To obtain this superiority, is to become more SPIRITUAL; for in that single word every feminine grace and Jewish requisite is comprised. Let a woman truly and sincerely love her God, feel that His image is in her heart, that she can bring Him so close to her, that her every thought, her every aspiration, her every joy, as well as every prayer and sorrow, can be traced up to Him, and we need not fear that she will ever fail in her duties either to Him or to man, in his service or in her home. Once this spiritual love is obtained, and a halo is thrown over her whole life, be it one of sorrow or of joy. His Law becomes part of her very being; she could not disobey it, without disobeying the gracious Father and Lord whom she loves better than herself. She will love all mankind, think evil of none (without mighty cause), for they are His children, created in His image. She will love the ties of home, her parents, husband, children, brothers and sisters, with intensest and most endearing love, for He has granted them, and filled her glowing heart with the sweet emotions which *love in Him* creates . . .

This is to be spiritual – this is to be an Israelite – this is to be WOMAN! We are quite aware that many of our English readers will exclaim, 'Why, this is to be Christian!' and refuse to believe that such emotions can have existence in a Jewish heart. While our Jewish readers will, in consequence, refuse to seek its attainment, because, if it resembles Christianity, it cannot be Jewish; both parties choosing to forget that the SPIRIT of their widely differing creeds has exactly the same origin, the word of God; whence all of Christianity, save its doctrine of belief, originally came.

(London: Groombridge and Sons, 1845, Vol. II,
pp. 344–345, 387–389)

7.6   Constance Rothschild Battersea, *Reminiscences* (1922)

To begin with, in nearly every case we were most courteously received – indeed from some the greeting was affectionate. Thus I was generally called 'My dear,' and was often given a caressing pat on my arm, or a gentle pressure of the hand. When the children were home from school I found them wonderfully un-shy and ready to make friends; they would stand close to me, touch my dress, and stare at me with their wide-open wondering eyes. They generally had thick, closely curling hair, dark, almost black, or else of a red golden colour. They looked very intelligent, and when questioned about their school and their studies would give (especially the older ones) very ready and good answers. The women were mostly short in stature, and, like all Eastern races, mature at a somewhat early age.

Many of the men were engaged in tailoring and shoe-making. There were families who only talked Yiddish, which would have made conversation difficult, if not impossible, had it not been for the kind offices of some of the neighbours, who would generally be called in to translate questions and answers. They all belonged to the very orthodox form of Judaism; they all had 'Mezuzah' on their door-posts [a small piece of parchment, on which is written Deut vi. 4–9 and xi. 13–21, beginning 'Hear, O Israel'; and which is hung in the upper right hand part of the door-post and reverently touched wherever the threshold is crossed].

According to the custom, the married women concealed their hair, not under a veil, as they would have done in the East, but under a front of false hair – 'Sheitel', as it is called. They still keep a special set of cooking utensils and crockery for the Passover holy days, when a great scrubbing and cleaning takes place, so that it is a pleasure to visit them at that time. An old woman, whom I found reading her Hebrew prayer-book one Friday evening, assured me that she never looked at a book in any other language on the Sabbath, and I gathered that this was not uncommon in the days of which I am speaking.

We encountered various difficulties when visiting: we might climb the little, half-broken, rickety stair in some old house, looking for one of our cases, who perhaps happened to be living on the ground floor or in rooms at the back of the building; and, indeed, it was sometimes a morning's work to find the man or woman whose name might be on our list. . . . I suppose that at times we used to look fagged or worried, for the women would say in compassionate tones, 'Poor dears! are you very tired?' and occasionally we might be offered a cup of coffee. Singularly hospitable, friendly, and unceremonious were these women – not respectful of class distinction, but with a kind of genial familiarity, originating in a strong racial fellow-feeling for their visitors.

On one occasion, learning from a *very* respectable Jewish woman that her son had been appointed Reader in one of the City synagogues, and seeing that son well dressed walking down the street, I could not help saying to his mother: 'I hope your son will do more than merely read prayers in synagogue; I hope he will visit amongst our people, and do other spiritual and religious work where it is so much wanted.'

'But why?' said the mother in a shocked tone of voice; 'we are not like the *goyem* (Gentiles), we do not want to be talked to or taught, we do not drink, and we know how to bring up our children religiously and soberly.'

I did not like to argue the question, and left the woman very indignant at the suggestion.

I do not know that my East End visiting – which extended over thirty years – led to any marked results as regards the poor people amongst whom I went, but I am confident that I learned much from this experience, and that I felt far humbler about my own powers, and also more eager to bring a little sunshine into the lives of those who so often lived under hard or difficult conditions. I learned to know many of the courts and alleys about Commercial Road and Mile End, and would trudge down some of the most disreputable streets, quiet and harmless in the daytime, but warranted dangerous at night.

(London: Macmillan, 1922, pp. 415–417)

7.7   Lily H. Montagu, *My Club and I: the Story of the West Central Jewish Club* (1941)

Most of my girls in the early years of the Club were tailoresses in domestic workshops. The employers had to carry on their work near the big, fashionable West End retail shops. Rents were inordinately high, and it was necessary to live near the 'shop', so that rooms had to be used for both living and working purposes. The average working hours were 8 a.m. to 8 p.m., with an hour for dinner and half an hour for tea. In hot weather the men often worked stripped to the waist, and the atmosphere created by over-heated bodies was anything but pleasant. Many of our elegantly clothed men friends would have been surprised and shocked if they had seen some of the places in which their clothes were produced. They were under the impression that the workrooms in which the workers sat were somewhere at the back of the pleasant shops in which they gave their orders and received assurances that their garments would be faithfully delivered on a given day. It would seem, indeed, that the outfitters regarded it as a joy and a privilege to have the garments produced as required by the customer. The purchaser knew nothing about the real conditions and did not enquire. Many of our girls worked for very long hours as dressmakers and milliners. It seemed remarkable that children could survive the strain of such protracted sedentary occupation. It is not surprising that they were glad of the chance to make a noise in their Club in the evening, or that they talked loudly in the streets. . . .

Quite early in our Club history, we realised the importance of securing for our young girls at least the minimum legal standard of working conditions. We knew that bad employers, by evasion of the law, could get an unfair advantage over those who benefited their employees by keeping the law. The first necessity for us leaders was to know the law. We had the assistance on our Council of Miss Clementina Black. At one time she made a skilful rhyme of the Factory Act. She knew that the Law, as printed on paper, and hung on the walls of the factory and workshop, was most unattractive reading to the average worker whom it concerned. Moreover, the girl would draw considerable suspicion on herself if she stood gazing at the Factory Act in her leisure time and tried to disentangle its enactments. I don't know whether the rhyme ever proved very instructive, but I know it roused considerable mirth among the members of our Club.

In order to obtain the confidence of the workers and convince them it was their responsibility to report evasions of the Factory Act, we founded the Clubs' Industrial Association. Club leaders and delegates from affiliated clubs met on Saturday nights once in two months and listened to lectures and joined in lively discussion afterwards. We had lectures from factory inspectors, especially the senior inspector, Miss Anderson (afterwards Dame), and Mrs. S. Webb, and since we had the girls' confidence we could easily discover illegal over-time, and other evasions of the Factory Acts. We knew the injured-looking worker who always looked as if she were lifeless. Her spirit had been suppressed by bad working conditions. When, after considerable effort, we could get that girl to tell us some of her troubles, we might discover that she was among the sufferers whose hardship was caused by illegal employment. If we had knowledge, we could take appropriate action, and, without risk to the girl, report to the Factory Inspector, who, through her visits of investigation, could right the wrongs for our girls and also for many of their fellow workers.

Under the presidency of Mrs. Sidney Webb, we formed the Industrial Law Association, in connection with the Women's Industrial Council. . . . Girls became unafraid to tell of the many ruses which bad employers used to outwit the inspector. I remember hearing how a girl's young man was called in to assist the inspector. An official had often called at a certain workshop, suspecting that work was being carried on in the upper floors, and would mount the stairs to the first landing, but did not dare to proceed further because of the complete darkness which prevailed. The innocent caretaker had no knowledge of anything beyond the passage immediately connected with the front door which she opened. The young man heard from his girl that on a certain night some late work would be called for, three knocks would be given, and from the dark building would emerge girls delivering the promised work. The boy, having made his entry in the prescribed way, watched with the inspector in the passage. The work was brought down, and the illegality was then easy to prove.

(London: Herbert Joseph, 1941, pp. 60–66)

7.8   *Nocturnal Revels: or the History of King's Place, and other Modern Nunneries* (1779)

Before we proceed to enumerate the fair Beauties of these Nunneries, we shall give a little sketch of Black HARRIOTT, while she still remains upon this voluptuous spot. She was purchased amongst other slaves when very young upon the Coast of Guinea, and carried to Jamaica: she was, as usual, put up to public sale, and purchased by a capital Planter of Kingston. As she approached nearer to maturity, she discovered a lively genius, and a penetration far superior to the common run of Europeans, whose minds had been cultivated by learning. Her master now took particular notice of her, and removed her so far from her late menial capacity, as to make her a super-intendent of the other female negroes. He gave HARRIOTT a master to teach her to write, read, and do much of arithmetic as enabled her to keep the domestic accounts. He soon after distinguished her still farther from the rest of the slaves; he being a widower, used frequently to admit her to his bed: this honour was accompanied by presents which soon testified she was a great favourite. In this situation she remained for near three years, during which time she bore him two children. His business calling him to England, HARRIOTT accompanied him; and notwithstanding the Beauties of this Island often attracted his attention, and he frequently gave a loose to his natural appetites with his own country-women, still she remained unrivalled on a constant flame. Nor was it, in some respect, extraordinary: for though her complexion might not be so engaging as that of the fair daughters of Albion, she had many attractions that are not often met with in the Female World who yield to prostitution. She was faithful to his bed, careful of his domestic concerns, exact in her accounts, and would not suffer any of the other servants to impose upon their master; and in this respect she favoured him some hundreds a-year. Her person was very alluring; she was tall, well made, and genteel; and since her arrival in England, she had given her mind to reading, and at her master's recommendation, had perused several useful and entertaining books, calculated for women; whereby she had considerably improved her understanding, and had attained a degree of politeness scarce to be paralleled in an African female.

Such was her situation for many months; but unfortunately her master, or friend, which you please, had never had the small-pox; and having caught it, this malady proved fatal to him, and he paid the great and final mortal tribute upon the occasion. She had made some small provision for herself, with regard to clothes, and some trifling trinkets; but she had acted in so upright and generous a manner towards her departed master, that she had not amassed five pounds in money, though she might easily, and without detection, have been the mistress of hundreds.

The scene was soon changed, and from being the superintendent of a noble table, she found herself reduced to a scanty pittance, and even that pittance could not last long, if she did not find some means of speedily recruiting her almost exhausted finances . . .

HARRIOTT, notwithstanding she had read some pious books, and many moral books . . . found it necessary to make the most of her jetty charms, and accordingly applied to Lovejoy to be properly introduced into company. She was quite a new face, in every sense of the word, upon the Town, and a perfect phenomenon of her kind. He despatched immediately a messenger to Lord S—who instantly quitted the arms of Miss R—y for this black beauty. The novelty so struck him, with her unexpected improved talents, that he visited her several successive evenings, and never failed giving her at least a twenty pound Bank-note.

She was resolved to vend her charms as dear as possible; and she now rolled in money, and finding that she had attractions sufficient to draw the commendations and applause of so great a connoisseur in female merit as his Lordship, she found that the caprice of mankind was so great, that she could command almost any price.

In the course of a few months she could class among her list of admirers, at least a score of Peers and fifty Commoners, who never presented her with any thing less than soft paper commonly called a bank note . . .

(London: M. Goadby, 1779, second edition, Vol. II, pp. 98–103)

7.9 The History of Mary Prince, A West Indian Slave, Related by Herself (1831)

Oh dear! I cannot bear to think of that day, – it is too much. – It recalls the great grief that filled my heart, and the woeful thoughts that passed to and fro through my mind, whilst listening to the pitiful words of my poor mother, weeping for the loss of her children. I wish I could find words to tell you all I then felt and suffered. The great

God above alone knows the thoughts of the poor slave's heart, and the bitter pains which follow such separations as these. All that we love taken away from us – Oh, it is sad, sad! and sore to be borne! – I got no sleep that night for thinking of the morrow; and dear Miss Betsey was scarcely less distressed. She could not bear to part with her old playmates, and she cried sore and would not be pacified.

The black morning at length came; it came too soon for my poor mother and us. Whilst she was putting on us the new osnaburgs in which we were to be sold, she said, in a sorrowful voice, (I shall never forget it!) 'See, I am shrouding my poor children; what a task for a mother!' – She then called Miss Betsey to take leave of us. 'I am going to carry my little chickens to market,' (these were her very words,) 'take your last look of them; may be you will see them no more.' 'Oh, my poor slaves! my own slaves!' said dear Miss Betsey, 'you belong to me; and it grieves my heart to part with you.' – Miss Betsey kissed us all, and, when she left us, my mother called the rest of the slaves to bid us good bye. One of them, a woman named Moll, came with her infant in her arms. 'Ay!' said my mother, seeing her turn away and look at her child with the tears in her eyes, 'your turn will come next.' The slaves could say nothing to comfort us; they could only weep and lament with us. When I left my dear little brothers and the house in which I had been brought up, I thought my heart would burst.

Our mother, weeping as she went, called me away with the children Hannah and Dinah, and we took the road that led to Hamble Town, which we reached about four o'clock in the afternoon. We followed my mother to the market-place, where she placed us in a row against a large house, with our backs to the wall and our arms folded across our breasts. I, as the eldest, stood first, Hannah next to me, then Dinah; and our mother stood beside, crying over us. My heart throbbed with grief and terror so violently, that I pressed my hands quite tightly across my breast, but I could not keep it still, and it continued to leap as though it would burst out of my body. But who cared for that? Did one of the many by-standers, who were looking at us so carelessly, think of the pain that wrung the hearts of the negro woman and her young ones? No, no! They were not all bad, I dare say, but slavery hardens white people's hearts towards the blacks; and many of them were not slow to make their remarks upon us aloud, without regard to our grief – though their light words fell like cayenne on the fresh wounds of our hearts. Oh those white people have small hearts who can only feel for themselves.

At length the vendue master, who was to offer us for sale like sheep or cattle, arrived, and asked my mother which was the eldest. She said nothing, but pointed to me. He took me by the hand, and led me out into the middle of the street, and, turning me slowly round, exposed me to the view of those who attended the vendue. I was soon surrounded by strange men, who examined and handled me in the same manner that a butcher would a calf or a lamb he was about to purchase, and who talked about my shape and size in like words – as if I could no more understand their meaning than the dumb beasts. I was then put up to sale. The bidding commenced at a few pounds, and gradually rose to fifty-seven*, when I was knocked down to the highest bidder; and the people who stood by said that I had fetched a great sum for so young a slave. I then saw my sisters led forth, and sold to different owners; so that we had not the sad satisfaction of being partners in bondage. When the sale was over, my mother hugged and kissed us, and mourned over us, begging of us to keep up a good heart, and do our duty to our new masters. It was a sad parting; one went one way, one another, and our poor mammy went home with nothing.

*Bermuda currency; about £38 sterling.

(Reprint: edited by Moira Ferguson, Ann Arbor: University of Michigan Press, 1993, pp. 50–53)

7.10   *The Wonderful Adventures of Mrs Seacole in Many Lands* (1857)

That the officers were glad of me as a doctress and nurse may be easily understood. When a poor fellow lay sickening in his cheerless hut and sent down to me, he knew very well that I should not ride up in answer to his message empty-handed. And although I did not hesitate to charge him with the value of the necessaries I took him, still he was thankful enough to be able to *purchase* them. When we lie ill at home surrounded with comfort, we never think of feeling any special gratitude for the sick-room delicacies which we accept as a consequence of our illness; but the poor officer lying ill and weary in his crazy hut, dependent for the merest necessaries of existence upon a clumsy, ignorant soldier-cook, who would almost prefer eating his meat raw to having the trouble of cooking it (our English soldiers are bad campaigners), often finds his greatest troubles in the want of those little delicacies with which a weak stomach must be humoured into retaining nourishment. How often have I felt at the sight of poor lads who in England thought attending early parade a hardship, and felt harassed if their neck-cloths set awry, or the natty little boots would not retain their polish, bearing, and bearing so nobly and bravely, trials and hardships to which the veteran campaigner frequently succumbed. Don't you think, reader, if you were lying, with parched lips and fading appetite, thousands of miles from mother, wife, or sister, loathing the rough food by your side, and thinking regretfully of that English home where nothing that could minister to your great need would be left untried – don't you think that you would welcome the familiar figure of the stout lady whose bony horse has just pulled up at the door of your hut, and whose panniers contain some cooling drink, a little broth, some homely cake, or a dish of jelly or blanc-mange – don't you think, under such circumstances, that you would heartily agree with my friend *Punch*'s remark:–

> 'That berry-brown face, with a kind heart's trace
> Impressed on each wrinkle sly,
> Was a sight to behold, through the snow-clouds rolled
> Across that iron sky.'

I tell you, reader, I have seen many a bold fellow's eyes moisten at such a season, when a woman's voice and a woman's care have brought to their minds recollections of those happy English homes which some of them never saw again; but many did, who will remember their woman-comrade upon the bleak and barren heights before Sebastopol.

(London: Falling Wall Press, 1984 [1857]), pp. 166–168)

7.11   Joseph Salter, *The Asiatic in England: Sketches of Sixteen years' Work among Orientals* (1873)

Let us now visit the chief rendezvous of these men. We are about to enter Satan's stronghold, and shall observe how shamelessness has its premuim and admirers, and honesty, truth, and self-respect are trampled in the dust. The locality is by the river-side, and is a turning in High Street, Shadwell, with other smaller turnings running out of it. Here disease and death, decked in gaudy tinseled robes, allure the victim to the grave . . .

We are now fairly in the Oriental quarter; there are several houses here devoted to the Asiatics, presided over by the Chinese, Malays, and Indians, according to the country of the Asiatic seeking companionship. Each of the proprietors is assisted by an English mistress, some of whom have lived so long in this element, that they use the Oriental vernacular, and have even been known to act as interpreters at the Police-courts when the oft-repeated quarrels of Asiatics have brought them into trouble. We have indications here of their position in the names which the women bear; names, indeed, which they have earned for themselves, such as Mrs. Mohammed, Mrs. Peeroo, Mrs. Janoo, oriental names derived from the proprietors of the houses above referred to; or Chinese Emma, Calcutta Louisa, and Lascar Sally, names which in themselves may justly be considered to suggest the mode of life adopted. Let us enter the first house in this colony of evil spirits. It is a house of three rooms, and is kept by a stalwart Chinese, aided by Emma. This is a Chinese gambling-house, and these celestials are so earnest in their dangerous play, that they are by no means troubled by our presence. At one end of the table they are gambling with dice, which they cast with much energy into a glass, whirl it violently round, and toss the dice out again with fevered excitement. The money is rapidly changing hands, poverty and destitution will soon be the heritage of the gamblers. At the other end of the table they are equally in earnest, though at a different, still equally as dangerous a game. Here they are playing with Chinese cards: these are about three inches long and three-quarters of an inch broad, embellished with Chinese pictures and reading. The flashing eye, the rapid and excited accent of the tongue, tell us that things are becoming desperate. . . . Above is the opium-room, which serves for fraud and robbery as well as the gambling room. In this house about twenty Chinese are accommodated. The proprietor is a native of Amoy, a very friendly and easy-going Chinese, but, roused to action and out of temper, he is a very desperate man, and his Emma in her drunken fits tries him to the uttermost. Her life, on these occasions, has several times been in imminent danger. Some years past, two speculating Chinese brought a dancing girl here, whom they had bought in China at a low price, hoping to make great gain by her in the metropolis of sight-seers, but they quarrelled over their interests, and one of the speculators stabbed the other, and while one was in the hospital suffering from his wounds, and the other in prison expiating his offence, a servant of Christ snatched the girl from her perilous position. Christian sympathy educated her; the Saviour, who blessed little children, put his hand on her heart, and she returned to China to teach her pagan countrymen the way of eternal life.

What a triumph of sovereign grace it would be, should the Lord touch Chinese Emma's heart, and exalt her to her proper position in society. . . .

In my report for 1858, SING SUNG, a Chinese woman is referred to in the following words: – 'Sing Sung was a native of Ningpo, China. She came to England as a nurse to a returning missionary's wife and children. She could talk no English, and was an heathen, one of two widows of the same husband. She lived in my house, and before she left she made some advance in the English language, and requested to join us in our family devotions. Halooh, a Christian Chinese, from Shanghae, was in the Home at the time, and he repeatedly came into my house, and read and prayed with her in Chinese. She left the Home with a copy of the Scriptures in Chinese.' Sing Sung left England in the service of the Bishop of Hong-Kong. I scarcely expected to hear of her again, but recently I have seen Dr McGowan and his kind lady, both of whom had, not long before, arrived from China. Mrs. McGowan had conversed with Sing Sung since her return to China from England, and had heard from her own lips her determination to worship idols no more. One can but value this small piece of intelligence in reference to such a character as Sing Sung after a period of more than two years; and which perhaps gains some interest from the distance which it comes: and cannot fail to remind us of the promise, 'Cast thy bread upon the waters, for thou shalt find it after many days.'

(London: Seeley, Jackson and Halliday, 1873,
pp. 26–28, 106–108)

7.12   Excerpts from letters from Pandita Ramabai to Sister Geraldine, CSMV, Wantage, October 1884, and to Canon Butler, Wantage, 3 July 1885

Dear Ajeebai,

I am so very sorry I cannot have a talk with you and express my feelings. I could not fully understand Sister Eleanor's letter. The two things which I can make out are these that the colour is approved by

Father Goreh, and that she wishes us (that is for the Sisters of the Indian Community) a cross like yours with Latin words on it and not Sanskrit. I am really surprised at Father Goreh's approval (as you are). I did not expect it so . . . Father Goreh no doubt is good, old and wise, and perhaps he thinks right (I have not received his letter yet, so I cannot tell what he thinks about those words), but I am sorry to say in some things I cannot agree with him. Whatever may be in others' opinion, all the good, old things are *very, very* dear to me, and if I do not find anything in them that is contrary to our blessed Religion, I will not and must not part with them. I do not want to take from others what is not wanted, and also what is not good for my country.

As for the Cross, you know very well why I do not like to have that great sign. It is all right with you, who are Christians from generations, and with Father Goreh who does not or will not sympathise with Indian feelings, but I am just plucked down from (as Indians say) Hinduism and Brahmoism, so I know very well and sympathise their feelings. So I am not inclined to do any such thing, which will lead my fellow (Indian) Christians into wrong ideas.

Well now for a moment I put aside my opinion, and take Sister Eleanor's. Suppose we are going to have a cross as she wishes us to do: then why should it not be inscribed with Sanskrit words, instead of the Latin? Here again I am obliged to be a Conservative. Do you think that Latin language has something better in it than our old Sanskrit or have you the same feeling for the Latin as the Brahmins have for the Sanskrit (i.e. think it to be the Sacred Language and spoken by God and Angels)? I stick fast to Sanskrit, not because I think it to be sacred or the language of gods, but because it is the most beautiful, and the oldest language of my dear native land. And, therefore, if I must have a cross, I should like to see Sanskrit words words written upon it instead of the Latin words. Moreover, I do not myself understand Latin, neither do my countrywomen (with some exception). And even also Latin is not the mother tongue of Marathi [people], so our Indian Sisters will not find a single word in it that they know or is like to some word that is known to them. Then why should we be kept in ignorance of our professed text? . . .
Yours mischevious,
Mary Rama

. . .

You, my dear Father in Christ, and Sister Geraldine, and my other Christian friends, are too learned, too spiritual, too wise, and too faithful to your faith which you profess from your childhood, to

understand my difficulties in accepting wholly the religion taught by
you. You have never gone through the same experience of choosing
another religion for yourself, which was totally foreign to you, you
cannot interpenetrate my poor feelings. You will, I trust, not be
offended if I say so, for no man is omniscient, you do me injustice if
you apply such parables to me as you did last time when I asked you
questions and say in a roundabout way (or lead me to understand
so) that I was not humble and in a teachable spirit when I came to
you. If a Hindoo theologian – however learned and holy and good
he may be – comes and tells you that your religion was a false one,
and that you were to accept humbly everything that he taught, could
you do it? . . .

(A. B. Shah (ed.), *The Letters and Correspondence of
Pandita Ramabai, Compiled by Sister Geraldine*
(Bombay: Maharashtra State Board for Literature
and Culture, 1977), pp. 27–29, 72–77)

Chapter Eight

British women and the empire

'British' history can be said to have happened not only within the British Isles, but in much of the rest of the world.[1] The empire took British men and women overseas as colonial administrators, slave traders, missionaries, etc. and brought people to Britain as workers, students and sometimes as slaves. Until very recently, the empire has been seen as both separate from British domestic social history and as a site of male adventure and exploration, to where men travelled to win territory and engage in distant administration. But British women were also on the imperial scene. Their contributions to empire-building included promoting and guiding female emigration and settlement in the White settler colonies, supporting church-building and missionary work, providing juvenile imperialist education, and offering hospitality for colonial visitors from other countries. As leading imperialists of the late nineteenth century were increasingly turning their attention away from military conquest towards building a settled, 'civilising' Empire, women were seen to have a vital role.[2] The documents in this chapter look at three main areas of British imperial endeavour in which women were involved: as missionaries and abolitionists; wives and others associated with colonial administration; and as emigrants. Historians now tend to concur that rather than 'softening' imperialism, women's participation served to place domestic and familial concerns onto the imperial reform agenda.[3]

8.1 Hannah Kilham, *Missionary Register* (July and September 1824)

The overseas mission formed an early site of encounter between British men and women and those of other cultures. Beginning in the 1790s with the formation of the Baptist, London (largely Independent) and Church Missionary Societies in England, and the Glasgow and Edinburgh Missionary Societies in Scotland, missionary men and women travelled throughout the world. Their primary aim was to inculcate Christian belief and practice. Christianity was for missionaries part of a broader conception of civilization, however, influenced by eighteenth-century Enlightenment thought, which centred on the adoption of values and cultural practices associated with the British evangelical middle class. In these excerpts, Hannah Kilham (1774–1832), Quaker missionary in West Africa in the 1820s and 1830s, articulates the widespread belief that cruelty to women and domestic disorder were signifiers of an uncivilised state, and could be changed by educating men and by girls' acquisition of domestic skills. Through this emphasis on domestic reform, women such as Kilham were able to carve out a specialist role for female missionaries, as only they could enable the domestic transformation believed to be so critical to wider social and religious change.

8.2 Mary Slessor, letter to Miss Crawford (1912)

By the later nineteenth century, single women missionaries outnumbered males. Mary Slessor (1848–1915), a Presbyterian from Dundee, became a celebrated missionary to Old Calabar (today part of south-eastern Nigeria) from 1876. Slessor, who settled among the Okoyong people, was not interested in the tea parties or genteel entertaining that frequently formed the routine of the missionary wives. As revealed by these excerpts from a letter to Miss Crawford of 1912, she ran schools, took in babies, and preached to the people. She was especially concerned with issues pertaining to the status of women: she worked to undermine opposition to girls' education, the practices of bride price and fattening ceremonies, the ostracism of mothers of twins and the seclusion of widows. (A slight digression concerns the marginalia discovered in one of Slessor's Bibles. At the passage so beloved of nineteenth-century evangelicals, as St Paul advocates the subjection of wives to husbands (Ephesians

5:22), Slessor had scribbled: 'Na! Na! Paul, laddie! This will no do!'[4])

8.3 Josephine Butler, *The Storm-Bell* (June 1898)

In the second half of the nineteenth century, their commitment to anti-slavery took women beyond campaigns concerning Africa and the Caribbean to other parts of the world. In this excerpt from *The Storm-Bell* (June 1898), Josephine Butler (1828–1906) emphasises the oppression of Indian women who, she believed, like the animals she also campaigned on behalf of as an anti-vivisectionist, were in need of rescue by western women. She compares their situation to that of women in Britain oppressed by the Contagious Diseases Acts. In taking upon themselves the moral responsibility for the uplift of Indian womanhood, British women represented themselves as important imperial citizens and so furthered their own claims for citizenship. At the same time, they contributed to a representation of 'eastern' women as particularly downtrodden, and in need of the intervention of their 'sisters' in the west.

8.4 Anna Maria Falconbridge, *Two Voyages to Sierra Leone* (1794)

Women travelled to the empire as wives and other family members of colonial administrators. Anna Maria Falconbridge, the young wife of Alexander Falconbridge, travelled to Sierra Leone in 1791 in the wake of the apparent disaster of the 1787 Settlement Scheme. Organised by Granville Sharp and other abolitionists and philanthropists, this had a number of motivations, one of which was the repatriation of black inhabitants of London. The settlement was not a success, due to a combination of disease, war and the ravages of the slave trade. By the time of the arrival of the Falconbridges, only 60 people were living as part of the settlement. This excerpt from Anna Maria Falconbridge's *Two Voyages to Sierra Leone* (1794), written in the form of a letter to a friend, describes her first meeting with King Naimbana and combines discussion of Falconbridge's diplomatic skills with observations of the king's marital and domestic life.[5]

8.5 Maria Graham, *Journals of a Residence in India* (1812)

Maria Graham's writing on India came perhaps a little too early in the nineteenth century to fulfil the stereotype of the socially aloof woman of the Raj. Graham (nee Dundas) travelled to India with her father in 1809 and in the same year married Lt. Thomas Graham, whom she had met on the journey. Her writing, especially *Letters on India* (1814), is elegant and scholarly, revealing her knowledge of Indian history, literature, languages, religion and culture.[6] In this engaging excerpt from her *Journals of a Residence in India* (1812), Graham describes a social gathering of English residents in Bombay.

8.6 Flora Annie Steel and Grace Gardiner, *The Complete Indian Housekeeper and Cook* (1898)

By the mid-nineteenth century, the women of the Raj played a key role in the maintenance of social distinctions between themselves and the 'natives', upholding English dress and social occasions such as sports and hunting, dinner parties and attending the Club. Flora Annie Steel and Grace Gardiner's *The Complete Indian Housekeeper and Cook* aimed to help young British memsahibs who found themselves in India and beyond all 'the familiar landmarks' of British housewifery. Steel, who had arrived in India in 1867 (to remain until 1889) as the young wife of a member of the Indian Civil Service, was quite a character. Living mainly in the Lahore district of the Punjab, she learned local vernaculars, helped her husband write his reports, took up gardening, taught girls, organised the local Municipal Council, drew and submitted a design for the local Town Hall, wrote a successful novel set during the mutiny, and published *The Complete Indian Housekeeper and Cook*, which drew upon her many years' experience in India. (In her capacity as the Inspector of Schools for the Punjab, she upset the government with the suggestion that Lahore University was selling degrees. The government moved her husband to a more remote place in a bid to silence her, and asked him to control his wife, his apparent reply being: 'Take her for a month and try').[7] In this excerpt, Steel is clearly stating that Indian servants are lazy and therefore need constant vigilance in order that they perform their duties according to British standards of cleanliness. However, the possibility that even after several centuries of British presence in India, the 'mistress' has only to be absent for a few days and the servants revert to their own forms of subversive behaviour, makes a rather different point about the precariousness of colonial rule.

8.7 Letter from Elizabeth Gaskell to Charles Dickens (1850)

Women travelled to the empire as emigrants. As these letters from Elizabeth Gaskell to Charles Dickens (1850) reveal, the motivation for individual cases of emigration were often very personal. Dickens and Angela Burdett-Coutts had developed the Urania Cottage Project (from 1846) which aimed to help 'fallen women' emigrate to Australia. The subject of Mrs Gaskell's letters was a Miss Pasley, an orphan and a dress-maker, who had been 'seduced' by a doctor called out to her when she was ill. Gaskell hoped that emigration, and preferably a placement with a respectable working-class family, would enable the unfortunate young woman to 'redeem herself' and to start afresh in a new environment.

8.8 Dora Gore Browne, 'To England's Daughters' (1904)

Between 1884–1914 over 20,000 women emigrated, the majority to Canada and South Africa,[8] many of them supported by the pro-liferating female emigration societies. It was hoped that they might find not only employment, but a husband: the latter were in short supply in England, where there were considerably more women than men of marriageable age. As Dora Gore Browne's poem suggests, it was important that 'the right sort of women' chose to populate the white settler colonies: she should be able to spread the 'English way of life', have a 'civilizing influence' through her womanly care and education, and be fit to become a mother of the next generation of settlers and of the imperial race.

8.9 Mary Kingsley, *Travels in West Africa* (1897)

Mary Kingsley (1862–1900) travelled to Africa in the 1890s, initially with the intention of finishing a book begun by her recently-deceased father. She learned necessary skills in survival from Angolan people and went off alone – an untravelled Victorian spinster – on adventures that involved travelling through dense forests and wading through swamps and being attacked in her canoe by a crocodile. Her book *Travels in West Africa* (1897) was an immediate best-seller. She was much in demand as a lecturer on her return and was outspoken in her criticism of missionaries and settlers, and of aspects of British imperialism. In this excerpt from *Travels in West Africa*, Kingsley describes tracking through inhospitable terrain with her west African companions.

8.10 Empire Day, Sheffield (1906)

Imperialism was abundantly present in popular culture at the end of the nineteenth century. Music hall songs, cigarette cards, packets of soap, children's toys, etc. all drew upon imperial imagery. While there is no doubt that for the organisers of Empire Day in Sheffield in 1906 this was intended to enhance support for colonial expansion and pride in an identity as a colonial power, participation for the (largely) working-class crowd might have had a variety of meanings: from full-blown support for imperialism to the enjoyment of seeing children on a school parade.

8.1   Hannah Kilham, *Missionary Register* (July and September 1824)

I have visited many of the huts here, and have seen with grief in what a state of extreme degradation and immorality the people live. Their wretched habits lead to much misery; and those domestic bonds which should endeavour to unite to each other the father, the mother, and the children of one family, are here supplanted by jealousy, con- fusion, and in many instances, great cruelty. When writing the last sentence, I was called upon to visit a poor woman, who had been so inhumanly beaten by her husband, that she was in danger of suffering greatly, if not of dying, in consequence of his treatment; and although time was pressing, I immediately went. On my way, I was informed that the king of Barra, some time ago, wishing to dismiss one of his wives, had ordered her legs to be broken, which was the cause of her death. All these things reminded me of the easy complacency with which I had heard some people in England talk of leaving the uncivilized part of the world to themselves, saying, that they were very happy as they were, and much more INNOCENT than was imagined; but, indeed, from all the accounts which we hear from those who have really had a near view of the state of the uncivilized, it is evident that the innocency, that is talked of at a distance, is not found in them. On the contrary, all that we see, or hear, calls aloud for the help of those who have been favoured with the blessings of a Christian Education, and the advantages of civilized and improved society.

I am fully convinced it is not any inferiority in the African Mind or natural capacity that has kept them in so depressed a state in the scale of society; but the lack of those advantages, which are, in the usual order of Providence, made use of as instruments for the advancement and improvement of human beings. Those dis- advantages, which they, in common with other civilized nations, have suffered, have with them been cruelly increased, by that oppression, which, wherever exercised, has a natural tendency to fetter, to depress, and to blunt the powers of the mind; and it is very unfair, and a great aggravation of the cruelty, to reflect on the victims of it, as LACKING ABILITY for any other station than that which they have been suffered to fill.

– The wives of the Missionaries find no insurmountable difficulty in teaching the African Girls to be clever cooks, house-maids, and laundresses. I had the gratification to see one of the poor girls who was rescued from the iron-hearted slave-dealer, who had confined his two remaining victims in a cask on board. One of the girls is now married; the other is a chief monitor in the church Missionary school, at Leopold, which consists of from 80 to 90 boys and girls; and is conducted with much attention, by Phoebe Davey, the Wife of the Superintendent of that village . . .

– the Missionaries have succeeded, better than most others that we have seen, in training young people to manage domestic business well; and their houses exhibit more of domestic order and comfort, than we have generally met with.

– There is one thing particularly pleasant in the Schools: the children generally look clean, and healthy, and cheerful.

– In the School at Leopold was a little boy, who, in the course of six months, had learned to read in the Testament; and, in the neighbouring town of Charlotte, was a very little girl, apparently not more than five or six years of age, who read to me the account of the sick and the palsy restored, very agreeably, and had only had about fifteen months' instruction.

– The European Colonists of Sierra Leone have several times remarked, that people in England are under a great mistake, in supposing that a Native Youth, with very little instruction in the Schools, would be sufficient to teach as a Master, and as an Instructor of the people in the neighbouring villages. They say, on the contrary, that very acute reasoners are found among the Natives, and especially the Mahomedans who would soon baffle an inexperienced youth in this way.

8.2   Mary Slessor, Letter to Miss Crawford (23 March 1912)

Ikpe Ikot Nkon
23rd March 1912
My dear Miss Crawford.
. . . As a rule the Sabbath school comprises the whole company of the Xtian [Note 1] section. It is always well attended & only mothers with babies & elderly men come after the Church bell at the close. The Church is always quite full before school is over. One section of boys, about 60 of them, who cant read in the Bible, have been going

thoroughly through the Catechisms, & they get Marks, & a small Prize to the 2 best on the 1st Sabbath of the month. A crowded Class of boys & lads who can read the New Testament have been committing John 14 to memory & for the last 3 months they too have been getting a Prize & Marks for memorizing. A girls & young womens class taught by Alice have been learning Psalm 103, & a Hymn from the Hymn Book in use at service, while the old & staid men learn from the Old Testament. They have learned Isaiah 53rd & etc. etc. & the tinies [Note 2] get a Hymn.... The rest is very generally composed of singing(?) [Note 3]. The wildest stretch of imagination can hardly call it harmony! & any thing that will lessen this outpour of the crudest & most wonderful Christian (rhetoric) [Note 4] this is wrongly spelt, you know what I mean! seems to me a boon & discipline. Since they have begun to learn how very little they know, there have not been the forwardness to take the 'Chair' & the 'Prayers' that there used to be. Instead there have been many questions on many subjects, & quiet knowing looks at one another when answers were received. Names of Catechumens [Note 5] came in steadily, the greater number with the pathetic announcement that they saw no hope of full membership in view, as the wives betrothed to them by their parents, were either not willing to become Christians & go into Christian Marriage, or their parents were not favourable to their giving up girls thus betrothed to them, telling them they must stick to their bargain, church or no church. However things are bit by bit coming round, & several young girls are willing, & several wives are willing to be one wife in Christian marriage, where a number are already in the Yard. Some parents are very obstinate, so are some husbands where wives wish to leave the Harem & be Baptised & in these cases the young people can do nothing as they cannot pay back the dowry, so must hold to the wife, or to the husband, in the choosing of whom they had no share. The dowry is much higher here than lower down river. But parents must come round as the years march with their progresses, & God is for them, so that is the great point. I have found their fathers fighting shy of me, because they have not the courage to say to me that they will not do God's way, but some of them laugh & say, wait a little Ma, till the work time is over, & we have proved the lads & women & we shall see. They are afraid lest this upset the very roots of their life, by allowing the old ground work of all their existence to be taken away. And there are dangers too, that unworthy women & men may make Church membership a mere excuse for breaking Home ties & giving licence to vice. So I am not in a hurry to give into the lads, or to blame the Chiefs & parents, even if it keep the Communion Roll low in numbers. For this very reason of conserving Home relations, as they know them, I have met girls privately, & do not call their names at class. . . .

Now dear Miss Crawford I shall close, with every possible wish & desire for your wellbeing, & for your home, & your work. May God bless & INDWELL [Note 8] you more & more for His glory. I am ever your loving friend

Mary M Slessor

EDITORIAL NOTES:

1] Xtian = Christian
2] the tinies = the youngest children
3] Miss Slessor's own question mark
4] rhetoric. Miss Slessor had two tries at the spelling of this word
5] Catechumens = those being taught the basics of Christianity before being baptised
8] indwell = dwell or abide within spiritually

(GD.X.260.11, *Dundee City Archives, Mary Slessor Letters and Documents*, transcription by Leslie A. Mackenzie, edited by Ruth E. Riding, February 1999)

8.3   Josephine Butler, *The Storm-Bell* (June 1898), pp. 59–60

Mrs Andrew spoke of the Queen's daughters in India, the poor Indian women sacrificed by our rulers to the base theory of the necessity of sinful indulgence for our army in India, as being ground between 'upper and the nether millstone'; on the one hand the native Indian laws and customs which oppress and degrade their women – the child marriages, child widowhood, the condition of the widow as a despised outcast, &c.; and on the other hand, the foul and heavy-handed injustice exercised towards them by the English authorities in India (backed by the English Home Government) in entrapping and enslaving them, oppressing and tormenting them, and doing them to death under their unlawful system of officially regulated fornication.

They are indeed between the upper and the nether millstone, helpless, voiceless, hopeless. Their helplessness appeals to the heart, somewhat in the same way in which the helplessness and suffering of an animal does, under the knife of the vivisector.

We have heard of the meekness and patience of dogs, (the dearest and noblest of beasts), under the human tortures of the great vivisector; – even of their licking the hand which held the scalpel, in a mute appeal for pity. It is that dumbness, that impossibility of resistance, the complete helplessness of the subjected animal which appeals to our hearts (some of our hearts at least), with a sense of peculiar pain, and of a resentment against their tormenters, which in its way is unique.

The tortured human being, we hope, we believe, has, in some instances the intelligence, dim as that may be, of a Divine power above all earth's cruelty, which may be exercised on behalf of the tortured.

The Martyr Saints at the stake or on the rack, however terrible their sufferings, were enabled to rise above them, and even to rejoice and sing in the midst of their anguish.

Somewhere, half way between the Martyr Saints and the tortured 'friend of man' the noble dog, stand, it seems to me, these pitiful Indian women, girls, children, as many of them are. They have not even the small power of resistance which the western woman may have, under the tyranny of the executive of this base system. The western woman may have some clearer knowledge of a just and pitiful God to whom she may make her mute appeal. She has occasionally perhaps the consciousness that among her countrymen and those outside his tyranny there are some who are pleading her cause. This, I believe, has brought to some a faint hope, though it is no more than a vague hope for the future rather than for the present.

I recall the wail of a spirited woman, crushed under the wheels of the Juggernaut of State organized vice in England, before the repeal, a wail expressed in such words as these, which no doubt echo the half conscious feeling of that world of cruelly subjected womanhood. 'If it were a man insulting me in that way on his own responsibility, a base fellow guilty of a private assault, I would use all the strength I have of muscle and sinew to resist and defeat him. I would fight with him, for my person, my honour, and my life, even if I was killed in doing so. But O! Madam, when you know that that man, guilty of that foul assault, has the House of Lords, the *Queen*, the *Law*, all at his back, you feel as if your heart died within you; you cannot fight against all these. It seems to you then as if God himself is against you.'

These are awful words, awful in their strict truth and reality. And this horrible pressure, – the pressure of *authority* doing the devil's work, – weighs more heavily on the poor Indian woman than on others; she bends under it more hopelessly, more helplessly, a broken reed, trodden down by unholy feet . . .

8.4   Anna Maria Falconbridge, *Two Voyages to Sierra Leone* (1794)

Letter III, Bance Island, 10 February 1791, pp. 58–59

. . .

After setting nigh half an hour, Naimbana made his appearance, and received us with seeming good will: he was dressed in a purple embroidered coat, white satin waistcoat and breeches, *thread stockings*, and his left side emblazoned with a flaming star; his legs to be sure were *harlequined*, by a number of holes in the stockings, through which his black skin appeared.

Compliments ended, Mr Falconbridge acquainted him with his errand, by a repetition of what he wrote the day before: and complained much of King Jemmy's injustice in driving the settlers away, and burning their town. . . .

Having prefaced his arguments with a small donation of some rum, wine, a cheese, and a gold laced hat, which Naimbana seemed much pleased with, Falconbridge began, by explaining what advantages would accrue to his *majesty*, and all the inhabitants round about, by such an establishment as the St George's Bay Company were desirous of making; – the good they wished to do – *their disinterestedness in point of obtaining wealth*, and concluded by expostulating on the injustice and imposition of dispossessing the late settlers of the grounds and houses they occupied, which had been honestly and honourably purchased by Captain Thompson of the Navy, in the name of our gracious Sovereign, his Britannic Majesty. . . .

The King said he liked the English in preference to all white men, tho' he considered every white man as a *rogue*, and consequently saw them with a jealous eye; yet, he believed the English were by far the honestest, and for that reason, notwithstanding he had received more favours from the French than the English, he liked the latter much best.

He was decidedly of the opinion, that all contracts or agreements between man and man however disadvantageous to either party should be binding; but observed, he was *hastily drawn in* to dispose of land to Captain Thompson, *which in fact he had not a right to sell,* because says he, 'this is a great country, and belongs to many people – where I live belongs to myself – and I can live where I like; nay, can appropriate any uninhabited land within my dominions to what use I please; but it is necessary for me to obtain the consent of my people, or rather the head man of every town, before I sell any land to a white man, or allow strangers to come and live among us.' . . .

They then shook hands heartily, and Naimbana retired, I suppose to his Pegininee woman's house, but presently returned dressed in a suit of black velvet, except the stockings, which were the same as before.

I often had an inclination to offer my services to close the holes: but was fearful least my needle might blunder into his Majesty's leg, and start the blood, for drawing the blood of an African King, I am informed, whether occasioned by accident or otherwise, is punished with death: the dread of this only prevented me. . . .

I saw several of his wives, but his *Pegininee* woman is a most beautiful young girl of about fourteen. None of them are titled to the appellation of *Queen*, but the oldest, who I was introduced to, and by whom the King has several children; one of the daughters, named Clara, is wife to Elliotte, and a son named Bartholomew, is now in France for his education. . . .

We were now led to the garden, which was only furnished with African plants, such as pines, melons, pumpkins, cucumbers, &c. &c.

The King cut two beautiful pines and presented to me . . .

Having been seen as the raree-shows in Robana, we returned to the Queen's house to dinner, which was shortly after put on a table covered with a plain calico cloth, and consisted of boiled and broiled fowls, rice, and some greens resembling our spinage.

But I should tell you, before dinner, Naimbana again changed his dress for a scarlet robe embroidered with gold.

Naimbana, Elliott, Falconbridge, and myself, only set down; the Queen stood behind the King eating an onion I gave her, a bite of which she now and then indulged her *royal Consort* with: silver forks were placed on the King's plate, and mine, but no where else . . .

On the whole I was much pleased with the occurrences of the day; indeed, methinks, I hear you saying, 'Why the weak mind of this giddy girl will be quite intoxicated with the courtesy and attention paid to her by such great folks;' but believe me, to whatever height of self-consequence I may have been lifted by aerial fancies, over-powering sleep prevailed, and clouding all my greatness – I awoke next morning without the slightest remains of fancied importance.

(Deirdre Coleman (ed.), *Maiden Voyages and Infant Colonies: Two Women's Travel Narratives of the 1790s* (Leicester: Leicester University Press, 1999), pp. 58–63)

8.5   Maria Graham, *Journal of a Residence in India* (1812)

October 20th 1809

With regard to the Europeans in Bombay, the manners of the inhabitants of a foreign colony are in general so well represented by those of a country town at home, that it is hopeless to attempt making a description of them very interesting. However, as it may be gratifying to know how little there is to satisfy curiosity, I shall endeavour to describe our colonists. On our arrival we dined with the governor, and found almost all the English of the settlement invited to meet us. There were a good many very pretty and very well dressed women, a few ancient belles, and at least three men for every woman. When dinner was announced, I, as the stranger, though an unmarried woman, was handed by the governor into a magnificent dining-room, formally the chapel of the Jesuit's college, at one end of which a tolerable band was stationed to play during dinner. We sat down to table about eight o'clock, in number about fifty, so that conversation, unless with one's neighbour, was out of the question. After dinner, I was surprised that the ladies sat so long at the table; at length, after everybody had exhibited repeated symptoms of weariness, one of the ladies led the way into the saloon, and then I discovered that, as the stranger, I was expected to move first. Does not this seem a little barbarous? I found our fair companions like the ladies of all the country towns I know, under-bred and over-dressed, and, with the exception of one or two, very ignorant and very grossiere. The men are, in general, what a Hindoo would call of a higher caste than the woman; and I generally find the merchants the most rational companions. Having, at an early age, to depend on their own mental exertions, they acquire a steadiness and sagacity which prepare their minds for the acquisition of a variety of information, to which their commercial intercourse lends.

The civil servants to government being, in Bombay, for the most part young men, are so taken up with their own imaginary importance, that they disdain to learn, and have nothing to teach. Among the military I have met with many well-informed and gentleman-like persons, but still, the great number of men, and the small number of rational companions, make a deplorable prospect to one who anticipates a long residence here.

The parties in Bombay are the most dull and uncomfortable meetings one can imagine. Forty or fifty persons assemble at seven o'clock, and stare at one another until dinner is announced, when the ladies are handed to table, according to the strictest rules of precedency, by a gentleman of rank corresponding to their own. At table there can be no general conversation, but the different couples who have been paired off, and who, on account of their rank, invariably sit together at every great dinner, amuse themselves with remarks on the company, as satirical as their wit will allow; and woe be to the stranger, whose ears are certain of being regaled with the catalogue of his supposed imperfections and misfortunes, and who has the chance of learning more of his own history than in all probability he ever knew before. After dinner the same topics continue to occupy the ladies, with the addition of lace, jewels, intrigues, and the latest fashions; or if there be any newly-arrived young women, the making and breaking of matches for them furnish employment for the ladies of the colony until the arrival of the next cargo. Such is the company of an English Bombay feast. The repast itself is as costly as possible, and in such profusion that no part of the table-cloth remains uncovered. But the dinner is scarcely touched, as every person eats a hearty meal called tiffin, at two o'clock, at home. Each guest brings his own servant, sometimes two or three; these are either Parsees or Musselmans. It appears singular to a stranger to see behind every white man's chair a dark, long bearded, turbaned gentleman, who usually stands so close to his master, as to make no trifling addition to the heat of the apartment; indeed, were it not for the *punka*, (a large frame of wood covered with cloth), which is suspended over every table, and kept constantly swinging, in order to freshen the air, it would scarcely be possible to sit out the melancholy ceremony of an Indian dinner.

(Edinburgh, 1812, pp. 27–30)

8.6   Flora Annie Steel and Grace Gardiner, *The Complete Indian Housekeeper and Cook* (1898)

Housekeeping in India, when once the first strangeness has worn off, is a far easier task in many ways than it is in England, though it none the less requires time, and, in this present transitional period, an almost phenomenal patience; for, while one mistress enforces cleanliness according to European methods, the next may belong to the opposite faction, who, so long as the dinner is nicely served, thinks nothing of it being cooked in a kitchen which is also used as a latrine; the result being that the servants who serve one and then the other stamp of mistress, look upon the desire for decency as a more personal and distinctly disagreeable attribute of their employer, which, like a bad temper or stinginess, may be resented or evaded.

And, first, it must be distinctly understood that it is not necessary, or in the least degree desirable, that an educated woman should waste the best years of her life in scolding and petty supervision. Life holds higher duties, and it is indubitable that friction and over-zeal is a sure sign of a bad housekeeper. But there is an appreciable difference between the careworn Martha vexed with many things, and the absolute indifference displayed by many Indian mistresses, who put up with a degree of slovenliness and dirt which would disgrace a den in St Giles, on the principle that it is no use attempting to teach the natives.

They never go into their kitchens, for the simple reason that their appetite for breakfast might be marred by seeing the *khitmugar* using his toes as an efficient toast-rack (*fact*); or their desire for dinner weakened by seeing the soup strained through a greasy turban.

The ostrich, who, according to the showman, ' 'ides 'is head in the sand and thinks as 'e can't see no-one, nobody can't see 'e', has, fortunately, an exceptional faculty of digestion. With this remark we will leave a very unpleasant subject.

Easy however as the actual housekeeping is in India, the personal attention of the mistress is quite as much needed here as at home. The Indian servant, it is true, learns more readily, and is guiltless of the sniffiness with which Mary Jane receives suggestions; but a few days of absence or neglect on the part of the mistress, results in the servants falling into their old habits with the inherited conservatism of dirt. This is of course disheartening, but it has to be faced as a necessary condition of life, until a few generations of training shall have started the Indian servant on a new inheritance of habit. It must never be forgotten that at present those mistresses who aim at anything beyond keeping a good table are in the minority, and that pioneering is always arduous work.

The first duty of a mistress is, of course, to be able to give intelligible orders to her servants; therefore it is necessary she should learn to speak Hindustani. No sane Englishwoman would dream of living, say, for twenty years in Germany, Italy, or France, without *making the attempt*, at any rate, to learn the language. . . . The next duty is obviously to insist upon her orders being carried out. . . . The secret lies in making rules, and *keeping to them*. The Indian servant is a child in everything save age, and should be treated as a child; that is to say, kindly, but with the greatest firmness.

(London: William Heinemann, 1911 [1898]), pp. 1–3)

8.7   Letter from Elizabeth Gaskell to Charles Dickens (1850)

121, Upper Rumford Street
Manchester Janry 8. [1850]
My dear Sir,
In the first place I am going to give you some trouble, and I must make an apology for it; for I am very sorry to intrude upon you in your busy life. But I want some help, and I cannot think of any one who can give it to me so well as you. Some years since I asked Mr Burnett to apply to you for a prospectus of Miss Coutts' refuge for Female prisoners, and the answer I received was something to the effect that you did not think such an establishment could be carried out successfully anywhere, *unless connected with a scheme of emigration, as Miss Coutts was*. (As I have written it it seems like a cross question & crooked answer, but I believe Mr Burnett told you the report was required by people desirous of establishing a similar refuge in Manchester.)

I am just now very much interested in a young girl, who is in our New Bayley prison. She is the daughter of an Irish clergyman who died when she was two years old; but even before that her mother had shown most complete indifference to her; and soon after the husband's death, she married again, keeping her child out at nurse.

The girl's uncle had her placed at 6 years old in the Dublin school for orphan daughters of the clergy; and when she was about 14, she was apprenticed to an Irish dress-maker here, of very great reputation for fashion. Last September but one this dress-maker failed, and had to dismiss all her apprentices; she placed this girl with a woman who occasionally worked for her, and who has since succeeded to her business; this woman was very profligate and connived at the girl's seduction by a surgeon in the neighbourhood who was called in when the poor creature was ill. Then she was in despair, & wrote to her mother, (*who had never corresponded with her all the time she was at school and an apprentice*;) and while awaiting the answer went into the penitentiary; she wrote 3 times but no answer came, and in desperation she listened to a woman, who had obtained admittance [to the penitentiary] solely as it turned out to decoy girls into her mode of life, and left with her; & for four months she has led the most miserable life! in the hopes, as she tells me, of killing herself, for 'no one had ever cared for her in this world,' – she drank, 'wishing it might be poison', pawned every article of clothing – and at last stole. I have been to see her in prison at Mr Wright's request, and she looks quite a young child (she is but 16,) with a wild wistful look in her eyes, as if searching for the kindness she has never known, – and she pines to redeem herself; her uncle (who won't see her, but confirms fully the account of the mother's cruel hardness,) says he has 3O£ of her father's money in his hands; and she agrees to emigrate to Australia, for which her expenses would be paid. But the account of common emigrant ships is so bad one would not like to expose her to such chances of corruption; and what I want you to tell me is, how Miss Coutts sends out her protegees? under the charge of a matron? and might she be included among them? I want her to go out with as free and unbranded a character as she can; if possible, the very fact of having been in prison &c to be unknown on her landing. I will try and procure her friends when she arrives; only how am I to manage about the voyage? and how soon will a *creditable* ship sail; for she comes out of prison on Wednesday, & there are two of the worst women in the town who have been in prison with her, intending to way-lay her, and I want to keep her out of all temptation, and even chance of recognition. Please, will you help me? I think you know Miss Coutts. I can manage all except the voyage. She is a good reader [,] writer, and a beautiful needlewoman; and we can pay all her expenses &c.

Pray don't say you can't help me for I don't know any one else to ask, and you see the message you sent about emigration some years

ago has been the mother of all this mischief. Will you give my love to Mrs Dickens & Miss Hogarth & believe me.
Yours very truly
E C Gaskell
(*The Letters of Mrs Gaskell,* ed. J. A. V. Chapple and Arthur Pollard (Manchester: Manchester University Press, 1997 [1966]), pp. 98–99)

8.8   Dora Gore Browne, 'To England's Daughters', *The Imperial Colonist* (1904)

Do you feel the heart of England beating high with love and yearning
As her daughters gather round her, ere they sever from her knee?
'Oh, my children!' hear her speaking, 'when your steps from home are turning,
See you keep my fame unsullied, be you true to God and me.
For I bid you to remember how from days of ancient story
Every loyal English daughter, who was worthy of the name,
In whose heart the glow was kindled for her country's highest glory.
Bore aloft the torch of freedom, adding lustre to the flame.
And to you 'tis now entrusted, with a meaning, larger, higher,
You, my daughters, as you go to join your kinsfolk o'er the foam,
'Tis for you to keep the flaming torch of loyalty on fire,
In the land of your adoption, for the honour of your home.
Yes! For God and for your country now 'tis yours to make the story
You, the future nursing mothers of the English race to be.
In your arms His love will lay them, and He looks for England's glory
You her loyal sons and daughters in her homes beyond the sea.
'God be with you, then, and speed you, as you cross the heaving waters,
God be with you, as you land upon our kinsmen's distant shore.
Let them feel that Mother England sends the noblest of her daughters,
Forges living links of Empire, links to bind us more and more.
'Keep your anchor firmly grounded in the steadfast Rock of Ages;
Keep your eyes upon His cross who died to save us in His love;
Seek the Holy Spirit's guiding, as life's ocean round you rages,
He will lead you to the heaven, to the Father's home above.'
(In *The Imperial Colonist: The Official Organ of the British Women's Emigration Association and the South African Colonisation Society*, Vol. III, No. 36, December 1904)

8.9   Mary H. Kingsley, *Travels in West Africa* (1897)

The first day in the forest we came across a snake – a beauty with a new red-brown and yellow-patterned velvety skin, about three feet six inches long and as thick as a man's thigh. Ngouta met it, hanging from a bough, and shot backwards like a lobster, Ngouta having among his many weaknesses a rooted horror of snakes. This snake the Ogowe natives all hold in great aversion. For the bite of other sorts of snakes they profess to have remedies, but for this they usually have none. If, however, a native is stung by one he usually conceals the fact that it was this particular kind, and tries to get any chance the native doctor's medicine may give. The Duke stepped forward and with one blow flattened its head against the tree with his gun butt, and then folded the snake up and got as much of it as possible into the bag, while the rest hung dangling out. . . . We had the snake for supper, that is to say the Fan and I; the others would not touch it, although a good snake, properly cooked, is one of the best meats one gets out here, far and away better than the African fowl.

The Fans also did their best to educate me in every way: they told me their names for things, while I told them mine. . . . They also showed me many things . . .

On one occasion, between Egaja and Esoon, [Wiki] came back from one of these quests and wanted me to come and see something, very quietly; I went, and we crept down into a rocky ravine, on the other side of which lay one of the outermost Egaja plantations. When we got to the edge of the cleared ground, we lay down, and wormed our way, with elaborate caution, among a patch of Koko; Wiki first, I following in his trail.

After about fifty yards of this, Wiki sank flat, and I saw before me some thirty yards off, busily employed in pulling down plantains, and other depredations, five gorillas: one old male, one young male, and three females. One of these had clinging to her a young fellow, with beautiful wavy black hair with just a kink in it. The big male was crouching on his haunches, with his long arms hanging down on either side, with the backs of his hands on the ground, the palms upwards. The elder lady was tearing to pieces and eating a pine-apple, while the others were at the plantains destroying more than they ate.

They kept up a sort of a whinnying, chattering noise, quite different from the sound I have heard gorillas give when enraged, or from the one you can hear them giving when they are what the natives call 'dancing' at night. I noticed that their reach of arm was immense, and that when they went from one tree to another, they squattered across the open ground in a most inelegant style, dragging their long arms with the knuckles downwards. I should think the big male and female were over six feet each. The others would be from four to five. I put out my hand and laid it on Wiki's gun to prevent him from firing, and he, thinking I was going to fire, gripped my wrist.

I watched the gorillas with great interest for a few seconds, until I heard Wiki make a peculiar small sound, and looking at him saw his face was working in an awful way as he clutched his throat with his hand violently.

Heavens! think I, this gentleman's going to have a fit; it's lost we are entirely this time. He rolled his head to and fro, and then buried his face into a heap of dried rubbish at the foot of a plantain stem, clasped his hands over it, and gave an explosive sneeze. The gorillas let go all, raised themselves up for a second, gave a quaint sound between a bark and a howl, and then the ladies and the young gentleman started home. The old male rose to his full height (it struck me at the time this was a matter of ten feet at least, but for scientific purposes allowance must be made for a lady's emotions) and looked straight towards us, or rather towards where that sound came from. Wiki went off into a paroxysm of falsetto sneezes the like of which I have never heard; nor evidently had the gorilla, who . . . went off after his family with a celerity that was amazing the moment he touched the forest, and disappeared as they had, swinging himself along through it from bough to bough, in a way that convinced me that, given the necessity of getting about in tropical forests, man has made a mistake in getting his arms shortened. I have seen many wild animals in their native wilds, but never have I seen anything to equal gorillas going through bush; it is a graceful, powerful, superbly perfect hand-trapeze performance.

After this sporting adventure, we returned, as I usually return from a sporting adventure, without measurements or the body.

(London: Macmillan, 1897, pp. 265–268)

8.10 Empire Day, Sheffield (May 1906)

Chapter Nine

Feminisms

As historians have noted, it is the suffrage campaign that has traditionally dominated histories of nineteenth-century feminism, no doubt due in part to its high-profile militancy. Suffrage was, however, embedded in a wider feminist culture and in many ways was the least successful of a range of feminist initiatives.[1] Documents in this chapter focus on organised feminism: the campaigns for marriage reform, for the extension of education and employment opportunities; issues of public morality and the Contagious Diseases Acts; suffrage; the big working-class women's movement of the late nineteenth century, the Women's Co-operative Guild; and the 'woman question' in relation to the trades unions and the socialist movement. We should note, however, that 'feminism' is a term that was used from the 1890s. Prior to then, the usual terminology was 'the Woman Question'. While it may be anachronistic to refer to feminism in the 1860s, that decade saw the beginnings of what has (since) been termed 'equal rights feminism', as women analysed inequalities in their position in society when compared to men.[2]

9.1 Barbara Leigh Smith, *A Brief Summary, in plain language, of the most important laws of England concerning Women, together with a few observations thereon* (1854)

Barbara Leigh Smith's *Brief Summary* challenged the doctrine of 'coverture', by which married women had no separate legal identity and were forced into economic dependence upon men. Women were considered to be property themselves, and upon marriage their property, including any earnings from paid labour, passed to the husband; this was the case unless a trust had been set up, a practice which was only available to the very wealthy. The publication launched one of the most important and far-reaching sites of the feminist battle: the campaign for marriage reform. It led to the formation in 1855 of a committee to campaign and petition in support of the Married Women's Property Bill which was then before Parliament. The 'Ladies of Langham Place', as they were known, also inaugurated early campaigns for single women's access to occupations other than needlework and governessing and the extension of girls' and women's education and suffrage. These were promoted through the *Englishwomen's Journal*, which Leigh Smith (1827–1891) edited with Bessie Raynor Parkes between 1858 and 1864. It was not until 1870 and 1882 – after decades of lobbying by women nationwide – that married women finally gained any control over their earnings, certain investments and small legacies.

9.2 Caroline Norton, *Plain Letter to the Lord Chancellor on the Infant Custody Bill* (1839)

The movement for the reform of the custody laws of the 1880s had a precedent in the case of Caroline Norton (1808–1877) who in 1837 had campaigned for the law in England to recognise the bond between mother and children. After their separation, George Norton had sued Caroline for adultery, of which she was cleared; he then went on to withhold permission for her to see her three young sons, aged two, four and six years. Norton used her political connections to see through the passing of the 1839 Infant Custody Bill, but this was a limited victory as it only entitled women to see their children and to have custody rights for infants under seven years of age. The Plain Letter to the Lord Chancellor discusses her own case, and numerous others, including that of Mrs Greenhill, who eventually left the country in a bid to prevent her daughters being separated from her. The mother in this case was prepared to accept that the children were to reside with the father; what she could not accept was that she would not be allowed to see them. The 1886 Guardianship of Infants Act took account of the mother's wishes, though did not reduce the father's authority.

9.3 *Frances Power Cobbe*, 'What shall we do with our old maids' (1862)

The mid-nineteenth century saw an unprecedented number of single women in Britain: in 1851, 30 per cent of all women between the ages of 20 and 40 were unmarried; this was despite the fact that in this age group there were only about 6 per cent more women than men. The high numbers of spinsters were due to men marrying later and to male emigration. One solution to the pleasantly-titled 'surplus-' or 'redundant-woman' question, suggested by W. R. Greg in his famous article 'Why are women redundant?' (*National Review*, 1862), was to encourage them to emigrate. This essay by Frances Power Cobbe (1822–1904) was written in response to Greg's argument that marriage should be promoted at all cost, including that of sending women to the colonies in pursuit of a husband. After making the point that it was labouring women, rather than the middle-class 'redundant' women, who were wanted in colonies, she develops the opposing argument: that marriage should be a positive choice; and should be one opportunity for happiness and fulfilment alongside others, including employment and education.

9.4 Elizabeth Garrett Anderson, 'Sex and Mind in Education: a Reply' (1874)

Anxieties over the 'unsexing' of women permeated debates about women's access to higher education. Henry Maudsley predicted nervous disorders as a result of girls having an education during puberty (see chapter 1). Elizabeth Garrett Anderson (1836–1917), Britain's first woman physician, shared with Maudsley the belief that there were basic differences between the sexes, but argued that healthy femininity required that women (and girls) were active, both physically and mentally. The causes of women's illnesses were not physiological, she argued, but social; boredom and idleness led to disaffection and even madness. Elsewhere in the text, she humorously challenges Maudsley's suggestion that young men were 'intellectual athletes'. She concludes that the health of young women would be best served by giving women an education and discouraging early marriage and motherhood.

9.5   The Ladies' Protest against the Contagious Diseases Acts, *Daily News*, 1 January 1870

The Contagious Diseases Acts, passed in 1864 and expanded in 1866 and 1869, gave magistrates in garrison towns the power to inspect (by internal examination, with a speculum, on a fortnightly basis) and treat (with a dose of mercury) any woman suspected of prostitution. If doctors found evidence of venereal disease, the woman could be detained, for three to nine months, in a lock hospital. The Acts came out of anxieties at the time of the Crimean War, when doctors voiced their fears that British soldiers were becoming syphilitic and enfeebled. The assumption was that prostitution was a necessary evil. Whereas women's 'sexuality' was naturally expressed in motherhood, the male sex drive was 'innate' and 'clean' prostitutes were required both to enable the natural expression of male sexual energy and to maintain the purity of the domestic woman. The campaign against the CD Acts saw women as prominent participants for the first time in debates about prostitution. In 1869, the Ladies' National Association for the Repeal of the Contagious Diseases Acts (LNA) was founded and its campaign was launched with the publication in the *Daily News* of the famous Ladies' Protest against the Acts on New Year's Day 1870. The LNA exposed the 'double-standard' supported by the Acts, which placed the spread of syphilis with the prostitute rather than the men who visited her. They also criticised the violation of inspection and the compromise to the freedom of all women, including the non-prostitutes accidentally rounded up by the police.

9.6   Christabel Pankhurst, *The Great Scourge and How to End It* (1913)

With its call for 'Votes for Women, Chastity for Men', Christabel Pankhurst's *The Great Scourge* has been a controversial pamphlet, for both her contemporaries and for recent historians. The pamphlet – in which Pankhurst (1880–1958) used erroneous statistics compiled by doctors – concerns the widespread existence of venereal disease in Edwardian England. Acquired by men prior to marriage, gonorrhoea was passed to their unwitting wives, causing pelvic and uterine diseases, still-birth and abnormalities in children. The pamphlet was part of the feminist attack upon the 'sex-slavery' by which husbands had rights to sexual intercourse and women were continually child-bearing; with few alternatives to marriage, women were merely legal-ised prostitutes. Historians have contributed greatly to our under-standing of such 'puritanism' not as a simple prudish prohibitionism, as many male historians have liked to portray it, but as 'a political analysis of the workings of a double standard which ruled [women's] lives with considerable force.'[3]

9.7 Elizabeth Blackwell, 'On the Abuses of Sex – II. Fornication' (1902)

Elizabeth Blackwell, a gynecologist and obstetrician who had been the first woman to earn a medical degree in the United States in 1849, presents a very different perspective on female sexuality from that held by her male colleagues (see William Acton, chapter 1). In this excerpt, she argues that women were not passionless but enjoyed sexual relations that did not just focus on penetration. She also suggests that enjoyment of sex was for many women profoundly affected by the fear of pregnancy, or residual pain from a bad experience of childbirth.

9.8 John Stuart Mill, Speech to the House of Commons on the subject of women's suffrage (1867)

The mid-nineteenth-century campaign to extend the franchise to women began with a petition to Parliament drawn up in 1865 by Barbara Bodichon and Emily Davies. They were supported by the liberal intellectual and Member of Parliament, John Stuart Mill. Mill's argument in this 1867 speech, that the denial of citizenship to women was incompatible with a civilised society based on individual-ism and in which men and women were companions, became central to the claim for suffrage and pre-empted *Subjection of Women* (1869), the most famous statement on women's rights in the nine-teenth century (see chapter 1).

9.9 Barbara Bodichon, *Reasons For and Against the Enfranchisement of Women* (1869)

In *Reasons For and Against the Enfranchisement of Women* (1869), Barbara Bodichon dismissed the various arguments against the enfranchisement of women: that they didn't want the vote (she argued that some did and not all men did); that women had other duties (so did men); that women were ignorant of politics (there was no evidence that this did not apply to the mass of the existing voters); and that it caused family dissension (she questioned whether it really was 'essential that brothers and sisters and cousins shall all vote on the same side'.) Bodichon explored the different reasons for granting women the vote, arguing that it was a natural right, a necessary protection for women and, as shown by the excerpt here, of benefit to public life.

9.10 Sylvia Pankhurst, *The Suffragette Movement: An Intimate Account of Persons and Ideals* (1931)

It is the militant suffragists who engaged in the high-profile campaigns of the late 1900s and 1910s who both symbolise suffragism in the public mind and were the focus of much early women's history. The Women's Social and Political Union (WSPU), formed in 1903, and associated with Emmeline and Christabel Pankhurst, the Women's Freedom League (WFL) (1907) and Sylvia Pankhurst's East London Federation of Suffragettes (1912) all orchestrated militant campaigns. Sylvia Pankhurst (1882–1960), who disagreed with the WSPU's growing distance from the labour movement and was committed to furthering both causes, describes a range of militant actions undertaken by suffragists.

9.11 'A Guildswoman', in Margaret Llewellyn Davies (ed.), *Life as We Have Known It* (1931)

The Women's Co-operative Guild, which emerged in 1883 out of 'The Women's Corner' section of the Co-op newspaper *The Co-operative News*, was to become the largest political organisation of working-class women and by 1930 had 1,400 branches and 67,000 members. Most women co-operators were the wives of male co-operators, who were usually skilled, relatively well-paid artisans. The co-operators aimed to provide cheap, unadulterated food for their members and to share out their profits through what became known as the 'divi', the dividend, this making society more just and enabling working-class people to help themselves collectively. They established education societies, and took an interest in wider social and political issues. Under the leadership of Margaret Llewellyn Davies from 1889, the Women's Co-operative Guild increasingly encouraged women to take a role in the movement's wider campaigns and to organise for themselves rather than be instructed by philanthropic ladies. As this excerpt reveals, some women found this to be a refreshing change from the 'mother's meetings'. Gillian Scott has argued that the Guild 'rapidly became a source of a new and emancipatory discourse about working-class femininity', through its emphasis on women's capacity for public service, their responsibilities and rights as citizens beyond the confines of the home, and their entitlement to protection from domestic abuse. Llewellyn Davies and the Assistant General Secretary, Mrs Barton, were invited on behalf of the Guild's membership to give evidence to the 1909 Royal Commission on Divorce Law Reform. Most of the membership were opposed to divorce law which continued to enshrine the double standard: the wife had to prove adultery plus cruelty, bigamy, incest or bestiality, whereas adultery alone was grounds enough for the husband to divorce his wife.[4]

9.12 'Women's Trades Unions – II', Woman's Corner, *The Co-operative News* (18 April 1891)

Women played an important role in the new attempts at trade union organisation with the founding of unions for women (and run by women). The excerpt from 'Woman's Corner' of *The Co-operative News* (1891) concerns the Confectioners' Union founded in 1889. It refers to the mechanics of starting a union, as well as the difficult relationship between men and women workers.

9.13 Isabella Ford, *Women and Socialism* (1906)

Women were active in the new socialist parties, the Social Democratic Federation (1884) and the Independent Labour Party (ILP), formed in 1893. Women participated in the ILP as speakers, writers, organisers and fundraisers. Although it is often seen as being a woman-friendly organisation, however, the Party struggled with the women's movement.[5] This is evident in the writing of many socialist-feminists, such as Isabella Ford (1855–1924), who was involved with the Leeds Women's Suffrage Society and the ILP in the 1890s. In *Women and Socialism* (1906), Ford continued her campaign against the prejudices against women's suffrage which divided the Labour movement, arguing that suffrage was necessary for social transformation.

9.14 Enid Stacy, 'A Century of Women's Rights' (1897)

Enid Stacy (1868–1903) saw feminism as a 'middle-class fad', and reflects the hostility to the women's movement of some within the Labour movement. In this excerpt, Stacy describes the impact of the labour movement on feminism, and in so doing caricatures the early feminists as middle-class man-haters who needed to extend their vision to include hardships facing 'ordinary' (working- or lower middle-class and, above all, married) women.

9.1   Barbara Leigh Smith, *A Brief Summary, in Plain Language, of the Most Important Laws of England Concerning Women, Together with a Few Observations Thereon* (1854)

Married women no legal existence.
A man and wife are one person in law; the wife loses all her rights as a single woman, and her existence is, as it were absorbed in that of her husband. He is civilly responsible for her acts; and in some cases for her contracts; she lives under his protection or cover, and her condition is called coverture.

A husband has a right to the person of his wife.
In theory, a married woman's body belongs to her husband; she is in his custody, and he can enforce his right by writ of *habeas corpus*; but in practice this is greatly modified. . . .

Her personal property vests in her husband.
A wife's personal property before marriage (such as stock, shares, money in hand, money at the bank, jewels, household goods, clothes, &c.), becomes absolutely her husband's, unless when settled in trust for her, and he may assign or dispose of it at his pleasure, whether he and his wife live together or not.

He takes her chattels real.
A wife's chattels real (i.e., estates held during a term of years, or the next presentation to a church living, &c.) become her husband's by his doing some act to appropriate them; but, if he does not and the wife survives, she resumes her property. . . .

Equity.
While the Common Law gives the whole of a wife's personal property to her husband, the Courts of Equity, when he proceeds therein to recover property in right of his wife, oblige him to make a settlement of some portion of it upon her, if she be unprovided for and virtuous.

A wife's debts.
A husband is liable for the price of such goods as he allows his wife, as his agent, to order; she may have more power than any other

agent, but her power is of the same kind; for if a wife orders goods without the knowledge of the husband, it is not at all certain that a legal decision will oblige him to pay for them; it mainly depends on what the jury thinks are domestic necessaries, or requisite for the position of the family.

Her right to support.

Neither the Courts of Common Law nor of Equity, have any direct power to oblige a man to support his wife. But the Divorce of Matrimonial Court, granting a judicial separation may decree that the husband shall pay *alimony* to the wife for her support, and when a wife becomes chargeable to the parish, the magistrates may, upon application of the parish officers direct the husband to pay for her maintenance. A wife, whose husband without valid reason refuses to support her, may rent lodgings, take up goods &c., suitable to her station, for which the creditors can compel the husband to pay.

Husband's power over his wife's real property.

A husband has the possession and usafruct of his wife's freehold property during the joint existence of himself and her; that is to say, he has absolute possession of them as long as they both live. If the wife dies without children, the property goes to his heir; but if she has borne a child capable of inheriting her husband holds possession until his death, when it passes to her heir; but on surviving her husband, her freehold reverts to her.

A married woman's earnings not her own but her husband's.

Money earned by a married woman belongs absolutely to her husband; that and all source of income, excepting those mentioned above, are included in the term personal property. And her receipt for the earnings is not legal. The husband can claim the money notwithstanding such payment.

A wife's will.

By the express permission of her husband, a wife can make a will of her personal property; for by such a permission he gives up his right. But he may revoke his leave at any time before *probate* (i.e., the exhibiting and proving a will in Court).

A mother's rights over children.

The legal custody of children belongs to the father. During the life time of a sane father, the mother has no rights over her children, except limited power over infants, and the father may take them from her and dispose of them as he thinks fit. If there be a legal separation of the parents, and there be neither agreement nor order in Court, giving the custody of the children to either parent, then the *right to the custody of the child* (except for the nutriment of infants) belongs legally to the father.

(London: John Chapman, 1854, pp. 6–7)

9.2 Caroline Norton [Pearse Stevenson Esq], *A Plain Letter to the Lord Chancellor on the Infant Custody Bill* (1839)

The other case in which Serjeant Talfourd was employed (as counsel for the husband), was that of Mrs. Greenhill, who afterwards presented a petition to the House of Commons, and the report of whose painful history may be briefly copied here. . . .

On the morning of Thursday, the 5th November, the petition in Chancery was heard by the Vice-Chancellor, and six affidavits were read before him, the substance of which was as follows: –

That Mr. Greenhill had, as already stated, carried on an adulterous connection with Mrs. Graham, for more than a twelvemonth; and that *he positively refused to part with her* (although he affirmed, that he had expressed his regret and contrition to his wife, and made overtures of reconciliation); that on being told by his wife that she had heard he had taken a house for three years for this woman, he replied, 'it was no business of *hers* if he had taken it for ten years;' that he allowed Mrs. Graham to take his wife's name, and call herself 'Mrs. Greenhill;' and at other times *he* called himself 'Mr. Graham;' and that he desired the servant, who also occasionally waited on his wife, to wait on this woman, and drive her out in his cab; that he left his wife at Weymouth, to go and live with Mrs. Graham at Portsmouth; and that he took her with him in his yacht, &c.: in short, that as to the act of adultery it was neither attempted to be concealed or denied; but, on the contrary, he had admitted it to his wife's uncle and other relatives, and expressed his determination to persist in the intimacy he had formed.

That Mrs. Greenhill firmly believed, that her children, if taken from her, would be *prevented from seeing her*, and delivered over to her husband's mother, Mrs. Mary Tyler Greenhill; that the said Mrs. Mary Tyler Greenhill had not only abused and quarrelled with her daughter-in-law, and refused to see her grandchildren, but that she had been at law for years *with her own son*; and that so bitter was their estrangement, that Mr. Greenhill had said to a friend who advised him to be reconciled to his mother, that such reconciliation was *impossible*; and that they were, in fact, *only drawn together by the anger of Mr. Greenhill against his wife, and since the quarrel between the parties.* That for these, and other reasons, neither Mrs. M. Tyler Greenhill, nor Mr. Greenhill himself, were fit persons to have the custody of these infant children, and that their mother *was* a fit and proper person, and *neither her husband, nor any other person, alleged anything to the contrary, nor had there been at any time a shadow of imputation against her.* That Mrs. Greenhill's own mother, Mrs. Macdonald (who had always been on good terms with her son-in-law, and had shewn him great affection, especially in nursing him through the cholera, when every one else, from fear or prudence, withdrew from the house), *was willing to receive his wife and children; to give them a permanent home with her; and was also willing that the father should come and visit his children, at her house, as often as he pleased.* That Mrs. G. was fondly and devotedly attached to her little girls, and had never been separated from them; and that the father had always been in the habit of leaving them under her sole custody and control during his absence from home; and though it was affirmed, on the one hand, that Mr. Greenhill was a fond and attentive father, yet it was sworn in contradiction, that one of the little children being brought into the room with several strangers, asked Mrs. Greenhill's uncle, 'if *he* was papa,' from which it was argued, that they had *not* been in the frequent habit of seeing him, since his connection with Mrs. Graham. Finally, it was sworn, that Mrs. Greenhill had always fulfilled, to the utmost, her duties as a wife and mother; and that there was no possible ground for depriving her of her three little girls, but, on the contrary, every reason why she should be permitted the care of them; and that her health, already very delicate, had suffered so much from the terror, agony, and sorrow, which she had lately endured, that it was expected she would sink under the blow (if inflicted) of that forcible separation.

All this having been sworn, the Vice-Chancellor gave an adverse decision, and dismissed the petition; the mother's separate claim not being acknowledged by the Court.

(London: James Ridgway, 1839, pp. 60–65)

9.3   Frances Power Cobbe, 'What shall we do with our old maids?' (1862)

There is, however, an actual ratio of thirty percent of women now in England who never marry, leaving one-fourth of both sexes in a state of celibacy. This proportion further appears to be constantly on the increase. It is obvious that these facts call for a revision of many of our social arrangements. The old assumption that marriage was the sole destiny of woman, and that it was the business of her husband to afford her support, is brought up short by the statement that one woman in four is certain not to marry, and that three millions of women earn their own living at this moment in England. We may view the case two ways: either –

1st. We must frankly accept this new state of things, and educate women and modify trade in accordance therewith, so as to make the condition of celibacy as little injurious as possible; or, –

2nd. We must set ourselves vigorously to stop the current which is leading men and women away from the natural order of Providence. We must do nothing whatever to render celibacy easy or attractive; and we must make the utmost efforts to promote marriage by emigration of women to the colonies, and all other means in our power.

The second of these views we shall consider first. It may be found to colour the ideas of a vast number of writers and to influence essentially the decisions made on many points – as the admission of women to university degrees, to the medical profession, and generally to free competition in employment. Lately it has met a powerful and not unkindly exposition in an article in a contemporary quarterly, entitled, 'Why are Women Redundant?' Therein it is plainly set forth that all efforts to make celibacy easy for women are labours in the wrong direction, and are to be likened to the noxious exertions of quacks to mitigate the symptoms of disease, and allow the patient to persist in his evil courses. The root of the malady should be struck at, and marriage, the only true vocation for women, promoted at any cost, even by the most enormous schemes for the deportation of 44,000 females. . . .

A little deeper reflection, however, discloses a very important point which has been dropped out of the argument. Marriage is, indeed, the happiest and best condition for mankind. But does anyone think that all marriages are so? When we make the assertion that marriage is good and virtuous, do we mean a marriage of interest, a marriage for wealth, for position, for rank, for support? Surely nothing of the kind. Such marriages as these are the sources of misery and sin, not of happiness and virtue; naturally, their moral character, to be fitly designated, would require stronger words than we care to use. There is only one kind of marriage which makes good the assertion that it is the right and happy condition for mankind, and that is a marriage founded on free choice, esteem, and affection – in one word, on love. . . .

Let the employments of women be raised and multiplied as much as possible, let their labour be as fairly remunerated, let their education be pushed as high, let their whole position be made as healthy and happy as possible, and there will come out once more, here as in every other department of life, the triumph of the Divine laws of our nature. Loving marriages are (we cannot doubt) what God has designed, not marriages of interest. When we have made it less women's interest to marry, we shall indeed have less and fewer interested marriages, with all their train of miseries and evils. But we shall also have more *loving* ones, founded on free choice and free affection. Thus we arrive at the conclusion that for the very end of promoting marriage – that is, such marriage as it is alone possible to promote – we should pursue a precisely opposite course to that suggested by the reviewer or his party. Instead of leaving single woman as helpless as possible, and their labour as ill-rewarded – instead of dinning into their ears from childhood that marriage is their one vocation and concern in life, and securing afterwards if they miss it that they shall find no other vocation or concern; – instead of this, we shall act exactly on the reverse principle. We shall make single life so free and happy that they shall not have one temptation to change it save the only temptation which *ought* to determine them – namely, love. . . .

(In Frances Power Cobbe, *Essays on the Pursuits of Women,*
reprinted from Fraser's and Macmillan's Magazines
(London: Emily Faithfull, 1863), pp. 58–101, here pp. 59–64)

9.4 Dr Elizabeth Garrett Anderson, 'Sex and Mind in Education: a Reply', *The Fortnightly Review*, Vol. XV (1874)

Is it true, or is it a great exaggeration, to say that the physiological differences between men and women seriously interferes with the chances of success a woman would otherwise possess? We believe it to be very far indeed from the truth. When we are told that in the labour of life women cannot disregard their special physiological functions without danger to health, it is difficult to understand what is meant, considering that in adult life healthy women do as a rule disregard them almost completely. It is, we are convinced, a great exaggeration to imply that women of average health are periodically incapacitated from serious work by the facts of their organization. Among poor women, where all the available strength is spent upon manual labour, the daily work goes on without intermission, and, as a rule, without ill effects. For example, do domestic servants, either as young girls or in mature life, show by experience that a marked change in the amount of work expected from them must be made at these times unless their health is to be injured? It is well known that they do not . . .

The case is, we admit, very different during early womanhood, when rapid growth and the development of new functions have taxed the nutritive powers more than they are destined to be taxed in mature life. At this age a temporary sense of weakness is doubtless much more common than it is later in life, and where it exists wise guardians and teachers are in the habit of making allowances for it, and of encouraging a certain amount of idleness. This is, we believe, as much the rule in the best English schools as it is in private school-rooms and homes. . . . While, too, we would not deny that very great pressure of mental work at this age is to be deprecated, we believe that practically the risk of injury from undue or exceptional physical fatigue at an inopportune moment is much greater. Riding, long standing, lifting heavy weights – e.g. young brothers or sisters – dancing, and rapid or fatiguing walks are, we believe, the chief sources of risk to delicate girls at these times, and of them all riding is probably much the most serious. The assertion that, as a rule, girls are unable to go on with an ordinary amount of quiet exercise or mental work during these periods, seems to us to be entirely contradicted by experience. . . .

Even were the dangers of continual mental work as great at Dr Maudsley thinks they are, the dangers of a life adapted to develop only the socially and consciously feminine side of the girl's nature would be much greater. From the purely physiological point of view, it is difficult to believe that study much more serious than that usually pursued by young men could do a girl's health as much harm as a life directly calculated to over-stimulate the emotional and sexual instincts, and to weaken the guiding and controlling forces which these instincts so imperatively need. The stimulus found in novel-reading, in the theatre and ball-room, the excitement which attends a premature entry into society, the competition of vanity and frivolity, these involve far more real dangers to the health of young women than the competition for knowledge, or for scientific and literary honours, ever has done, or is ever likely to do. And even if, in the absence of a real culture, dissipation be avoided, there is another danger still more difficult to escape, of which the evil physical results are scarcely less grave, and this is dullness. It is not easy for those whose lives are full to overflowing of the interests which accumulate as life matures, to realize how insupportably dull the life of a young woman just out of the schoolroom is apt to be, nor the powerful influence for evil this dullness has upon her health and morals. There is no tonic in the pharmacopoeia to be compared with happiness, and happiness worth calling such is not known where the days drag along filled with make-believe occupations and dreary sham amusements.

(London: Chapman and Hall, 1874, pp. 582–594, here pp. 585–591)

9.5   The Ladies' Protest Against the Contagious Diseases Acts, *Daily News*, 1 January 1870

There are two Acts of Parliament – one passed in 1866, the other in 1869 – called the Contagious Diseases Acts. These Acts are in force in some of our garrison towns, and in large districts around them. Unlike all other laws for the repression of contagious diseases, to which both men and women are liable, these two apply to women only, men being wholly exempt from their penalties. The law is ostensibly framed for a certain class of women, but in order to reach these, all the women residing in the districts where it is in force are brought under the provisions of the Acts. Any woman can be dragged into court, and required to prove that she is not a common prostitute. The magistrate can condemn her, if a policeman swears only that he 'has good cause to believe' her to be one. The accused has to rebut, not positive evidence, but the state of mind of her accuser. When condemned, the sentence is as follows: To have her person outraged by the periodical inspection of a surgeon, through a period of twelve months; or, resisting that, to be imprisoned, with or without hard labour – first for a month, next for three months – such imprisonment to be continuously renewed through her whole life, unless she submit periodically to the brutal requirements of this law. Women arrested under false accusations have been so terrified at the idea of encountering the public trial necessary to prove their innocence, that they have, under the intimidation of the police, signed away their good name and their liberty by making, what is called a 'voluntary submission', to appear periodically for twelve months, for surgical examination. Women who, through dread of imprisonment, have been induced to sign the 'voluntary submission', which enrols them in the ranks of common prostitutes, now pursue their traffic under the sanction of Parliament; and the houses where they congregate, so long as the Government surgeons are satisfied with the health of their inmates, enjoy, practically, as complete a protection as a church or school.

We, the undersigned, enter our solemn protest against these Acts.

1st. – Because, involving as they do such a momentous change in the legal safeguards hitherto enjoyed by women in common with men, they have been passed, not only without the knowledge of the country, but unknown, in a great measure, to Parliament itself; and we hold that neither the Representatives of the People, nor the Press, fulfil the duties which are expected of them, when they allow such legislation to take place without the fullest discussion.

2nd. – Because, so far as women are concerned, they remove every guarantee of personal security which the law has established and held sacred, and put their reputation, their freedom, and their persons absolutely in the power of the police.

3rd. – Because the law is bound, in any country professing to give civil liberty to its subjects, to define clearly an offence which it punishes.

4th. – Because it is unjust to punish the sex who are the victims of a vice, and leave unpunished the sex who are the main cause, both of the vice and its dreaded consequences; and we consider that liability to arrest, forced medical treatment, and (where this is resisted) imprisonment with hard labour, to which these Acts subject women, are punishments of the most degrading kind.

5th. – Because, by such a system, the path of evil is made more easy to our sons, and to the whole of the youth of England; inasmuch as a moral restraint is withdrawn the moment the State recognises, and provides convenience for, the practice of a vice which it thereby declares to be necessary and venial.

6th. – Because these measures are cruel to the women who come under the action – violating the feelings of those whose sense of shame is not wholly lost, and further brutalising even the most abandoned.

7th. – Because the disease which these Acts seek to remove has never been removed by any such legislation. The advocates of the system have utterly failed to show, by statistics or otherwise, that these regulations have in any case, after several years' trial, and when applied to one sex only, diminished disease, reclaimed the fallen, or improved the general morality of the country. We have, on the contrary, the strongest evidence to show that in Paris and other Continental cities where women have long been outraged by this system, the public health and morals are worse than at home.

8th. – Because the conditions of this disease, in the first instance, are moral, not physical. The moral evil through which the disease makes its way separates the case entirely from that of the plague, or other scourges, which have been placed under police control or sanitary care. We hold that we are bound, before rushing into experiments of legalising a revolting vice, to try to deal with the *causes* of the evil, and we dare to believe that with wiser teaching and more capable legislation, those causes would not be beyond control.

(Published in Josephine Butler, *Personal Reminiscences of a Great Crusade* (London: Horace Marshall and Son, 1896), pp. 17–19)

9.6   Christabel Pankhurst, *The Great Scourge and How to End It* (1913)

For women the question of venereal disease has a special and a tragic interest. It strikes at them in their own person and through their children. A woman infected by syphilis not only suffers humiliation and illness which may eventually take the most revolting form, but is in danger of becoming the mother of deformed, diseased, or idiot children. Why are such children born into the world? Women have often cried in despair. The answer is – Syphilis! Miscarriage is frequently caused by the same disease. Indeed nothing, as one doctor says, is so murderous to the offspring as syphilis.

Rather different, though hardly less terrible where women are concerned, is the effect of gonorrhoea. In future chapters we deal more fully with this matter. Here we may say that gonorrhoea is one of the most prevalent of all diseases. It is acquired before marriage by 75 per cent. or 80 per cent. of men, and it is very often contracted after marriage by men as are not entirely faithful to their wives. To men the disease gives comparatively little trouble, and in the old days the doctors made very light of it.

But to a woman, owing to their physiological structure, it is one of the gravest of all diseases. A very large number are infected by their husbands with gonorrhoea. The common result is sterility, which prevents the birth of any child, or may prevent the birth of more than one child. Race suicide!

Generally speaking, the female ailments which are urged by some ignoble men as a reason against the enfranchisement of women are not due to natural weakness, but – to gonorrhoea. Women – and there are so many of them – who 'have never been well since they married', are victims of gonorrhoea.

An enormous percentage of the operations upon women are necessitated by this disease, which in many cases so affects the organs of maternity as to necessitate their complete removal. Race Suicide again.

These are awful truths, so awful that the woman's instinct is to keep them hidden, until she realises that only by making these truths known can this appalling state of affairs be brought to an end.

Women have suffered too much from the conspiracy of silence to allow that conspiracy to last one minute longer. It has been an established and an admitted rule in the medical profession to keep a wife in ignorance of the fact that she has become the victim of venereal disease. A bride struck down in illness within a few days, or within a few weeks, of her wedding day is told by her husband and the doctor that she is suffering from appendicitis, and under cover of this lie her sex organs are removed without her knowledge. Women whose husbands contract syphilis, and are in turn infected, are kept in ignorance of this, and are thus unable to protect themselves and to do their duty by the future. . . .

Sexual disease, we say again, is due to the subjection of woman. It is due, in other words, to the doctrine that woman is sex and beyond that nothing. Sometimes this doctrine is dressed up in the saying that women are mothers and beyond that nothing. What a man who says that really means is that women are created primarily for the sex gratification of men, and secondarily, for the bearing of children if he happens to want them, but of no more children than he wants.

As the result of this belief the relation between man and woman has centred in the physical. What is more, the relation between man and woman has been that of an owner and his property – of a master and his slave – not the relation of two equals.

From that evil has sprung another. The man is not satisfied to be in relation with only one slave; he must be in relation with many. That is to say, sex promiscuity has arisen, and from that has in its turn come disease.

And so at the beginning of the twentieth century in civilised Britain we have the doctors breaking through the secrecies and traditions of long years, and sounding the note of alarm. This canker of venereal disease is eating away the vitals of the nation, and the only cure is Votes for Women, which is to say recognition of the freedom and human equality of women.

(London: E. Pankhurst, 1913, pp. 16–21)

9.7   Elizabeth Blackwell, 'On the Abuses of Sex – II. Fornication' (1902)

One of the first subjects to be investigated by the Christian physiologist is the truth or error of the assertion so widely made, that sexual passion is a much stronger force in men than in women. Very remarkable results have flowed from the attempts to mould society upon this assertion. A simple Christian might reply, 'Our religion makes no such distinction; male and female are as one under guidance and judgment of the Divine law.' But the physiologist must go farther, and use the light of principles underlying physical truth in order to understand the meaning of facts which arraign and would destroy Christianity . . .

The affectionate husbands of refined women often remark that their wives do not regard the distinctively sexual act with the same intoxicating physical enjoyment that they themselves feel, and they draw the conclusion that the wife possesses no sexual passion. A delicate wife will often confide to her medical adviser (who may be treating her for some special suffering) that at the very time when marriage seems to unite them most closely, when her husband's welcome kisses and caresses seem to bring them into profound union, comes an act which mentally separates them, and which may be either indifferent or repugnant to her. But it must be understood that it is not the special act necessary for parentage which is the measure of the compound moral and physical power of sexual passion; it is the profound attraction of one nature to the other which marks passion, and delight in kiss and caress – the love-touch – is physical sexual expression as much as the special act of the male.

It is well known that terror or pain in either sex will temporarily destroy all physical pleasure. In married life, injury from childbirth, or brutal or awkward conjugal approaches, may cause unavoidable shrinking from sexual congress, often wrongly attributed to absence of sexual passion. But the severe and compound suffering experienced by many widows who were strongly attached to their lost partners is also well known to the physician, and this is not simply a mental loss that they feel, but an immense physical deprivation. It is a loss which all the senses suffer by the physical as well as moral void which death has created.

Although physical sexual pleasure is not attached exclusively, or in women chiefly, to the act of coition, it is also a well-established fact that in healthy loving women, uninjured by the too frequent lesions which result from childbirth, increasing physical satisfaction attaches to the ultimate physical expression of love. A repose and general well-being results from this natural occasional intercourse, whilst the total deprivation of it produces irritability. . . .

The comparison so often drawn between the physical development of the comparatively small class of refined and guarded women, and the men of worldly experience whom they marry, is a false comparison. These women have been taught to regard sexual passion as lust and as sin – a sin which it would be a shame for a pure woman to feel, and which she would die rather than confess. She has not been taught that sexual passion is love, even more than lust, and that its ennobling work in humanity is to educate and transfigure the lower by the higher element. The growth and indications of her own nature she is taught to condemn, instead of to respect them as foreshadowing that mighty impulse towards maternity which will place her nearest to the Creator if reverently accepted. But if the comparison be made between men and women of loose lives – not women who are allowed and encouraged by money to carry on a trade in vice, but men and women of similar unrestrained loose life – the unbridled impulse of physical lust is as remarkable in the latter as in the former. The astounding lust and cruelty of women uncontrolled by spiritual principle is a historical fact. . . .

In forming a wiser judgment for future guidance, it must be distinctly recognised that the assertion that sexual passion commands more of the vital force of men than of women is a false assertion, based upon a perverted or superficial view of the facts of human nature. Any custom, law, or religious teaching based upon this superficial and essentially false assertion, must necessarily be swept away with the prevalence of sounder physiological views.

(From *Essays in Medical Sociology* (London: Ernest Bell, 1902), Vol. 1, pp. 44–59, here pp. 47, 52–55, 58)

9.8   J. S. Mill, Speech to the House of Commons on the subject of women's suffrage, 20 May 1867

... We talk of political revolutions, but we do not sufficiently attend to the fact that there has taken place around us a silent domestic revolution: women and men are, for the first time in history, really each other's companions. Our traditions respecting the proper relations between them have descended from a time when their lives were apart – when they were separate in their thoughts, because they were separate equally in their amusements and in their serious occupations. In former days a man passed his life among men; all his friendships, all his real intimacies, were with men; with men alone did he consult on any serious business; the wife was either a plaything, or an upper servant. All this, among the educated classes, is now changed. The man no longer gives his spare hours to violent outdoor exercises and boisterous conviviality with male associates: the two sexes now pass their lives together; the women of a man's family are his habitual society; the wife is his chief associate, his most confidential friend, and often his most trusted adviser. Now, does a man wish to have for his nearest companion, so closely linked with him, and whose wishes and preferences have so strong a claim on him, one whose thoughts are alien to those which occupy his own mind – one who can neither be a help, a comfort, nor a support, to his noblest feelings and purposes? Is this close and almost exclusive companionship compatible with women's being warned off all large subjects – being taught that they ought not to care for what it is men's duty to care for, and that to have any serious interests outside the household is stepping beyond their province? Is it good for a man to live in complete communion of thoughts and feelings with one who is studiously kept inferior to himself, whose earthly interests are for-cibly confined within four walls, and who cultivates, as a grace of character, ignorance and indifference about the most inspiring sub-jects, those among which his highest duties are cast? Does any one suppose that this can happen without detriment to the man's own character? Sir, the time is now come when, unless women are raised to the level of men, men will be pulled down to theirs. The women of a man's family are either a stimulus and a support to his highest aspirations, or a drag upon them. You may keep them ignorant of politics, but you cannot prevent them from concerning themselves with the least respectable part of politics – its personalities; if they do not understand and cannot enter into the man's feelings of public duty, they do care about his personal interest, and that is the scale into which their weight will certainly be thrown. They will be an influence always at hand, co-operating with the man's selfish promptings, lying in wait for his moments of moral irresolution, and doubling the strength of every temptation. Even if they maintain a modest forbearance, the mere absence of their sympathy will hang a dead-weight on his moral energies, making him unwilling to make sacrifices which they will feel, and to forego social advantages and successes in which they would share, for objects which they cannot appreciate. Supposing him fortunate enough to escape any actual sacrifice of conscience, the indirect effect on the higher parts of his own character is still deplorable. Under an idle notion that the beauties of character of the two sexes are mutually incompatible, men are afraid of manly women; but those who have considered the nature and power of social influences well know, that unless there are manly women, there will not much longer be manly men. When men and women are really companions, if women are frivolous, men will be frivolous; if women care for nothing but personal interest and idle vanities, men in general will care for little else: the two sexes must now rise or sink together. It may be said that women may take interest in great public questions without having votes; they may, certainly; but how many of them will? Education and society have exhausted their power in inculcating on women that their proper rule of conduct is what society expects from them; and the denial of the vote is a proclamation intelligible to every one, that whatever else society may expect, it does not expect that they should concern them-selves with public interests. Why, the whole of a girl's thoughts and feelings are toned down by it from her schooldays; she does not take the interest even in national history which her brothers do, because it is to be no business of hers when she grows up. If there are women –

and now happily there are many – who do interest themselves in these subjects, and do study them, it is because the force within is strong enough to bear up against the worst kind of discouragement, that which acts not by interposing obstacles, which may be struggled against, but by deadening the spirit which faces and conquers obstacles.

> (Reprinted in Ann P. Robson and John M. Robson, *Sexual Equality: Writings by John Stuart Mill, Harriet Taylor Mill, and Helen Taylor* (Toronto: University of Toronto, 1994) pp. 234–246, here pp. 238–240)

9.9   Barbara Bodichon, *Reasons For and Against the Enfranchisement of Women* (1869)

There are now a very considerable number of open-minded, unprejudiced people, who see no particular reason why women should not have votes, if they want them; but, they ask, what would be the good of it? What is there that women want which male legislators are not willing to give?

. . . [A]mong all the reasons for giving women votes, the one which appears to me the strongest, is that of the influence it might be expected to have in increasing public spirit. Patriotism, a healthy, lively, intelligent interest in everything which concerns the nation to which we belong, and an unselfish devotedness to the public service, – these are the qualities which make a people great and happy; these are the virtues which ought to be most sedulously cultivated in all classes of the community. And I know no better means, at this present time, of counteracting the tendency to prefer narrow private ends to the public good, than this of giving to all women, duly qualified, a direct and conscious participation in political affairs. Give some women votes, and it will tend to make all women think seriously of the concerns of the nation at large, and their interest having once been fairly roused, they will take pains, by reading and by consultation with persons better informed than themselves, to form sound opinions. As it is, women of the middle class occupy themselves but little with anything beyond their own family circle. They do not consider it any concern of theirs, if poor men and women are ill-nursed in the workhouse infirmaries, and poor children are ill-taught in workhouse schools. If the roads are bad, the drains neglected, the water poisoned, they think it is all very wrong, but it does not occur to them that it is their duty to get it put right. These farmer-women and business-women have honest, sensible minds and much practical experience, but they do not bring their good sense to bear upon public affairs, because they think it is men's business, not theirs, to look after such things. It is this belief – so narrowing and deadening in its influence – that the exercise of the franchise would tend to dissipate. The mere fact of being called upon to enforce an opinion by a vote, would have an immediate effect in awakening a healthy sense of responsibility. As far as experience goes, the power women have had as householders to vote at the School Board Elections has been an unmixed good. It has certainly drawn public attention to the education of girls, and, in many places, has awakened an ardent interest in new subjects among women themselves, by the simple fact that they have had to discuss the different opinions of the candidates. There is no reason why these women should not take an active interest in all the social questions – education, public health, prison discipline, the poor laws, and the rest – which occupy Parliament, and they would be much more likely to do so, if they felt that they had importance in the eyes of members of Parliament, and could claim a hearing for their opinions.

. . . Everything, I say again, should be done to encourage this most important and increasing class to take their place in the army of workers for the common good, and all the forces we can bring to bear for this end are of incalculable value. For by bringing women into hearty co-operation with men, we gain the benefit not only of their work, but of their intelligent sympathy. Public spirit is like fire: a feeble spark of it may be fanned into a flame, or it may very easily be put out. And the result of teaching women that they have nothing to do with politics, is that their influence goes towards extinguishing the unselfish interest – never too strong – which men are disposed to take in public affairs.

(Published in London, 1872, pp. 3, 5–9)

9.10 Sylvia Pankhurst, *The Suffragette Movement: An Intimate Account of Persons and Ideals* (1931)

The brief truce before the withdrawal of the Reform Bill and its amendments, was followed by destructive militancy on a hitherto unparalleled scale, petty injuries and annoyances continuing side by side with large-scale damage. Street lamps were broken, Votes for Women was painted on the seats at Hampstead Heath, keyholes were stopped up with lead pellets, house numbers were painted out, chairs flung in the Serpentine, cushions of railway carriages slashed, flower-beds damaged, golf greens all over the country scraped and burnt with acid. A bowling green was cut in Glasgow, the turf in Duthie Park, Aberdeen. A mother and daughter, bearing an ancient name, spent much of their time travelling in trains in order to drop pebbles between the sashes of carriage windows, hoping the glass would smash on being raised. Old ladies applied for gun licences to terrify the authorities. Bogus telephone messages were sent calling up the Army Reserves and Territorials. Telegraph and telephone wires were severed with long-handled clippers; fuse boxes were blown up, communication between London and Glasgow being cut for some hours. There was a window-smashing raid in West End club-land; the Carlton, the Junior Carlton, the Reform Club and others being attacked. A large envelope containing red pepper and snuff was sent to every Cabinet Minister; the Press reported that they all fell victims to the ruse. Boat-houses and sports pavilions in England, Ireland and Scotland, and a grand-stand at Ayr race-course were burnt down. Mrs. Cohen, a Leeds member of the deputation to Lloyd George, broke the glass of a jewel-case in the Tower of London. Works of art and objects of exceptional value became the target of determined militants. Thirteen pictures were hacked in the Manchester Art Gallery. Refreshment pavilions were burnt down in Regent's Park and Kew Gardens, where the glass in three orchid houses was smashed, and the plants, thus exposed, were broken and torn up by the roots. Empty houses and other unattended buildings were systematically sought out and set on fire, and many were destroyed, including Lady White's house near Staines, a loss of £4,000, Rough-wood House, Chorley Wood, and a mansion at St Leonard's valued at £10,000. There were fires at several houses in Hampstead Garden Suburb, at the Suburb Free Church, at Abercarn Church, Monmouthshire, in the Shipcoat Council Schools, at South Bromley Station on the London underground, and in a wood yard at Walham Green. Hugh Franklin set fire to an empty railway carriage; he was imprisoned and forcibly fed. An old cannon was fired near Dudley Castle, shattering glass and terrifying the neighbourhood. Bombs were placed near the Bank of England, at Wheatley Hall, Doncaster, at Oxted Station, and on the steps of a Dublin Insurance Office. Lloyd George's new house in process of erection at Walton-on-the-

Hill was injured beyond repair by a bomb explosion. The story of a motor-car passing through the village at 4 a.m., two broken hat-pins, a hairpin, and a galosh indisputably feminine, found on the site, were the only traces of the incendiaries, Emily Wilding Davison and others, all of whom escaped undiscovered. That this was the work of the Suffragettes was usually made evident by literature deposited in the vicinity. In most cases the culprits had altogether disappeared and no clue to their identity was left. Where a capture was effected, the punishment varied considerably: up to nine months for breaking windows or the glass covering pictures; eighteen months or two years for arson.

(London: Longmans, 1931, pp. 433–435)

9.11 'A Guildswoman', in Margaret Llewellyn Davies (ed.), *Life as We Have Known It* (1931)

Another Guildswoman wrote: 'I used for a short time to attend a Mothers' Meeting, and did so more from a point of duty than any-thing, but after joining the Guild I did not feel to have patience to listen to the simple childish tales that were read at the former, and did not like to feel we had no voice in its control. There is such a different feeling in speaking of trials and troubles to Guilders (where they are real) than to speak to the ladies of the Mothers' Meeting. You know that they have a fellow-feeling being all on an equality, but there is the feeling in speaking to the ladies that after consulting this one, that one and somebody else, a little charity might be given – the tradesman perhaps who has always had your custom in better circumstances, he knows all about your business when you present your charity ticket. This sort of thing to honest working people hurts their feelings of independence, but when co-operators help them it is done in a different way.'

... The education I got in the Guildroom made me understand more about the laws of the country. So when I was ready to buy my house I had put the mortgage in my name. This caused a little friction between my husband and myself. He thought that although I had earned and saved the money, the house should certainly be bought in his name. He said it did not look respectful for a woman's name to be put on the deeds when she had a husband alive. I thought different, and so the house is mine.

Sometimes my husband rather resented the teachings of the Guild. The fact that I was determined to assert my right to have the house in my name was a charge against the Guild. The Guild, he said, was making women think too much of themselves. I did not quite agree with him there, though I did and still do think the Guild has been the means of making its members think more of themselves than they ever did before. The Guild's training altered the whole course of my life. When I look back and think what my life might have been without its training and influence, I shudder. I was living in a house with two other families who only ideas in life were work and sleep, and, for recreation, a visit each evening to the public-house or a cheap music hall. They tried very hard to induce me to go with them, and possibly, if I had not been connected with the Guild, when my baby died I might have fallen a victim to the drink habit. It is impossible to say how much I owe the Guild. It gave me education and recreation. The lectures I heard gave me so much food for thought that I seldom felt dull, and I always had something to talk to my husband about other than the little occurrences of daily life. Then I learnt in the Guild that education was to be the workers' best weapon, and I determined if it were at all possible that my son should have as good an education as I could give him. From a shy, nervous woman, the Guild made me a fighter. I was always willing to go on a deputation if there was a wrong to be righted, or for any good cause, local or national.

(*Life as We Have Known It*, by Co-operative Working Women, ed. Margaret Llewellyn Davies (London: Virago, 1982 [1931]), pp. 47–48)

9.12   'Women's Trades Unions – II', Woman's Corner, *The Co-operative News*, 18 April 1891

The East London Confectioners' Trade Union was first formed in the summer of 1889, and it then included both men and women. Somehow this arrangement rarely seems to work well, though it is not very easy to understand why it should not, since the interests of men and women are bound up together. I believe myself that in factories, as elsewhere, men have not yet learned to take women's work quite seriously; and, when a dispute arises among the men, they expect the women to stand by them as a matter of course – but they are not ready to risk anything, in their turn, for the women and girls. Also, as far as I have seen – but I am speaking only of lately-organised trades – the women have a higher notion of comradeship than the men, they have more imagination, they will stick closer together, and they have more pluck; this means that when they have once learned the meaning of discipline, they make better unionists. Mr. Burns, when working a girls' strike last summer, said he had only one complaint against the strikers, 'they couldn't hold their tongues', and even in this respect they have improved since then.

The Confectioners' Union started life as an apparently strong and healthy baby, but there must have been something seriously wrong with its constitution, or with the air into which it was born, for from the first it dwindled and pined until, when it was six months' old, it died. The union broke up and the members received their payments back again; this was in April of last year. But some of the girls had *got the idea*, and when they came up to the Women's Trade Union Association office to take back their money, first one and then another said she wished the union could start again 'without the men'. . . . This second start was a far more humble one than the first; the union was a very wee baby this time. I was not present at the reincarnation meeting, but I heard about it from Miss Black and Miss James; only twelve girls were there, and their fright lest their employer should hear of their doings was pitiful. For some time no one would be first to sign, but at last one exclaimed, 'I don't care, I've been fined a "bob" to-day, I'll sign!' Sign she did: the other eleven followed her, and the union was reconstituted for women and girls only. The very next day there broke out in the factory from which these twelve girls came one of the sudden strikes which are always frequent among ill-paid workers. Had there been no union, this strike would have been crushed in about twenty-four hours; had there been a strong union, it would probably never have happened; as it was, the girls had just the beginning of an organisation to fall back upon, and friends to appeal to for advice. But the strike is a separate story; its immediate effect was to make all the girls in the factory enthusiastic union members, so that from twelve the number rose to four hundred in what seemed no time; but on the other hand, its success made the new members inclined to think everything was going to be plain sailing, and perhaps the millennium had come – a serious mistake to make. So when the inevitable section of idle or stupid girls found that the union demanded honesty and intelligence from its members . . . some of the payments fell off, and many even of the older and steadier young women felt sorely disappointed when they realised that, although they had won a strike and founded a union, they could not yet do away with overwork and underpay. But Miss Black and Miss James preached and worked so well, that when Mr. Burns came over for the first quarterly meeting – and *how* the girls did welcome him – the union was six hundred strong, and so prosperous that it voted, with some triumph, £2 to help the men in starting a branch on their own account. This meeting was the first milestone safely passed, but very soon after it the bitter cold of this winter set in, and the work of extending the union had to stop, its strength was now taxed to stand firm. Work slackened at the factories, so the girls were 'put off' in batches; in July they had decided that no out-of-work pay should weaken the union funds, but it was one thing to make this resolution in July in all the flush of a successful strike, and another thing to stick to it in December and January, in that awful cold. . . . But the girls did stick and meantime the union had been doing its inevitable work of education, so that now there is a central body of young women who begin to understand what organisation is, and who mean business. . . .

March, 1891 Mary Simmons

9.13   Isabella Ford, *Women and Socialism* (1906)

. . . Socialism goes straight to the home, to the heart of the world, in its cry for freedom. Free the home, let the woman be no longer in political subjection, and free the worker, it says; bring light into all the dark homes of the earth so that each one like a torch may spread the light throughout all the world, and by that light we shall then see wisely and clearly how to bring about the social changes we so ardently desire. Reform coming thus from the heart of a nation, must be and will be, of the strongest and most enduring kind. . . .

Everywhere in England we see women fighting for reforms of the same kind as those for which the Labour Party is fighting, and arousing therefore the same opposition from those who prefer stagnation to reform. The women are, of course, generally unconscious as yet of the similarity of their respective aims, and, doubtless, the larger reforms we in the Socialist ranks desire, they do not always understand or wish for. Probably, the word Socialism arouses in some the same dread that it arouses within many men's minds. But, nevertheless, it was a non-Socialist woman Parish Councillor, the late Miss

Jane Escombe, who first lead the way in the direction of land nation-alisation in rural districts. She made her Council build and own cottages on their own land. Women's work is awakening people to see that society must be responsible for the welfare of the individual, because the individual, each one of us who fulfils a duty to the State, is the State (each for all, all for each, we say), and I am convinced they have thus helped immensely, even though unconsciously, to prepare the way for the growth of a Socialism of the best and most enduring kind. Unconscious reformers have sometimes achieved the strongest results. Mary Carpenter, who began the idea of reformatory schools for the young, was no more a Socialist than was Lord Shaftesbury.

The other two political parties know perfectly well that behind the women's demand for the vote lies the demand for a great economic and moral reform, and a reform which will immediately take its place amongst the practical politics of the day. Old-age pensions will not be left any longer on paper, adult suffrage will not have to wait another forty long years, temperance reform will mean something besides mere tinkering, industrial reform will come which will, doubtless, end, as in New South Wales, in a material improvement (unpleasant to the capitalist) in the conditions and wages of working women, when the women's voice is heard in Parliament. . . .

At the heart of every woman who now asks for the vote in all seriousness, lies the conviction that until women possess this power, the deepest moral evils against which the world is perpetually battling can never be crushed or even touched. This is chiefly due to the increasing knowledge of industrial life and conditions which women have gained through their work as Guardians, Factory Inspectors, Sanitary Inspectors, and so forth. It has shown them with a fearful distinctiveness, that the barbarous state of our marriage and divorce laws, of our laws concerning the custody of children, illegal mother-hood and fatherhood, the condition of our streets and factories, etc.: all press most heavily on the lives of *poor* women. It is this knowledge which has stirred in so many women's minds an enthusiasm strong as a religion – to many it is a religion – and a desperate determination that these things shall no longer continue, and, therefore, they have brought the question forward in such a manner that it now has acquired a position of enormous importance in all thinking minds.

(London: ILP, 1906, pp. 3, 8–11)

9.14   Enid Stacy, 'A Century of Women's Rights' (1897)

... The movement was thus in this earlier stage both middle class and individualistic, its chief strength lying in the claim of the individual woman to the right of fighting her way in life and supporting herself by her own exertions. As a natural result, the agitation was almost entirely carried out by unmarried women, and in much that was said and written by them or on their behalf a strong 'anti-man' and 'anti-marriage' tone was observable. The type of woman to be first affected by the movement was not the ordinary, home-loving, unthinking woman, but a more resolute, intellectual, and strongly-marked individual. ... It is not to be wondered at, therefore, that many pioneers of the movement, debarred from domestic life by choice or necessity, engaged in a harassing and uphill conflict with the world (a conflict in which the majority of men, with some honourable exceptions, proved their most bitter opponents), became somewhat hardened in manners and aggressive in tone, and lost occasionally some distinctive graces and charms of womanhood. The comic papers of that day would have been in sad plight had they had no angular, raw-boned, spectacled, gaunt, limply-clad, man-hating spinsters to jeer at. It was certainly unfortunate for the cause that some of its prominent fighters in the early days cared but little for the attractions of the 'outer woman', and it probably delayed progress. Under the circumstances, however, it was inevitable, and to us women of a later day, now enjoying some of the fruits of these brave women's labours, more than pardonable.

The movement was too great to long confine itself to the problem of opening out new careers for unmarried middle-class women. The more clear-sighted friends of the agitation saw that by the very nature of things the majority of women would always be wives and mothers, and that no movement of emancipation would be successful unless it touched the status of the married woman. ...

The results of the working-class agitation of late years upon the Women's Rights Movement have been most marked. It has practically broken it up into two divisions, which, for the sake of convenience, I shall call the Individual Rights and Social Duties sections respectively. The first section represents more of the older influences, which at first gave birth to the movement; it still stands for the ideal of the rights of the individual as against Society, and, applying this to the case of women, clamours for no more factory legislation to 'protect' women's labour, and no interference on the part of the State with a woman's right to earn her livelihood in the way and under the conditions she thinks best. In its attempts to obtain the suffrage for women, it is still concerned in making property ownership or direct taxpaying the sole conditions of citizenship, and the argument best beloved by its adherents is the injustice done to 'a lady of quality, social position, and education, in debarring her from the privilege of voting, whilst her uneducated gardener and dependent can have the right of electing the legislature which will frame the laws she has to obey, though allowed no voice in making them.' This pathetic appeal always enlists the sympathy of the 'ladies of property and education', who belong to this section of the emancipation movement! I do not think I shall be doing any injustice to the Individual Rights section if I call it practically a middle and upper middle class organisation, for I have failed to find that it has any hold upon any considerable section of women belonging to the lower middle or working classes. The second section can, perhaps, hardly be described as one definitely organised body. It is composed rather of many bodies of women, all more or less realising the importance of improving the status of women *in order that they may the better fulfil their duties to Society*. These sections, in their fight for the suffrage, desire it for working women as well as middle-class women, demanding the vote on the ground that wifehood and motherhood in themselves imply the most important civic duties and responsibilities, and to carry out such functions properly for the good of the community, as well as in the name of the individual, the State needs thoughtful, capable women, and that such women can not be obtained under social conditions that tend rather to foster dolls, ignoramuses, or despairing drudges. The franchise is claimed for women *as women*, whether in the capacity of industrial or domestic workers, but not as an end in itself, only as one of the means towards the end, an indispensable means truly, but still only a means.

(In Edward Carpenter (ed.), *Forecasts of the Coming Century* (Manchester: The Labour Press, 1897), pp. 86–102, here pp. 89–91, 94–96)

Notes and further reading

Introduction

1 Jane Austen, *The History of England from the reign of Henry the 4th to the death of Charles the 1st, By a partial, prejudiced, & ignorant Historian* (University of Alberta: Juliet Macmaster, 1995), pp. 1, 2, 6, 18.

2 Although as Miriam Burstein has recently suggested, 'far from being an "alternative" practice, writing about women in history was one of several ways of analyzing the *mainstream*: the progress of civilization, the spread of Christianity, the rise of British nationhood ...' Miriam Burstein, *Narrating Women's History in Britain 1770–1902* (Ashgate, 2004), pp. 1–2. We might therefore (following Lata Mani) see women as the grounds of such histories, rather than its subjects in their own right.

3 Johanna Alberti, *Gender and the Historian* (Harlow, 2002).

4 E. P. Thompson, *The Making of the English Working Class* (Middlesex, 1963).

5 Anna Davin, 'Redressing the balance or transforming the art? The British experience', in S. Jay Kleinburg (ed.), *Retrieving Women's History* (Oxford, 1988), pp. 60–78.

6 Jane Lewis, 'Women, lost and found: the impact of Feminism on history', in Dale Spender (ed.), *Men's Studies Modified* (Oxford, 1981).

7 Sheila Rowbotham, *Hidden from History* (London, 1973); Anne Oakley and Juliet Mitchell (eds), *The Rights and Wrongs of Women* (Middlesex, 1976).

8 Alberti: *Gender and the Historian*, p. 4.

9 Sheila Rowbotham, *Dreams and Dilemmas* (London, 1983), p. 170.

10 By the time of the publication of *Hidden from History*, Rowbotham had already written *Women, Resistance and Revolution* (London, 1972) and *Woman's Consciousness, Man's World* (London, 1973).

11 Martha Vicinus (ed.), *Suffer and Be Still* (Bloomington, 1972); Judith

Walkowitz, *Prostitution in Victorian Society* (Cambridge, 1980); Jane Lewis (ed.), *Labour and Love* (Oxford, 1986); Ellen Ross, *Love and Toil: Motherhood in Outcast London* (New York, 1993).

12 Carroll Smith-Rosenberg, 'The female world of love and ritual', *Signs* 1:3 (Autumn 1975), pp. 1–29; Nancy Cott, *The Bonds of Womanhood* (New Haven, 1977); Ellen Dubois, 'Politics and culture in women's history', *Feminist Studies* 6:1 (Spring 1980); Gerder Lerner, 'Placing women in history: definitions and challenges', *Feminist Studies*, 3:1 (1978), pp. 5–14, and *The Majority Finds Its Past* (Oxford, 1979).

13 Joan Kelly, 'The doubled vision of feminist theory', *Feminist Studies*, 5 (Spring 1979), pp. 216–227; Sheila Rowbotham, 'The trouble with patriarchy', *New Statesman* (December 1979), reprinted in Raphael Samuel (ed.), *People's History and Socialist Theory* (London, 1979), pp. 364–369; Sally Alexander and Barbara Taylor, 'In defence of patriarchy', ibid., pp. 370–373. See also: Sally Alexander, 'Women, class and sexual difference in the 1830s and 1840s: some reflections on the writing of a feminist history', *History Workshop Journal* 17 (Spring 1984), pp. 125–149; Sally Alexander, *Becoming a Woman and Other Essays on 19th and 20th century Feminist History* (London, 1994)

14 Joan Scott, 'Gender: a useful category of historical analysis', *American Historical Review*, 91:5 (1986), pp. 1053–1075; Joan Scott, *Gender and the Politics of History* (New York, 1988). See also: Denise Riley, *'Am I That Name?' Feminism and the Category of 'Woman' in History* (London, 1988).

15 Scott, *Gender and the Politics of History*.

16 Scott, 'Gender: a useful category of historical analysis'; Joan Scott, 'Experience', in J. Scott and J. Butler (eds), *Feminists Theorize the Political* (1992), pp. 22–40.

17 See: Laura Downs, 'If "woman" is just an empty category, why am I afraid to walk the street at night?' *Comparative Studies in Society and History* (1993) and Joan Scott's response and Downs' rejoinder (in the same volume); Karen Offen, Ruth Roach Pierson and Jane Rendall (eds), *Women's History: International Perspectives* (Basingstoke, 1991); Judith Bennet, 'Feminism and history', *Gender & History* 1:3 (1989), pp. 251–272; Judith Walkowitz, 'Patrolling the borders of feminist historiography and the new historicism', *Radical History Review*, 43 (1989), pp. 23–43; Gisela Bock, 'Women's history or gender history: aspects of an international debate', *Gender & History* 1:1 (Spring 1989), pp. 7–30. No. 3 (Autumn 1989); Catherine Hall, 'Politics, poststructuralism and feminist history', *Gender & History* 3:2 (1991), pp. 204–210.

18 Understanding of the ethnocentrism of women's history has come as much from the writing of Black women engaged in feminist politics as from post-structuralist drifts within academia. See: Valerie Amos and Pratibha Parmar, 'Challenging imperial feminism', *Feminist Review* 17

(Autumn 1984), pp. 3–19; Catherine Hall, introduction to *White, Male and Middle Class: Explorations in Feminism and History* (Oxford, 1992).

19 See: L. Bland and L. Doan (eds), *Sexology in Culture* (Cambridge, 1998).

20 See: K. Sangari and S. Vaid (eds), *Recasting Women: Essays in Colonial History* (New Delhi, 1989).

21 Clare Midgley, *Women against Slavery: the British Campaigns, 1780–1870* (London, 1992); Antoinette Burton, *Burdens of History*. See also, Burton, ' "History" is now: feminist theory and the production of historical feminisms', *Women's History Review* 1:1 (1992), pp. 25–39; 'Thinking beyond the boundaries: empire, feminism and the domains of history', *Social History* 26: 1 (January 2001), pp. 60–71.

22 Hall, *White, Male and Middle Class*; Clare Midgley, 'Ethnicity, "Race" and Empire', in J. Purvis (ed.), *Women's History: Britain 1850–1945* (London, 2000 [1995]).

23 Joan Hoff, 'Gender as a postmodern category of paralysis', *Women's History Review* 3:2 (1994), pp. 149–168; Susan Kingsley Kent, 'Mistrials and distribulations: a reply to Joan Hoff', *Women's History Review* 5:1 (1996), pp. 9–18; Caroline Ramazanoglu, 'Unravelling postmodern paralysis: a response to Joan Hoff', *Women's History Review* 5:1 (1996), pp. 19–23; Joan Hoff, 'A reply to my critics', ibid., pp. 25–31.

24 Kathleen Canning, 'Feminist history after the linguistic turn: historicizing discourse and experience', *Signs* 19:2 (Winter 1994), pp. 368–404; Mary Maynard, 'Beyond the "Big Three": the development of feminist theory in the 1990s', *Women's History Review* 4:3 (1995), pp. 259–281.

25 Leonore Davidoff and Catherine Hall, *Family Fortunes: Men and Women of the English Middle Class, 1780–1850* (London, 1987).

26 John Tosh, *A Man's Place. Masculinity and the Middle-Class Home in Victorian England* (London, 1999). See also Tosh, 'What should historians do with masculinity? *History Workshop Journal* 38 (Autumn 1994), pp. 179–202; and 'The Old Adam and the New Man: emerging themes in the history of English Masculinities, 1750–1850', Tim Hitchcock and Michele Cohen (eds), *English Masculinities 1660–1800* (London, 1999), pp. 217–238.

27 Helen Rogers, *Women and the People: Authority, Authorship and the Radical Tradition in Nineteenth-Century England* (Aldershot, 2000).

28 Catherine Hall, *Civilising Subjects: Metropole and Colony in the English Imagination 1830–1867* (Cambridge, 2002).

29 Joan Landes, *Women in the Public Sphere in the Age of Revolution* (New York, 1988).

30 Ann Rossiter, 'In search of Mary's past: placing nineteenth-century Irish immigrant women in British feminist history', Joan Grant (ed.), *Women, Migration and Empire* (Stoke-on-Trent, 1996), pp. 1–30.

31 For Scottish and Welsh women's history, see: Esther Breitenbach and

Eleanor Gordon (eds), *Out of Bounds: Women in Scottish Society, 1800–1945* (Edinburgh, 1992); Angela John, *Our Mother's Land: Chapters in Welsh Women's History* (Cardiff, 1991).

32 Rossiter: 'In search of Mary's past'. While I have included documents on Irish women migrants to England and Scotland, I have not focused on Ireland itself, largely because it is seen by many Irish historians as an appropriative gesture to include Irish history under the British umbrella during the period of political union. This decision was helped nonetheless by the existence of Maria Luddy's documentary history of Irish women (see below).

33 Maria Luddy (ed.), *Women in Ireland, 1800–1918: A Documentary History* (Cork, 1995); Alison Oram and Annmarie Turnbull, *The Lesbian History Sourcebook: Love and Sex Between Women in Britain, 1780–1970* (London, 2001); Ruth and Edmund Frow (eds), *Political Women 1800–1850* (London, 1989); Kathryn Gleadle, *Radical Writing on Women, 1800–1850* (Basingstoke, 2002).

34 *Benchmark Statement for History*, Quality Assurance Agency for Higher Education (2000), para. 18, p. 4.

Further reading

General

Abrams, Lynn, *The Making of Modern Woman* (Harlow, 2002).

Abrams, Lynn, Gordon, Eleanor, Simonton, Deborah and Yeo, Eileen (eds), *Gender in Scottish History* (Edinburgh, 2006).

Alexander, Sally, *Becoming a Woman and Other Essays in 19th and 20th Century Feminist History* (London, 1994).

Beddoe, Deirdre, *Out of the Shadows: A History of Women in Twentieth-century Wales* (Cardiff, 2001).

Breitenbach, Esther and Gordon, Eleanor, *Out of Bounds: Women in Scottish Society, 1800–1945* (Edinburgh, 1992).

Bruley, Sue, *Women in Britain since 1900* (Basingstoke, 1999).

Davidoff, Leonore, *Worlds Between: Historical Perspectives on Gender and Class* (Oxford, 1995).

Gleadle, Kathryn, *British Women in the Nineteenth Century* (Basingstoke, 2001).

John, Angela, *Our Mother's Land: Chapters in Welsh Women's History, 1830–1939* (Cardiff, 1991).

Lewis, Jane, *Women in England 1870–1950* (London, 1984).

Purvis, June, *Women's History: Britain, 1850–1914* (London, 1995).

Shoemaker, Robert, *Gender in English Society 1650–1850: The Emergence of Separate Spheres?* (London, 1988).

Steinbach, Susie, *Women in England, 1760–1914: A Social History* (London, 2004).

Researching and writing women's history

Alberti, Joanna, *Gender and the Historian* (Harlow, 2002).

Beddoe, Deirdre, *Discovering Women's History: A Practical Guide to Researching the Lives of Women Since 1800* 3rd edition (London, 1998).

Bock, Gisela, 'Women's history and gender history: aspects of an international debate', *Gender & History* 1 (1989), pp. 7–30; also in R. Shoemaker and M. Vincent (eds), *Gender & History in Western Europe* (London, 1998), pp. 25–42.

Burton, Antoinette, 'History is now: feminist theory and the production of historical feminisms', *Women's History Review* 1:1 (1992), pp. 25–38.

Davidoff, Leonore and Hall, Catherine, introduction to the revised edition, *Family Fortunes: Men and Women of the English Middle Class 1780–1850* (London, 2002 [1987]), pp. xiii–xlx.

Downs, L. L., *Writing Gender History* (Oxford, 2005).

Gallagher, A.-M., Lubelska, C. and Ryan, L. (eds), *Re-presenting the Past: Women and History* (Harlow, 2001).

Haggis, Jane, 'Gendering colonialism or colonising gender? Recent Women's Studies approaches to White women and the history of British colonialism', in L. Stanley (ed.), Special Issue: British Feminist Histories, *Women's Studies International Forum* 13:1/2 (1990), pp. 105–115.

Hall, Catherine, 'Feminism and feminist history', in *White, Male and Middle Class: Explorations in Feminism and History* (Cambridge, 1992), pp. 1–40.

Lesbian History Group, *Not a Passing Phase: Reclaiming Lesbians in History, 1840–1985* (London, 1988).

Midgley, Clare, 'Introduction. Gender and Imperialism: Mapping the Connections', in C. Midgley (ed.), *Gender and Imperialism* (Manchester, 1998), pp. 1–18.

Newton, Judith, Ryan, Mary and Walkowitz, Judith (eds), *Sex and Class in Women's History* (London, 1983):

Offen, Karen, Roach Pierson, Ruth and Rendall, Jane (eds), *Writing Women's History: International Perspectives* (Basingstoke, 1991).

Purvis, June, 'From "women worthies" to postructuralism? Debate and controversy in women's history in Britain', in J. Purvis (ed.), *Women's History: Britain, 1850–1945. An Introduction* (London, 1995), pp. 1–22.

Scott, Joan W., *Gender and the Politics of History* (New York, 1988).

Scott, Joan W., *Feminism and History* (New York, 1996).

Stanley, Liz, 'Romantic friendship? Some issues in researching lesbian history and biography', *Women's History Review* 1 (1992), pp. 193–216.

Vickery, Amanda, 'Golden Age to separate spheres? A review of the categories and chronology of English women's history', *Historical Journal* 36: 2 (1993), pp. 383–414.

I Making women: enlightenment, evangelical and medical perspectives

1 Henrietta Twycross-Martin, 'Woman supportive or woman manipula-tive? The "Mrs Ellis" woman', in Clarissa Campbell-Orr, *Wollstone-craft's Daughters: Womanhood in England and France, 1780–1920* (Manchester, 1996), pp. 109–120.
2 Sian Rhiannon Williams, 'The true "Cymraes": images of women in women's nineteenth-century Welsh periodicals', in Angela John, *Our Mother's Land: Chapters in Welsh Women's History* (Cardiff, 1991), pp. 69–92.
3 Virginia Woolf, 'Professions for women', reprinted in Michele Barrett (ed.), *Women and Writing* (London, 1979).
4 See Lindy Moore, ' "Education for the woman's sphere": domestic training versus intellectual discipline', in Esther Breitenbach and Eleanor Gordon (eds), *Out of Bounds: Women in Scottish Society, 1800–1945* (Edinburgh, 1992).

Further reading

Enlightenment, evangelicalism, medicine

Davidoff, Leonore and Hall, Catherine, *Family Fortunes: Men and Women of the English Middle Class 1780–1850* (London, 1987).

Jordanova, Ludmilla, *Sexual Visions: Images of Gender in Science and Medicine Between the Eighteenth and Twentieth Centuries* (London, 1989).

Knott, Sara and Taylor, Barbara (eds), *Women, Gender and the Enlighten-ment* (Basingstoke, 2005).

Laqueur, Thomas, *Making Sex: Body and Gender from the Greeks to Freud* (Cambridge, 1992).

Moscucci, O., *The Science of Woman: Gynaecology and Gender in England, 1800–1929* (Cambridge, 1990).

Outram, Dorinda, *The Enlightenment* (Cambridge, 1995).

Rendall, Jane, *The Origins of Modern Feminism: Women in Britain, France and the United states 1780–1860* (Basingstoke, 1985).

Russett, Cynthia E., *Sexual Science: the Victorian Construction of Woman-hood* (Cambridge, 1989).

Showalter, Elaine, *The Female Malady: Women, Madness and English Culture, 1830–1980* (London, 1987).

Vertinsky, P., *The Eternally Wounded Woman: Women, Exercise and Doctors in the Late Nineteenth Century* (Manchester, 1990).

Education

Davin, Anna, *Growing Up Poor: Home, School and Street in London 1870–1914* (London, 1996).

Delamont, Sara and Duffin, Lorna (eds), *Nineteenth-century Woman: Her Cultural and Physical World* (London, 1978).

Dyhouse, Carol, *Girls Growing Up in Late-Victorian and Edwardian England* (London, 1981).

Evans, W. Gareth, *Education and Female Emancipation: the Welsh Experience* (Cardiff, 1990).

Gomersall, Meg, *Working-class Girls in Nineteenth-century England: Life, Work, and Schooling* (Basingstoke, 1997).

Hunt, Felicity (ed.), *Lessons for Life: the Schooling of Girls and Women, 1850–1950* (Oxford, 1987).

Paterson, Fiona and Fewell, Judith (eds), *Girls in their Prime: Scottish Education Revisited* (Edinburgh, 1990).

Purvis, June, *A History of Girls' Education in England* (Milton Keynes, 1991).

Purvis, June, *Hard Lessons: The Lives and Education of Working Women in Nineteenth-century England* (Cambridge, 1989).

2 Middle-class and elite women: domesticity and 'separate spheres'

1   Davidoff and Hall: *Family Fortunes*.

2   Kathryn Gleadle, *British Women in the Nineteenth Century* (Basingstoke, 2001), p. 81.

3   See Alison Twells, 'Missionary domesticity and "woman's sphere" in early nineteenth century England', *Gender & History 18: 2* (2006).

4   Letter to Eliza Fox (1850), J. A. V. Chapple and Arthur Pollard (eds), *The Letters of Mrs Gaskell* (Manchester, 1997 [1966]), p. 106.

5   Roger Fulford, *Dearest Child: Letters Between Queen Victoria and the Princess Royal, 1858–1861* (London, 1964), p. 191.

6   For Joseph and Georgiana Coats, and for reflections on married life and gender roles more broadly, see Eleanor Gordon and Gwyneth Nair, *Public Lives: Women, Family and Society in Victorian Britain* (London, 2003), especially chapter 3, here p. 62.

7   Amanda Foreman, *Georgiana, Duchess of Devonshire* (London, 1998), p. 123.

8   Alison Oram, 'Telling stories about the ladies of Llangollen: the construction of lesbian and feminist histories', in Gallagher, Lubelska and Ryan (eds), *Representing the Past*.

Further reading

Marriage, motherhood and domesticity

Davidoff, Leonore and Hall, Catherine, *Family Fortunes: Men and Women of the English Middle Class, 1780–1850* (London, 1987).

Hammerton, A. James, *Cruelty and Companionship: Conflict in Nineteenth Century Married Life* (London, 1992).

Hughes, Kathryn, *The Short Life and Long Times of Mrs Beeton* (London, 2005).

Jalland, Pat and Hooper, John (eds), *Women from Birth to Death: The Female Life Cycle in Britain 1830–1914* (Brighton, 1986).

Langland, Elizabeth, *Nobody's Angels: Middle-Class Women and Domestic Ideology in Victorian Culture* (Ithaca, 1995).

Schneid Lewis, Judith, *In the Family Way: Childbearing in the British Aristocracy, 1760–1860* (New Brunswick, 1986).

Peterson, M. Jeanne, *Family, Love and Work in the Lives of Victorian Gentlewomen* (Bloomington, 1989).

Szreter, Simon, *Fertility, Class and Gender in Britain, 1860–1914* (Cambridge, 1996).

Vickery, Amanda, 'Golden age to separate spheres? A review of the categories and chronology of English women's history', *Historical Journal*, 36:2 (1993), pp. 383–414.

Love between women and life outside of marriage

Faderman, Lilian, *Surpassing the Love of Men: Romantic Friendship and Love Between Women from the Renaissance to the Present* (London, 1981).

Holden, Kath and Fink, Janet, 'Pictures from the margins of marriage: representations of spinsters and single women in the mid-Victorian novel, inter-war Hollywood melodrama and British film of the 1950s and 1960s', *Gender & History* 11:2 (July 1999), pp. 233–255.

Liddington, Jill, *Presenting the Past: Anne Lister of Halifax 1791–1840* (Hebden Bridge, 1994).

Oram, Alison, 'Telling stories about the Ladies of Llangollen: the construction of lesbian and feminist histories', in A.-M. Gallagher, C. Lubelska and C. Ryan (eds), *Re-presenting the Past: Women and History* (Harlow, 2001).

Vicinus, Martha, *Independent Women: Work and Community for Single Women, 1850–1920* (London, 1985).

3 Philanthropy and politics to 1860

1 Frank Prochaska, *Women and Philanthropy in Nineteenth Century England* (Oxford, 1980), p. 3.
2 Eileen Yeo, *The Contest for Social Science: Relations and Representations of Gender and Class* (London, 1996); Alison Twells, *The Civilising Mission and the English Middle Class, 1792–1857: the Heathen at Home and Overseas* (Basingstoke, forthcoming).
3 Elaine Chalus, ' "To serve my friends": women and political patronage in eighteenth century England', in Amanda Vickery (ed.), *Women, Privilege and Power: British Politics 1750 to the Present* (Stanford, 2001); Chalus, ' "That epidemical madness": women and electoral politics in the late eighteenth century', in H. Barker and E. Chalus (eds), *Gender in Eighteenth Century England* (London, 1997).
4 Kathryn Gleadle, *British Women in the Nineteenth Century* (Basingstoke, 2001), p. 160.
5 Jane Rendall, ' "Women that would plague me with rational conversation": aspiring women and Scottish Whigs, *c.*1790–1830', in Barbara Taylor and Sarah Knott (eds), *Women, Gender and the Enlightenment* (Basingstoke, 2005).

Further reading

Philanthropy

Stott, Anne, *Hannah More: The First Victorian* (Oxford, 2003).
Summers, Anne, *Female Lives, Moral States: Women, Religion and Public Life in Britain 1800–1930* (Berkshire, 2000).
Twells, Alison, *The Civilising Mission and the English Middle Class, 1792–1857: The Heathen at Home and Overseas* (Basingstoke, forthcoming).
Yeo, Eileen Janes, *The Contest for Social Science: Relations and Representations of Gender and Class* (London, 1996).

Politics

Gleadle, Kathryn and Richardson, Sarah (eds), *Women in British Politics 1760–1860: the Power of Petticoat* (Basingstoke, 2000), especially chapters by Cragoe, Gleadle, Morgan and Midgley.
Liddington, Jill, *Female Fortune: Land, Gender and Authority. The Anne Lister Diaries and Other Writings, 1833–36* (London, 1998).
Midgley, Clare, *Women Against Slavery: the British Campaigns, 1780–1870* (London, 1992).

Midgley, Clare, *Feminism, Philanthropy and Empire: Women Activists in Imperial Britain, 1790–1865* (London, forthcoming).

Reynolds, K. D., *Aristocratic Women and Political Society in Victorian Britain* (Oxford, 1998).

Richardson, Sarah, *Middle-class Women and Political Culture in early Nineteenth-Century England* (London, forthcoming).

Vickery, Amanda (ed.), *Women, Privilege and Power: British Politics 1750 to the Present* (Stanford, 2001).

4 Working women and the family wage

1   See Angela V. John, *By the Sweat of Their Brow: Women Workers at Victorian Coal Mines* (London, 1980)

Further reading

Alexander, Sally, 'Women's work in nineteenth-century London', in J. Mitchell and A. Oakley, *The Rights and Wrongs of Women* (Harmondsworth, 1976).

Berg, Maxine, 'What difference did women's work make to the industrial revolution?', *History Workshop Journal* 35 (1993), pp. 22–44.

Berg, Maxine, *The Age of Manufacture: industry, innovation, and work in Britain, 1700–1820* (Oxford, 1985).

Chinn, Carl, *They Worked All Their Lives: Women of the Urban Poor in England, 1880–1939* (Manchester, 1988).

Davidoff, Leonore, *Worlds Between: Historical Perspectives on Gender and Class* (Cambridge, 1995).

Gomersall, Meg, *Working-Class Girls in Nineteenth-Century England: Life, Work and Schooling* (Basingstoke, 1997).

Gordon, Eleanor and Breitenbach, Esther (eds), *The World is Ill-Divided: Women's Work in Scotland in the Nineteenth and Twentieth Centuries* (Edinburgh, 1990).

Higgs, Edward, 'Women, occupation and work in the 19th census', *History Workshop Journal* 23 (1986), pp. 59–80.

Honeyman, Katrina, *Women, Gender and Industrialisation in England, 1700–1870* (Basingstoke, 2000).

Hudson, Pat and Lee, W. R. (eds), *Women's Work and the Family Economy in Historical Perspective* (Manchester, 1990).

John, Angela (ed.), *Unequal Opportunities: Women's Employment in England 1800–1918* (Oxford, 1986).

Roberts, Elizabeth, *Women's Work, 1840–1940* (Basingstoke, 1988).

Rose, Sonya O., *Limited Livelihoods: Gender and Class in Nineteenth Century England* (London, 1992).

Sharpe, Pamela, *Adapting to Capitalism: Working Women in the English Economy, 1700–1850* (Basingstoke, 1995).

Sharpe, Pamela (ed.), *Women's Work: the English Experience, 1650–1914* (London, 1998).

Tilly, Louise A. and Scott, Joan W., *Women, Work and the Family* (London, 1989).

Valenze, Deborah, *The First Industrial Woman* (Oxford, 1995).

Verdon, Nicola, *Rural Women Workers in Nineteenth-Century England* (Woodbridge, 2002).

5 Working-class domestic life

1 Gleadle, *British Women in the Nineteenth Century.*
2 Helen Rogers, 'The father's rights are first in the house': working women on fathers and fatherhood', in H. Rogers and T. Broughton (eds), *Gender and Fatherhood in Britain 1780–1914* (Basingstoke, 2007).
3 Dot Jones, 'Counting the cost of coal: women's lives in the Rhondda, 1881–1911', in Angela John (ed.), *Our Mother's Land: Chapters in Welsh Women's History* (Cardiff, 1991)
4 Barbara Harrison, 'Women and Health', in June Purvis (ed.), *Women's History: Britain, 1850–1945* (London, 1995), p. 171.

Further reading

Bourke, Joanna, 'Housewifery in Working-Class England, 1860–1914', *Past and Present*, 143 (1994), pp. 167–97.

Davin, Anna, 'Imperialism and Motherhood', *History Workshop Journal 5*, (1978) pp. 9–65.

Davin, Anna, *Growing Up Poor: Home, School and Street in London 1870–1914* (London, 1996).

Lewis, Jane (ed.), *Labour and Love: Women's Experience of Home and Family 1850–1940* (Oxford, 1986).

McLaren, Angus, *Birth Control in Nineteenth-Century England* (London, 1978).

Roberts, Elizabeth, *A Woman's Place: An Oral History of Working-Class Women 1890–1940* (Oxford, 1984).

Ross, Ellen, *Love and Toil: Motherhood in Outcast London, 1870–1918* (Oxford, 1993).

Tebbutt, Melanie, *Woman's Talk. A Social History of 'Gossip' in Working-Class Neighbourhoods, 1880–1960* (Aldershot, 1995).

6 Community, politics and religion to 1860

1 See R. Jones, 'Women, community and collective action: the *Ceffyl Pren* tradition', in A. V. John (ed.), *Our Mothers' Land*, pp. 17–42.
2 Charles Redwood, *The Vale of Glamorgan: Scenes and Tales among the Welsh* (London, 1839), pp. 272, 276, 277, 285–286.
3 Catherine Hall, 'The home turned upside down? The working-class family in cotton textiles 1780–1850', in E. Whitelegg, M. Arnot and E. Bartels *et al.*, *The Changing Experience of Women* (Oxford, 1982).
4 See Helen Rogers, *Women and the People: Authority, Authorship and the Radical Tradition in Nineteenth-Century England* (Aldershot, 2000), chapter 3.
5 Clark, Anna, 'The rhetoric of Chartist domesticity: gender, language and class in the 1830s and 1840s', *Journal of British Studies* 31 (1992) pp. 62–88.
6 Deborah Valenze, *Prophetic Sons and Daughters: Female Preaching and Popular Religion in Industrial England* (Princeton, 1985).
7 Eileen Yeo, 'Christianity in Chartist Struggle 1838–1842', *Past & Present* 91 (1981) pp. 109–139.

Further reading

Radical Culture

Clark, Anna, *The Struggle for the Breeches: Gender and the Making of the British Working Class* (Berkeley, 1985).
Rogers, Helen, *Women and the People: Authority, Authorship and the Radical Tradition in Nineteenth-Century England* (Aldershot, 2000).
Schwarzkopf, Jutta, *Women in the Chartist Movement* (Basingstoke, 1992).
Taylor, Barbara, *Eve and the New Jerusalem: Socialism and Feminism in the Nineteenth Century* (London, 1983).

Religion

Malmgreen, Gail, *Religion in the Lives of Englishwomen, 1760–1930* (London, 1986).
Valenze, Deborah, *Prophetic Sons and Daughters: Female Preaching and Popular Religion in Industrial England* (Princeton, 1985).
Walker, Pamela J., *Pulling the Devil's Kingdom Down: The Salvation Army in Victorian Britain* (Berkeley, 2001).

7 Women in diaspora: Irish, Jewish, Black and Asian women in Britain

1   Ann Rossiter, 'In Search of Mary's Past', in J. Grant (ed.), *Women, Migration and Empire* (Stoke-on-Trent, 1996).
2   Lara Marks, *Model Mothers: Jewish Mothers and Maternity Provision in East London, 1870–1939* (Oxford, 1994).
3   Eileen Janes Yeo, 'Gender and Diaspora – Home and Homeland among the Jews in Britain and America', especially pp. 17–24. Copy in author's possession.
4   See Judith Walkowitz, *City of Dreadful Delight: Narratives of Sexual Danger in Late-Victorian London* (London, 1992).
5   Linda Gordon Kuzmack, *Woman's Cause: The Jewish Woman's Movement in England and the United States, 1881–1933* (Ohio, 1990).
6   Peter Fryer, *Staying Power: The History of Black People in Britain* (London, 1984).
7   Joan Grant, 'William Brown and other women: black women in London, *c*.1740–1840', in J. Grant, *Women, Migration and Empire*, pp. 51–72.

Further reading

Burman, Rickie, 'Jewish women and the household economy in Manchester, *c*.1890–1920', in D. Cesarani, *The Making of Modern Anglo-Jewry* (London, 1990).
Burman, Rickie, 'The Jewish woman as breadwinner: the changing value of women's work in a Manchester immigrant community', *Oral History* 10:2 (1982), pp. 27–39.
Burman, Rickie, ' "She looketh well to the ways of her household": the changing role of Jewish women in religious life, *c*.1880–1930', in G. Malmgreen (ed.), *Religion in the Lives of Englishwomen 1760–1930* (London, 1986).
Burton, Antoinette, *At the Heart of Empire: Indians and the Colonial Encounter in Late-Victorian Britain* (London, 1998).
Hollen Lees, Lynn, *Exiles of Erin: Irish Migrants in Victorian London* (Ithaca, 1979).
Gerzina, Gretchen, *Black England: Life Before Emancipation* (London, 1995).
Gerzina, Gretchen, *Black Victorians/Black Victoriana* (New Brunswick, 2003).
Midgley, Clare, 'Ethnicity, "Race" and Empire', in J. Purvis (ed.), *Women's History: Britain 1850–1945* (London, 1995), pp. 247–276.
Salih, Sara, '*The History of Mary Prince*, the black subject, and the black

canon', in B. Carey, M. Ellis, and S. Salih (eds), *Discourses of Slavery and Abolition: Britain and its Colonies, 1760–1838. An Anthology of Critical Essays* (Basingstoke, 2004).

Visram, Rosina, *Ayahs, Lascars and Princes: The Story of Indians in Britain, 1700–1947* (London, 1986).

8 British women and the empire

1 Antionette Burton, 'Rules of thumb: British history and imperial culture in nineteenth- and twentieth-century Britain', *Women's History Review* 3:4 (1994), pp. 483–500.
2 Julia Bush, *Edwardian Ladies and Imperial Power* (Leicester, 2000).
3 Jane Haggis, 'Gendering colonialism or colonising gender? Recent women's studies approaches to white women in the history of colonialism', *Women's Studies International Forum* 13 (1990), pp. 105–115; Haggis, 'White women and colonialism: towards a non-recuperative history', in C. Midgley (ed.), *Gender and Imperialism* (Manchester, 1998), pp. 45–75.
4 J. Buchan, *The Expendable Mary Slessor* (Edinburgh, 1980), p. 195.
5 See Deirdre Coleman's informative introduction to Anna Maria Falconbridge's *Two Voyages*, and the full text itself, in D. Coleman (ed.), *Maiden Voyages and Infant Colonies: Two Women's Travel Narratives of the 1790s* (Leicester, 1999), pp. 1–42.
6 For Maria Graham, see Jane Rendall's entry in E. Ewan, S. Innes, S. Reynolds and R. Pipes (eds), *Biographical Dictionary of Scottish Women* (Edinburgh, 2006).
7 Margaret Macmillan, *Women of the Raj* (London, 1999), p. 206.
8 A. James Hammerton, *Emigrant Gentlewomen* (London, 1979), p. 177.

Further reading

Blunt, Alison, *Travel, Gender and Imperialism: Mary Kingsley in West Africa* (New York, 1994).

Chaudhuri, Nupur and M. Strobel, Margaret, *Western Women and Imperialism: Complicity and Resistance* (Bloomington, 1992).

Hall, Catherine, *White, Male and Middle Class: Explorations in Feminism and History* (Cambridge, 1992).

Hall, Catherine, *Civilising Subjects: Metropole and Colony in the English Imagination 1830–1867* (Cambridge, 2002).

de Groot, Joanna, ' "Sex" and "Race": the construction of language and image in the nineteenth century', in S. Mendus and J. Rendall (eds),

Sexuality and Subordination: Interdisciplinary Studies in Gender in the nineteenth century (London, 1989).

Midgley, Clare (ed.), *Gender and Imperialism* (Manchester, 1998).

Midgley, Clare, *Women Against Slavery: the British Campaigns, 1780–1870* (London, 1992).

Midgley, Clare, *Feminism, Philanthropy and Empire: Women Activists in Imperial Britain, 1790–1865* (London, forthcoming).

Sangari, Kumkum and Vaid, Sudesh (eds), *Recasting Women: Essays in Indian Colonial History* (New Delhi, 1990).

Twells, Alison, *The Civilising Mission and the English Middle Class, 1780–1850* (Basingstoke, forthcoming).

Ware, Vron, *Beyond the Pale: White Women, Racism and History* (London, 1992).

9 Feminisms

1   Philippa Levine, *Victorian Feminism 1850–1900* (London, 1987).
2   Olive Banks, *Faces of Feminism. A Study of Feminism as a Social Movement* (Oxford, 1981).
3   Levine, *Victorian Feminism*, p. 149.
4   Gillian Scott, *Feminism and the Politics of Working Women: The Women's Co-operative Guild, 1880s to the Second World War* (London, 1988), p. 72.
5   Karen Hunt, *Equivocal Feminists: the Social Democratic Federation and the Woman Question, 1884–1911* (Cambridge, 1996).

Further reading

Bland, Lucy, *Banishing the Beast: English Feminism and Sexual Morality, 1885–1914* (London, 1995).

Bland, Lucy and Doan, Lucy, *Sexology in Culture: Labelling Bodies and Desires* (Cambridge, 1998).

Bland, Lucy and Doan, Lucy, *Sexology Uncensored: the Documents of Sexual Science* (Cambridge, 1998).

Caine, Barbara, *Victorian Feminists* (Oxford, 1992).

Dyhouse, Carol, *Feminism, Marriage and the Family in England, 1880–1939* (Oxford, 1989).

Dyhouse, Carol, *No Distinction of Sex? Women and British Universities 1870–1939* (London, 1995).

Eustance, Claire, Joan Ryan and Laura Ugolini (eds), *A Suffrage Reader: Charting Directions in British Suffrage History* (London, 2000).

Gordon, Eleanor, *Women and the Labour Movement in Scotland 1850–1914* (Oxford, 1991).

Hall, Lesley, *Sex, Gender and Social Change in Britain since 1880* (Basingstoke, 2000).

Hannam, June, 'Women and Politics', in J. Purvis (ed.), *Women's History: Britain 1850–1945* (London, 1995).

Holcombe, Lee, *Wives and Property: Reform of the Married Women's Property Law in Nineteenth Century England* (Toronto and Buffalo, 1985).

Stanley Holton, Sandra, *Suffrage Days* (London, 1998).

Stanley Holton, Sandra, *Feminism and Democracy: Women's Suffrage and the Reform Politics in Britain* (Cambridge, 1986).

Kingsley Kent, Susan, *Sex and Suffrage in Britain, 1860–1914* (Princeton, 1987).

Leneman, Leah, *A Guid Cause: the Women's Suffrage Movement in Scotland* (Aberdeen, 1991).

Levine, Philippa, *Feminist Lives in Victorian England: Private Roles and Public Commitment* (Oxford, 1990).

Liddington, Jill and Norris, Jill, *One Hand Tied Behind Us* (London, 1978).

Walkowitz, Judith, *Prostitution and Victorian Society* (Cambridge, 1980).

Walkowitz, Judith, *City of Dreadful Delight: Narratives of Sexual Danger in Late-Victorian London* (London, 1992).

Index

Jamaica 94, 178–179, 194; *see also* West
Indies
Jameson, Anna 80, 89–90
Jewish women 8–9, 174, 176–178,
188–193
John, Angela 267 n1
Jones, Dot 129
Jones, R. 269 n1

Kay, James Phillips (later Kay-
Shuttleworth) 174–175, 181–182
Kelly, Joan 5
Kilham, Hannah 204, 209–210
Kingsley, Mary 207–208, 222–223
Kuzmack, Linda 270 n5

Ladies' National Association 228,
240–242
Ladies of Llangollen 53, 76–77
Langham Place, Ladies of 226
Layton, Mrs 105, 124–125
Leeds 107, 115–116, 152, 178, 232, 250
legal status of women 22–23, 46, 48, 52,
75, 149, 155–157, 212–214,
225–226, 228–229, 231, 233–236,
240–242, 246–248, 251, 257
Leicester 81, 175
Leigh Smith, Barbara, *see* Barbara Leigh
Smith Bodichon.
lesbianism 5, 7, 10, 16–17, 37–39,
52–53, 75–77, 80
Levine, Philippa 272 n1, n3
Lewis, Jane 5
Lister, Anne 52–53, 75–77, 80, 91–92
Loane, Margaret 128, 136–137
London 8, 12, 15, 18, 73, 79, 87, 92,
103–104, 110, 119, 137–138, 147,
149–150, 162, 173, 175–180,
182–184, 191–193, 205, 230,
249–254
Luddy, Maria 10

MacGill, Patrick 176, 186–188
Manchester 61, 75, 81, 127, 135–136,
174–175, 181–182, 219, 250
Marks, Lara 177
marriage 4, 47–51, 58–63, 65–69, 104,
137, 142, 144–145, 207; as woman's
true vocation 16, 36–37; courtship

47, 56–58; marriage reform/critiques
of marriage 49, 62–63, 67, 149,
155–157, 204, 210–212, 225–229,
233–240, 242–246
Martineau, Harriet 17, 40–42, 52,
73–75
masculinity 6, 8, 11, 19, 22, 33, 37–38,
89–90, 94, 101, 109–110, 154–155,
185, 203, 228, 244–246
Maudsley, Henry 15–16, 34–36, 227,
240
Mayhew, Henry 103, 118–119, 175,
182–184
medical literature 11, 16, 33–39, 146,
228–229, 240–242
Methodism 151, 165–166
middle class women 8, 13, 17, 25–26,
39–42, 46–77, 78–79, 81, 104, 130,
176–177, 204, 227, 232, 248,
256–257; *see also* domestic life;
education; feminism
Midgley, Clare 7
midwives 50, 105, 124–125
migration 8, 128, 174; *see also*
emigration; immigration
militancy 225, 249
Mill, James 149
Mill, J.S. 13, 24–25, 229, 246–248
Millar, John 12, 20–22
mining 102–103, 114–117, 128–129,
139–140
missions: overseas missions 203–205,
209–212; criticisms of 208; London
City Mission 180, 198–200; to West
Africa 204–205, 209–212; to India
181, 205, 212–214; domestic
missionaries 87–88; Salvation Army
153, 173, woman's mission 65, 79,
81, 98; *Woman's Mission* 188
Mitchell, Hannah 130, 144–145
Mitchell, Juliet 3
Montagu, Lily 177–178, 192–193
More, Hannah 13, 25–26, 54, 78–79,
82–83
Morrison, Frances 150
Morrison, James 150
motherhood 3, 5, 9, 11–12, 14–16, 18,
19–20, 22–23, 29–30, 33–34, 36–37,
46–52, 58–59, 65–67, 72–73, 83–85,